# Optimize
# Criminal Law

# OPTIMIZE LAW REVISION

Titles in the series:
Contract Law
Criminal Law
English Legal System
Equity and Trusts
EU Law
Land Law
Public Law

Forthcoming:
Tort Law

The Optimize series' academic advisors are:

– **Michael Bromby**, Higher Education Academy Discipline Lead for Law 2011–2013, Reader in Law, GCU.

'The use of visualisation in Optimize will help students to focus on the key issues when revising.'

– **Emily Allbon**, Law Librarian and creator of Lawbore, City University.

'Partnering well-explained, comprehensive content with visual tools like maps and flowcharts is what makes the Optimize series so unique. These books help students take their learning up a notch; offering support in grappling with the subject, as well as insight into what will help make their work stand out.'

– **Sanmeet Kaur Dua**, Lecturer in Law, co-creator of Lawbore, City University.

'This series sets out the essential concepts and principles that students need to grasp in a logical way by combining memorable visual diagrams and text. Students will find that they will not easily forget what they read in this series as the unique aim higher and interaction points will leave a blueprint in their minds.'

– **Zoe Swan**, Senior Lecturer in Law, University of Brighton.

'The wide range of visual material includes diagrams, charts, tables and maps, enabling students to check their knowledge and understanding on each topic area, every step of the way ... When combined with carefully explained legal principles and solid, understandable examples, students will find this series provides them with a win–win solution to the study of law and developing revision techniques.'

# Optimize
# Criminal Law

John Hendy and Odette Hutchinson

Routledge
Taylor & Francis Group

LONDON AND NEW YORK

First published 2015
by Routledge
2 Park Square, Milton Park, Abingdon, Oxon OX14 4RN

and by Routledge
711 Third Avenue, New York, NY 10017

*Routledge is an imprint of the Taylor & Francis Group, an informa business*

*British Library Cataloguing in Publication Data*
A catalogue record for this book is available from the British Library

*Library of Congress Cataloging in Publication Data*
Hendy, John, 1980– author.
Optimize criminal law / John Hendy, Odette Hutchinson.
pages cm. — (Optimize series)
Summary: "Criminal Law volume of the new Optimize revision series"— Provided by publisher.
ISBN 978-0-415-85712-3 (paperback) — ISBN 978-1-315-84898-3 (ebk)   1. Criminal law—Great Britain.
I. Hutchinson, Odette.   II. Title.   III. Title: Criminal law.
KD7869.H46 2015
345.41—dc23
2014030106

ISBN: 978-0-415-85712-3 (pbk)
ISBN: 978-1-315-84898-3 (ebk)

Typeset in TheSans
by RefineCatch Limited, Bungay, Suffolk

Printed and bound by CPI Group (UK) Ltd, Croydon, CR0 4YY

# Contents

# Optimize – Your Blueprint for Exam Success

## Why Optimize?

In developing the *Optimize* format, Routledge have spent a lot of time talking to law students like you, and to your lecturers and examiners about assessment, about teaching and learning, and about exam preparation. The aim of our series is to help you make the most of your knowledge to gain good marks – to optimise your revision.

## Students

Students told us that there was a huge amount to learn, and that visual features such as diagrams, tables and flowcharts made the law easier to follow. Learning and remembering cases was an area of difficulty, as was applying these in problem questions. Revision guides could make this easier by presenting the law succinctly, showing concepts in a visual format and highlighting how important cases can be applied in assessment.

## Lecturers

Lecturers agreed that visual features were effective to aid learning, but were concerned that students learned by rote when using revision guides. To succeed in assessment, they wanted to encourage them to get their teeth into arguments, to support their answers with authority, and show they had truly understood the principles underlying their questions. In short, they wanted them to show they understood how they were assessed on the law, rather than repeating the basic principles.

## Assessment criteria

If you want to do well in exams, it's important to understand how you will be assessed. In order to get the best out of your exam or essay question, your first port of call should be to make yourself familiar with the marking criteria available from your law school; this will help you to identify and recognise the skills and knowledge you will need to succeed. Like course outlines, assessment criteria can differ from school to school and so if you can get hold of a copy of your own criteria, this will be invaluable. To give you a clear idea of what these criteria look like, we've collated the most common terms from 64 marking schemes for core curriculum courses in the UK.

research

reading

Evidence

# Understanding

Structure  Critical Argument

Evaluation

Engagement

Application  Use

Organisation

Analysis  Accuracy  Originality  sources

# Knowledge

Presentation

*Common Assessment Criteria, Routledge Subject Assessment Survey 2012*

## Optimizing the law

The format of this *Optimize Law* volume has been developed with these assessment criteria and the learning needs of students firmly in mind.

* ❖ **Visual format:** Our expert series advisors have brought a wealth of knowledge about visual learning to help us to develop the book's visual format.
* ❖ **Tailored coverage:** Each book is tailored to the needs of your core curriculum course and presents all commonly taught topics.
* ❖ **Assessment-led revision:** Our authors are experienced teachers with an interest in how students learn, and they have structured each chapter around revision objectives that relate to the criteria you will be assessed on.
* ❖ **Assessment-led pedagogy:** The Aim Higher, Common Pitfalls, Up for Debate and Case precedent features used in these books are closely linked to common assessment criteria – showing you how to gain the best marks, avoid the worst, apply the law and think critically about it.
* ❖ **Putting it into practice:** Each chapter presents example essay or problem questions and template answers to show you how to apply what you have learned.

Routledge and the *Optimize* team wish you the very best of luck in your exams and essays!

# Guide to Using the Book and the Companion Website

The Routledge *Optimize* revision series is designed to provide students with a clear overview of the core topics in their course, and to contextualise this overview within a narrative that offers straightforward, practical advice relating to assessment.

## Revision objectives

These overviews are a brief introduction of the core themes and issues you will encounter in each chapter.

## Chapter topic maps

Visually link together all of the key topics in each chapter to tie together understanding of key issues.

## Illustrative diagrams

A series of diagrams and tables are used to help facilitate the understanding of concepts and interrelationships within key topics.

## Up for Debate

Up for Debate features help you to critique current law and reflect on how and in which direction it may develop in the future.

## Case precedent boxes

A variety of landmark cases are highlighted in text boxes for ease of reference. The facts, principle and application for the case are presented to help understand how these courses are used in legal problems.

## Aim Higher and Common Pitfalls

These assessment-focused sections show students how to get the best marks, and avoid the most common mistakes.

# Case grid

This draws together all of the key cases from each chapter.

# Companion website

www.routledge.com/cw/optimizelawrevision

Visit the Optimize Law Revision website to discover a comprehensive range of resources designed to enhance your learning experience.

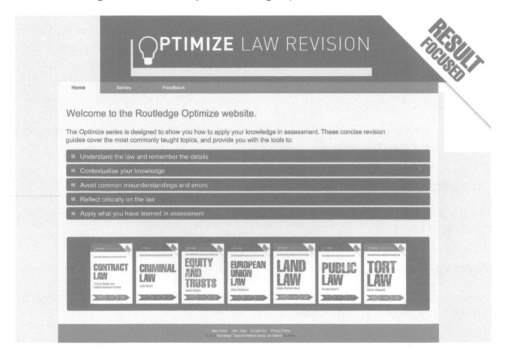

# Resources for Optimize Law Revision

❖ Up for Debate podcasts
❖ Aim Higher and Common Pitfalls podcasts
❖ Subject maps for each topic
❖ Downloadable versions of chapter maps and other diagrams

# Resources for Routledge Q&As

❖ MCQ questions
❖ Flashcard glossary
❖ The good, the fair and the ugly podcasts

# Table of Cases and Statutes

## ■ Cases

## ■ Statutes

# 1 Introduction – What is Criminal Law and What is a Crime?

**Understand the law**

- Do you understand the nature and purpose of the criminal law?
- Do you understand the general building blocks of criminal liability?

**Remember the details**

- Can you remember the meaning of the terms *actus reus* and *mens rea*?
- Can you remember the burden and standard of proof in criminal proceedings?

**Reflect critically on areas of debate**

- Do you understand the significance of the **Human Rights Act 1998** in relation to criminal proceedings?

**Contextualise**

- Are you able to contextualise your knowledge and identify overlap and distinctions in relation to civil law?

**Apply your skills and knowledge**

- Can you apply this knowledge to the rest of this text?

# Introduction to Criminal Law

Welcome to *Optimize Criminal Law*! Criminal law is a dynamic and fascinating area of law, and it is a subject that the majority of students enjoy studying. It is not however, a subject without challenges. The criminal law consists of a vast range of complex, sometimes conflicting and contradictory rules. The good news is that this textbook has been designed to support you in navigating this challenging but exciting area of law. *Optimize Criminal Law* is result-focused; we have one primary objective and that is to use our experience and knowledge to help you achieve an outstanding result in criminal law.

In the forthcoming chapters we will help you understand the substantive criminal law and how it is applied in real and hypothetical situations. We will show you how to break down individual offences into the core elements of criminal liability. You will learn how to construct criminal liability and how to identify relevant defences. We will illustrate how to maximise your marks by adopting a strategic and structured approach to answering problem questions. We will also support you in articulating and demonstrating a critical understanding of the criminal law in essay-style questions.

Throughout this book you will find a number of features, which will assist you in developing your knowledge and understanding of the criminal law. Some of these result-orientated features include:

- ❖ Aim Higher points;
- ❖ Tips and suggestions on how to answer problem questions;
- ❖ Suggested solutions to essay and problem questions;
- ❖ Examiner insight boxes, with contributions from experienced criminal law examiners;
- ❖ Read for success suggestions to enhance your critical understanding of the criminal law.

## Defining criminal law

Criminal law is a branch of public law. A straightforward way of understanding criminal conduct is by viewing it as conduct which gives rise to legal proceedings through the prospect of state punishment. In short:

1. The criminal law is enforced by the state;
2. Infringements of the criminal law are punishable by the state.

Professor Andrew Ashworth defines criminal conduct in the following terms:

> There are certain wrongs which are criminal in most jurisdictions, but in general there is no straightforward moral or social test of whether conduct is criminal. The most reliable test is the formal one: is the conduct prohibited, on pain of conviction and sentence?
>
> *Andrew Ashworth, Principles of Criminal Law*

## What functions does the criminal law perform?

The criminal law performs a number of different functions. Knowing and under-standing the functions that the criminal law performs is important, in so far as it provides students with a tool by which to critically evaluate cases, legislation and policy decisions.

Functions of the criminal law:

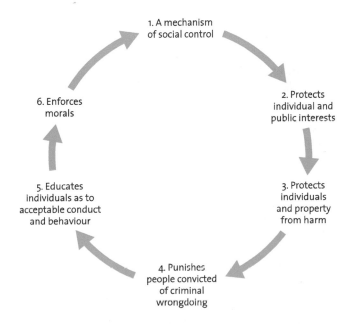

1. A mechanism of social control

2. Protects individual and public interests

3. Protects individuals and property from harm

4. Punishes people convicted of criminal wrongdoing

5. Educates individuals as to acceptable conduct and behaviour

6. Enforces morals

It is worth noting that functions 5 and 6 are particularly controversial. There is disagreement as to whether the criminal law is really an effective tool by which to educate members of society (point 5). There is also disagreement as to whether the criminal law should seek to enforce the morals and values of society (point 6). More detailed consideration of point 6 can be found in Martin and Storey, *Unlocking the Criminal Law*, 4th Edition, 2013, Routledge.

### Aim Higher

Every criminal law course is different. It is not unusual for there to be significant vari-ation between courses in terms of content and focus. One of the first things you should do is look at the syllabus for YOUR criminal law course! Do not assume that certain topics are included in your course, just because your course textbook contains material on these subjects! If you incorrectly make this assumption you may spend valuable time revising material that is not covered by your course and therefore material that is not examinable!

## Where does the criminal law come from?

There are a number of different sources of criminal law as illustrated in the following diagram.

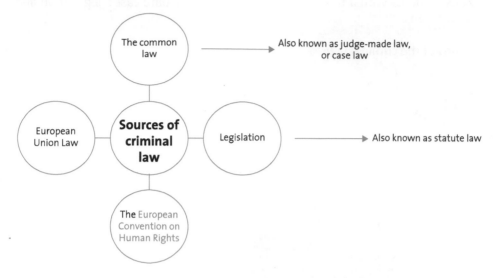

The most important sources of law, or at least the ones that you will be using most frequently throughout your criminal law studies, are:

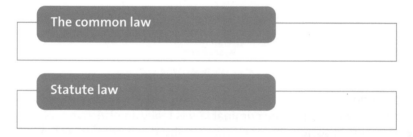

## Criminal liability versus civil liability

Criminal liability and civil liability can, and frequently do, cross over. An act or an omission (which simply means a failure to act) may give rise to civil and/or criminal liability. For example, if Odette hits Matt this could constitute the criminal offence of assault. It could also give rise to a civil action for trespass to the person (tort – civil law). Therefore, if Odette hits Matt and is convicted of a criminal offence Odette may have to pay a fine. She might be sentenced to a term in prison or receive some other form of punishment for the offence. Odette may also have to pay damages under civil law.

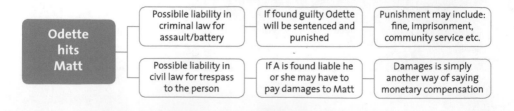

The important thing for you to remember, is that a criminal prosecution does not preclude a victim from pursuing a civil action against the wrongdoer and vice versa; that is, a civil action against a wrongdoer does not preclude the state from taking action against a defendant or defendants.

## Criminal liability

In simplistic terms, criminal liability exists where a defendant is responsible for conduct (this could take the form of an act, an omission or a state of affairs) that breaches the criminal law, and at the time the conduct was committed, or occurred, the defendant had a particular state of mind (there are some offences for which the defendant's state of mind is irrelevant; we refer to these as strict or absolute liability offences which we will discuss later); and, finally, the defendant has no valid defence.

Let's break this down in order to understand the building blocks of criminal liability more clearly. The building blocks of criminal liability consist of:

In criminal law some of the building blocks have special terms. For example, the conduct element of an offence is referred to as the *actus reus*; this Latin term means 'guilty act'. The state of mind element of criminal liability is referred to as the *mens rea*, this Latin term means 'guilty mind'. It is important that you use these Latin terms in your assessments. So let's re-draft the above diagram accordingly.

We will consider *actus reus* and *mens rea* in more detail in Chapter 1 and Chapter 2, but at the moment we simply want you to understand that these terms are the building blocks of criminal liability.

## Key points of criminal liability

Before you embark on your journey through the criminal law there are a number of key points that you need to be aware of at this juncture. When constructing criminal liability you must bear the following critical points in mind:

❖ The defendant's motive is irrelevant to the question of constructing criminal liability. Do not get caught up with or preoccupied with WHY the defendant committed the offence.

❖ The substantive criminal law is not concerned with HOW the prosecution will PROVE the defendant's guilt. Again if you spend time considering this you will be wasting valuable time!

❖ You are not the judge, or the jury. Your job is to construct criminal liability, not to determine whether the defendant will be convicted. That is for the jury, or magistrates to determine. In an assessment you must put forward arguments for both sides **unless** specifically asked to do otherwise.

**Common Pitfalls**

❖ Your role is to demonstrate to the examiner a detailed knowledge of the substantive criminal law. Many students spend valuable time focusing on the motive(s) of the defendant, or agonising over how the prosecution in practical terms will be able to prove the defendant's state of mind.

❖ These are both 'red herrings'. When answering a problem question your job is to identify potential offences and to construct liability for those offences, before considering likely available defences.

❖ If you decide to complete the professional stage of training through the Bar Professional Training Course (BPTC) or the Legal Practice Course (LPC) you will study criminal litigation and procedure. You will also study the complex rules of evidence. For now, at least, focus only on the substantive criminal law!

## Fundamental principles of criminal law

1. A key principle running throughout the criminal law is that the defendant is **innocent until proven guilty**.
2. Another key principle in English criminal law is that the **prosecution** (in most cases the Crown Prosecution Service) **bears the burden of proof**.
3. The standard of proof in criminal prosecutions is 'beyond a reasonable doubt'.

| The presumption of innocence |
| --- |
| This means that the defendant is innocent until proven guilty. This fundamental principle is protected by the common law *R v Woolmington* [1935] AC 462 and by Art 6 of The European Convention on Human Rights |

| The prosecution bears the burden of proof |
| --- |
| This means that the prosecution must prove the defendant committed the alleged offence. The defendant does not have to prove he, or she is innocent. |

| The burden of proof is 'beyond a reasonable doubt' |
| --- |
| This is a very high standard of proof, much higher than the civil standard of proof. |

## The burden and standard of proof

In practice the burden and standard of proof operates in the following way. If Amy kills Bob, the prosecution must prove beyond a reasonable doubt that Amy killed

Bob. If the prosecution succeeds in doing this, then the jury should convict Amy. If the jury are sure that Amy did not kill Bob, they must acquit Amy. If the jury are not sure either way, then the jury must acquit the defendant.

The prosecution bears the burden, then, of proving the defendant's guilt. It also bears the burden of disproving any defence that the accused may raise.

---

### Case precedent – *Woolmington* [1935] AC 462

**Facts:** In this case the defendant claimed that he had accidently shot his wife. The prosecution argued that the defendant must prove that the shooting was an accident. The defendant was convicted of murdering his wife.

**Principle:** On appeal the House of Lords held that a defendant is innocent until proven guilty. It is for the prosecution to prove beyond a reasonable doubt that the shooting was not an accident. It was not for the defendant to prove he was not guilty.

**Application:** Use this case to illustrate the principle that a defendant is innocent until proven guilty. You can also use this case to illustrate that the prosecution bears the burden of proof.

---

## Reverse burden of proof

In certain situations the burden of proof will shift from the prosecution to the defence. This can happen where the defence has raised a certain defence such as insanity or diminished responsibility. In the event that the accused raises one of these defences the standard of proof changes from 'beyond a reasonable doubt' to on the 'balance of probabilities'. The table below will help you break down these important points.

| | The burden of proof | The standard of proof | Rule | Authority |
|---|---|---|---|---|
| **The prosecution** | The prosecution bears the burden of proof in most criminal prosecutions. A defendant is innocent until proven guilty. This means they must prove that the defendant is guilty. It also means that the prosecution must disprove the existence of any defence that the accused raises. | Beyond a reasonable doubt | This is the general rule. It is often referred to as 'the golden thread running through the criminal law'. | *Woolmington* [1935] AC462 **Article 6 ECHR** |

|  | The burden of proof | The standard of proof | Rule | Authority |
|---|---|---|---|---|
| **The defence** | In the event that the defence raises the defence of insanity or diminished responsibility, the burden of proof shifts from the prosecution to the defence. | Where the burden of proof shifts, the standard of proof changes to the lower standard of proof, the civil standard – on the balance of probabilities. | This is an exception to the general rule that the prosecution bears the burden of proof. | **Diminished responsibility** – **s 2** Homicide Act 1957 as amended by **s 52** of the Coroners and Justices Act 2009 |
|  | The defence must prove the existence of the defence. The prosecution must then attempt to disprove it! |  |  | **Insanity** – Reverse burden of proof established by the common law rather than statute |
|  |  |  |  | In *Sheldrake v DPP* [2005] 1 AC 264 it was held that a reverse burden of proof does not automatically violate **Art 6** of the **ECHR** |

## Human rights and the criminal law

It is important to understand that the rules and processes of the criminal law do not exist in isolation and as such English criminal law is affected by the Legislation, which was incorporated into domestic law in the form of the Human Rights Act 1998.

The following provisions are particularly important in the context of the criminal law:

> Article 2: The right to life

> Article 6: The right to a fair trial

> Article 7: No punishment without law

# Key Points Checklist

| | |
|---|---|
| Criminal law is a branch of public law. The preoccupation of the criminal law is conduct which gives rise to legal proceedings through the prospect of state punishment. The criminal law is enforced by the state and punishable by the state. | ✔ |
| The criminal law performs a number of different functions including: the protection of individuals and property; the maintenance of social and public order; the enforcement of morals; the punishment of individuals who have committed criminal offences; education. | ✔ |
| The criminal law is derived from a number of different sources including: the common law; statute law; EU law. | ✔ |
| Criminal law differs from civil law. The terminology can be different. The standard and burden of proof are also different in criminal and civil proceedings. | ✔ |
| The building blocks of criminal liability are **actus reus** (guilty act), **mens rea** (guilty mind) and the absence of a valid defence. | ✔ |

---

@ **Visit the book's companion website to test your knowledge**

❖ Resources include a subject map, revision tip podcasts, downloadable diagrams, MCQ quizzes for each chapter, and a flashcard glossary

❖ www.routledge.com/cw/optimizelawrevision

# 2

# General Elements of Liability

**Understand the law**

- Can you define the terms *actus reus* and *mens rea*, and how they interact?
- Can you identify the *actus reus* and *mens rea* in different offences?

**Remember the details**

- Can you remember the different types of *actus reus* and *mens rea* and their meaning?
- Can you identify case law examples for each type of *actus reus* and *mens rea*?

**Reflect critically on areas of debate**

- Can you demonstrate that you understand the term strict liability and that you are able to offer examples of offences that are strict liability offences?
- Can you reflect on the meaning of intention and recklessness and the distinctions between recklessness and intention using case law to illustrate the differences?

**Contextualise**

- Do you understand the context in which *actus reus* and *mens rea* operate?
- Do you understand the significance of a break in the chain of causation?

**Apply your skills and knowledge**

- Can you complete the problem questions for *actus reus* and *mens rea* providing case law and statutory illustrations to support your answer?

# Chapter Map

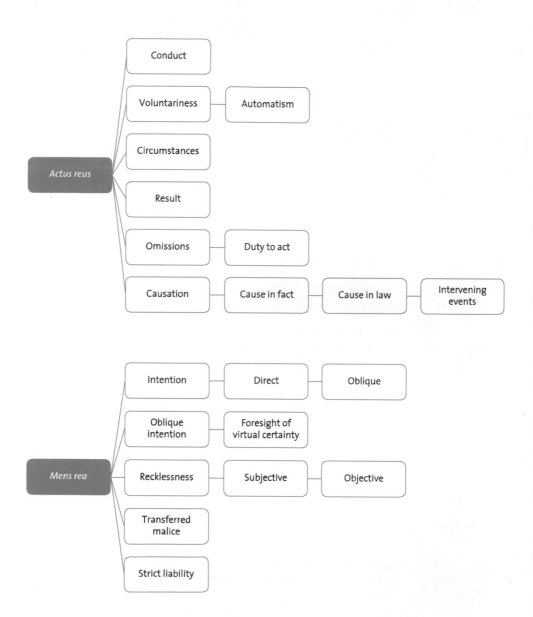

# Introduction

In the last chapter we considered two key terms: *actus reus* and *mens rea*. In this chapter we are going to consider these terms in more detail. In particular we are going to consider how these crucial elements come together to construct criminal liability.

The physical element of criminal liability is referred to as *actus reus*, a Latin term which translates as 'guilty act'. The term *mens rea* refers to the mental element of criminal liability. A literal translation of this Latin term is 'guilty mind'.

Therefore there are three ingredients to criminal liability.

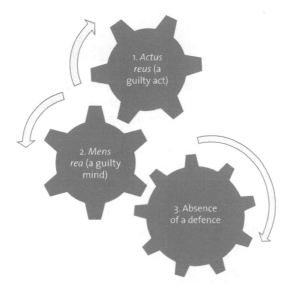

These first two elements will be considered in detail in this chapter. We will consider defences in relation to specific offences throughout the book. We will also consider general defences in the two chapters on general defences,

We will start our consideration of the substantive content in this chapter by considering *actus reus* as a concept.

## *Actus reus*

We are going to start this section of the chapter by considering the importance of voluntariness to the *actus reus* as a concept. Then we will move on to consider the different types of *actus reus* before considering failures to act, also known as omissions. The final *actus reus* topic we will consider together is key concept in criminal liability known as causation.

## Voluntariness

In order to construct liability for a criminal offence you will need to be satisfied that the defendant's conduct or omission was voluntary. As a general rule there can be no liability for serious criminal offences unless D's conduct was *voluntary*.

### Aim Higher

You should bear in mind that this is not applicable to state of affairs crimes, which are crimes committed when the defendant (D) finds themselves in a particular prohibited situation, such as in possession of a controlled substance (drugs). The nature of a state of affairs case is that it doesn't matter how D came to find himself in that situation. A good illustration can be found in the case of *Winzar v Chief Constable of Kent* The Times 28 March (1983).

Involuntary movements or conduct cannot form the basis of criminal liability. For example, let's imagine that Kaya has very severe hay fever, and as a result of the very high pollen count he begins to sneeze uncontrollably. Whilst sneezing he head-butts his friend Jack. Jack sustains a large bruise to his head. In this scenario Kaya could be argued to have committed the *actus reus* of the offence of battery or actual bodily harm. However, his sneezing is an involuntary action and as such, despite the fact that Jack has suffered physical harm, Kaya would not be liable for either battery or actual bodily harm.

The defendant's inability to control their movements may be the result of a number of different factors including:

❖ illness – physical or mental;
❖ reflex body actions;
❖ the result of injury – having been rendered in an unconscious state.

For example, in *Hill v Baxter* (1958), D lost control of the car that he was driving because he was attacked by a swarm of bees. Another case that you can use to illustrate this principle of law is *Burns v Bidder* (1967).

### Case precedent – *R v Quick & Paddison* [1973] 3 AER 397

**Facts:** D was affected by hypoglycaemia, and had a fit where he was not in control of his arms or legs. During this fit, D assaulted V.

**Principle:** Voluntariness and automatism

**Application:** D was found guilty, but on appeal the judge ruled that automatism was a possible defence open to D and that the critical part should have been considered in the original trial. As a result, D's conviction was quashed.

Now we are going to consider the different types of *actus reus* that exist in English criminal law.

## Types of *actus reus*

The *actus reus* of a criminal offence consists of all the external elements of that offence. The *actus reus* of a crime can be defined in a number of different ways, for example a conduct crime or a result crime. This has given rise to a typology of criminal offences, the most common of which are conduct crimes and result crimes.

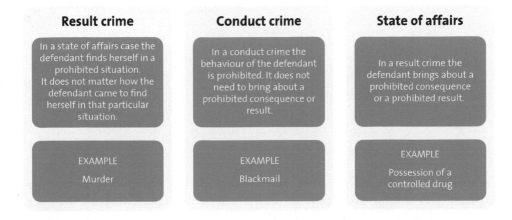

| Result crime | Conduct crime | State of affairs |
|---|---|---|
| In a state of affairs case the defendant finds herself in a prohibited situation. It does not matter how the defendant came to find herself in that particular situation. | In a conduct crime the behaviour of the defendant is prohibited. It does not need to bring about a prohibited consequence or result. | In a result crime the defendant brings about a prohibited consequence or a prohibited result. |
| EXAMPLE Murder | EXAMPLE Blackmail | EXAMPLE Possession of a controlled drug |

It is worth noting that some offences, such as arson under the **Criminal Damage Act 1971**, are both result and conduct offences.

In the case of a conduct crime it is the defendant's behaviour that is prohibited irrespective of the result or consequences.

For example:

> Cameron discovers some information about Ben and then demands money with menaces. This is blackmail – it is the **conduct which is prohibited**. As such it does not matter whether Ben goes to the police or pays the money.

> Ben is angry with Cameron for having blackmailed him. Intending to cause Cameron serious harm Ben hits Cameron on the head with a spade. The result is the unlawful death of Cameron – **the result is prohibited**. B caused C's death.

The term *actus reus* as we have seen, translates literally to mean 'guilty act'. The term is potentially misleading because it can give rise to an assumption that the *actus reus* of an offence must always be the result of a positive act. You need to be careful because this literal translation of the Latin term is potentially misleading because it suggests that the *actus reus* of an offence is always the result of a positive action. For example, Ben hitting Cameron on the head with a spade. In reality liability for a criminal offence can arise where the defendant fails to act. The term we use in criminal law to describe a failure to act is *omission*. We will now consider the circumstances in which a failure to act can give rise to criminal liability in English criminal law.

# Topic Map: Omissions

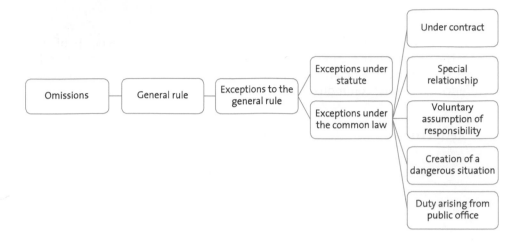

# Omission

The general rule in English criminal law is that failing to act cannot give rise to criminal liability. Whilst this is the general rule there are exceptions to this rule there are a number of situations in which a failure to act can give rise to criminal liability. Many of the textbooks give the following illustration of an omission.

A sees B drowning. In these circumstances A is under no legal obligation to assist B. It doesn't even matter if it would be perfectly safe for A to assist B. So where A is a strong swimmer or where B is a small child drowning in very shallow water. A is under no legal obligation to assist B.

## Aim Higher

It is important here to note that there is a difference between a legal and a moral obligation to assist a person in need. Most people would recoil at the concept of an adult standing by and watching a child – or indeed anyone – drown when they could have offered assistance without putting their own life in danger.

Having considered the general rule we are now going to consider the exceptions to the general rule.

## Exceptions

An exception to the general rule that there is no liability for a failure to act can arise under one of two headings:

1. An exception under statute
2. An exception under common law

We will consider each of these in turn.

## Exception under statute

A statute can impose liability for omissions to act. There are lots of examples of statutes imposing criminal liability for an omission to act. You can use the following to support this point in an essay or problem question.

❖ Section 170 of the Road Traffic Act – failure to report an accident;
❖ Section 7 of the Road Traffic Act – failure to provide a specimen of breath.

## Exceptions under the common law

There are a number of points that you need to be aware of in relation to exceptions created by the common law.

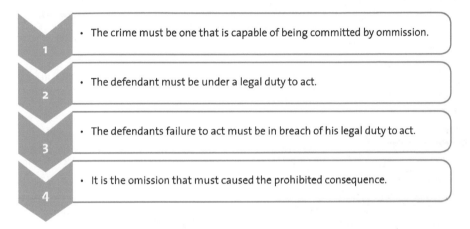

1 • The crime must be one that is capable of being committed by ommission.

2 • The defendant must be under a legal duty to act.

3 • The defendants failure to act must be in breach of his legal duty to act.

4 • It is the omission that must caused the prohibited consequence.

1. Not all crimes are capable of being committed by omission. Assault and Battery caused by omission are particularly tricky: in *Fagan v MPC* (1968) and *DPP v Santana-Bermudez* (2003).

### Case precedent – *DPP v Santana-Bermudez* [2003] EWHC 2908 (Admin)

**Facts:** In this case D failed to notify a police officer of the presence of hypodermic needles in his pockets despite having been asked this question prior to the search being carried out. The police office sustained a needle stick injury as a result of the defendant's omission.

**Principle:** Assault and Battery cannot normally be committed by omission. However, if the defendant creates a dangerous situation liability may arise.

**Application:** D created the danger by omitting to inform the police officer. D was convicted of ABH.

2. With regard to a duty, this could fall under a number of headings and examples.

## Common Pitfall

The general rule is that there can be no liability for failing to act, unless at the time of the omission the defendant was under a legal duty to act. It is important not to confuse this legal duty with a moral duty to act.

There are a number of situations defined by case law, which identify when a person has a legal duty to act. They are:

| | |
|---|---|
| **Duty arising from a contract** | • Where a person is under a positive duty to act because of his obligations under a contract, a failure to perform the contractual duty in question can form the basis of criminal liability. *Pitwood* **[1902]** |
| **Public office** | • A person holding a public office (such as a Police Officer) may be under a public duty to act. *Dytham* **[1979]** |
| **Voluntary assumption of responsibility** | • A common law duty to act can arise in circumstances where the D has voluntarily assumed responsibility to care for another person. *Stone and Dabinson* **[1977]** |
| **Creation of a dangerous situation** | • If the defendant accidentally commits an act that causes harm, and subsequently becomes aware of the danger he has created, there arises a duty to act reasonably to avert that danger. The D is under a legal duty to avert the danger he has created. *Miller* **[1983]** |
| **Duty arising from a special relationship** | • D may be liable for failing to act where there is a special relationship between V and D – this is generally a relationship of close family proximity. *Gibbins and Proctor* **[1918]** |

## Duty arising from contract

Where D is under a contractual obligation to act, a failure to do so can give rise to criminal liability. The key case that you need to remember in relation to this principle of law is the case of *Pitwood* (1902).

### Case precedent – *Pittwood* [1902] TLR 37

**Facts:** D was a level crossing keeper, but one day left the gate open when a train was approaching. The train hit a vehicle and killed the driver. D was charged with manslaughter.

**Principle:** Omission to act when D is under a contractual duty.

**Application:** D's employment contract created a duty to act, i.e. closing the gate, a duty which he failed to perform.

## Duty arising from public office

In circumstances where the defendant neglects their duty whilst in public office can give rise to criminal liability. In the case of *Dytham* (1979) the defendant who was an on duty police officer stood and watched as a man was attacked and beaten to death. The defendant made no attempt to intervene and he did not call for assistance. He was convicted of wilful misconduct in public office.

## Voluntary assumption of responsibility

In the case of *Instan* (1893) the defendant assumed caring responsibility for an elderly aunt. The aunt developed gangrene in her leg and she stopped eating. The defendant neglected to feed the aunt and did not call for assistance when it was clearly needed. The aunt died and the defendant was convicted of the aunt's manslaughter. The principle that voluntary assumption of responsibility can give rise to criminal liability also applied in the case of *Stone and Dobinson* (1977).

## Creation of a dangerous situation

In circumstances where a defendant creates a dangerous situation they are under a legal duty to avert further damage/harm. In the case of *Miller* (1983) the defendant fell asleep whilst smoking. He awoke to find that the mattress that he was sleeping on was on fire. Instead of calling the emergency services or attempting to put the fire out, he left the room and went to sleep in another room.

The principle in *Miller* was extended to manslaughter in *Evans* (2009), where the defendant supplied the victim with a controlled substance and failed to summon help the victim when he became unconscious and died.

## Duty arising from a special relationship

Where the defendant and the victim are in a relationship of close proximity the law may impose a duty to act. The most obvious relationship that gives rise to such a duty is the relationship between parent and child: *Gibbins and Proctor* (1918). The range of relationships to which this principle applies is not limited only to parent and child.

# Causation

In the case of a result crime it must be established that the defendant is the cause of the prohibited result, issues in relation to causation appear frequently in relation to homicide cases. You need to make sure that you understand the rules in relation to causation and how to apply them!

In this section we will consider:

In order to establish causation it must be demonstrated that D is the factual and the legal cause of the prohibited consequences.

Causation requires proof that D's conduct was:

The first step in establishing causation is to establish factual causation.

## Cause in fact (factual causation)

To be a cause *in fact* the defendant's conduct must satisfy the **'but for'** test. This means that we must be able to say that the consequence would not have occurred 'but for' the defendant's actions. This test is usually very easy to apply to a problem question; however, it does not adequately deal with situations where there are multiple causes, for example.

**Example**: Bob dislikes Nigel and wants to kill him. Bob puts rat poison in Nigel's coffee, but before Nigel can drink his coffee, Nigel suffers a heart attack and dies. Is Bob the factual cause of Nigel's death?

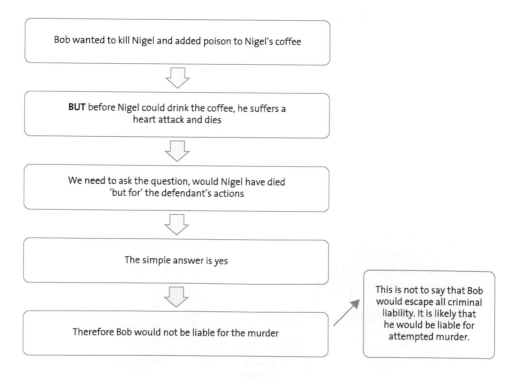

This scenario is drawn from the facts of a real case: *White* (1910).

## Common Pitfall

One of the most common mistakes that students make in relation to causation is that they fail to deal with factual and legal causation. More often than not students remember the test for factual causation and fail to discuss causation.

You must remember that factual causation is a necessary but insufficient test for establishing causation. You MUST deal with legal causation. If you do not you have not established a causal link and as a direct result you will limit the award of marks that the examiner can make.

Now consider the following example.

**Example**: Jody stabs Leon, and Leon is taken in an ambulance to hospital. As the ambulance is approaching the hospital, Laurence, who is driving a car, hits the ambulance and Leon is killed in the impact of the collision. Is Jody liable for the murder of Leon? Would your answer differ if the stab wound was only a minor injury?

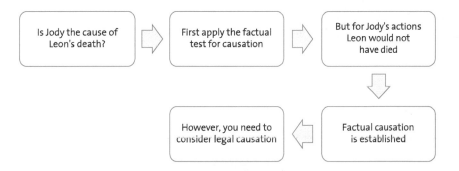

When you are looking at a problem question, it can sometimes be difficult to reach a final conclusion as to the cause of a victim's death – particularly when there are a number of possibilities! So in an exam, do not agonise over the conclusion. Show your working out and impress the examiner with your ability to work your way methodically through the alternatives.

## Common Pitfall

Students often form their own opinion about whether D should be held liable for a criminal offence. Do not let this cloud your ability to apply the law. It may be obvious to you that D is the cause of death, but the examiner will need to see your knowledge and application of law in relation to causation. We cannot give many marks at all for the expression of personal opinion alone!

We are now moving on to consider legal causation.

## Cause in law (legal causation)

In order to establish legal causation the prosecution must demonstrate that the defendant's actions were a 'substantial and operating' cause of the victim's death: *Smith* (1959). One of the key cases in relation to this principle is the case of Smith.

- ❖ One of the most important points to note about legal causation is that it does not require the defendant's actions or omissions to be the sole or even the main cause of the victim's death: *Hennigan* (1971).
- ❖ It is also important to note that D can be an indirect cause of V's death: *McKechnie* (1929).
- ❖ Another important rule in relation to causation is the 'thin skull' or 'eggshell skull' rule. This rule stipulates that the defendant must take the victim as he finds him. It is no defence to argue that V has a particular weakness rendering him more susceptible to death or injury. The leading case in relation to this rule is *Blaue* (1975). The pyramid below illustrates the operation of the Thin Skull Rule:

### Case precedent – *Blaue* [1975] 1 WLR 1411

**Facts:** D stabbed V, penetrating her lung. She was told at hospital that she needed a blood transfusion and surgery was necessary to save her life. She refused this transfusion as she was a Jehovah's Witness and it was against her religion. Medical evidence indicated that she would not have died had she had the transfusion.

**Principle:** Thin skull rule

**Application:** D argued that the victim's refusal of treatment broke the chain of causation. The Court of Appeal rejected this argument and extended the thin skull rule to 'the whole man, not just the physical man' (Lawton LJ p 1415).

But what happens when something happens between the time that the defendant inflicted the injury and the time that defendant dies? We will consider intervening events in the next section.

## Intervening events

The legal term for an intervening event is a *novus actus interveniens*. If the defence successfully establishes that there was a *novus actus interveniens* this will break the chain of causation.

> ### Common Pitfall
>
> You must be careful here with your use of language. If you say 'there are a number of intervening events' you are essentially saying the chain of causation has been broken. The correct thing to say is 'we will now consider **WHETHER** there has been an intervening event'.

Intervening events can take several forms:

| Naturally occurring events | • see *Environment Agency v Empress Car Co.* [1999] 2 AC 22 |
|---|---|

| Acts of third parties | • see *R v Jordan* (1956) 40 Cr App R 152 and *R v Cheshire* [1991] 1 WLR 844 |
|---|---|

| Acts of the victim | • see *R v Roberts* [1971] 56 Cr App R 95 |
|---|---|

## *Act of God*

In cases where it is the sole or immediate cause of the prohibited consequence. You can use the following case to support this principle of law: *Southern Water Authority v Pegrum* (1989).

## *Act of a third party*

The act or actions of a third party can only break the chain of causation where their acts or actions are free, deliberate and informed. The acts or actions of the third part must provide the immediate cause of the prohibited consequences in action.

> ### Case precedent – *R v Pagett* [1983] 76 Cr App R 279
>
> **Facts:** In this case the D used a women as a human shield and fired his gun at the police. The police returned fire and killed V. D was held liable for her death.
>
> **Principle:** Legal causation – acts of third parties

**Application:** D shot at the police first, causing the police to act in self-defence. Therefore D's act of shooting at the police and using the girl as a shield caused the death of V.

---

### Case precedent – *R v Jordan* [1956] 40 Cr App R 152

**Facts:** In this case the D stabbed V, but V's treatment at hospital was poor, and V died as a result of the treatment. The wound was no longer life-threatening.

**Principle:** Intervening act by a third party

**Application:** The judge in this case ruled that in order for medical treatment to break the chain of causation the medical treatment must be 'palpably wrong'. In this case the treatment was palpably wrong. However, in *R v Cheshire* [1991] 3 All ER 670 the judge said that the chain of causation would only be broken if D's act was not significantly important, *'so independent of D's acts, and in itself so potent in causing death'* (at 855).

## *R v Jordan*

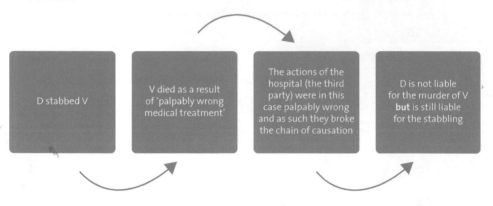

This case can be contrasted with the case of *R v Cheshire* (1991) in which, following an act of violence by the defendant the victim was sent to hospital. Whilst receiving medical treatment there were complications and the victim died as a result of the complications. In this case the complications were the natural consequence of the D's actions.

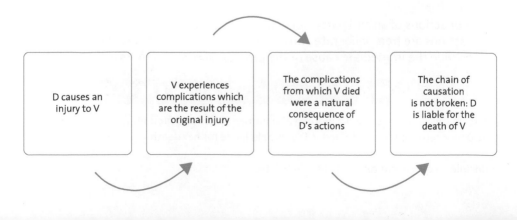

The decision in *Cheshire* was followed in the case of *Mellor* (1996) and the case of *Gowans* (2003). It is therefore safe to assert that it is highly unlikely that negligent medical treatment given which is the result of a D's violent actions will be permitted to break the chain of causation in future cases. The case of *Jordan* appears to be an exceptional case which would be unlikely to have the same outcome were it heard now.

> ### Aim Higher
>
> Read the following cases and look at the language the court uses in identifying the cause in law.
>
> *R v Pagett* [1983] 76 Cr App R 279
> *R v White* [1910] 2 KB 124
> *R v Roberts* [1971] 56 Cr App R 95
>
> You will notice the different language that the court uses – *substantial, operating and substantial, proximate, imputable, significant contribution* – these concepts are closely related.

The final category of intervening events that we need to consider is the actions or omissions of the victim and the extent to which these may break the chain of causation. The following principles apply in relation to this category:

❖ In circumstances where the V attempts to escape harm and is injured in the process the chain of causation will not normally be broken. Only in cases where the V's actions were 'so daft as to be unforeseeable' will the chain of causation be broken: *Roberts* (1972).
❖ If V's actions are not 'daft' then V will be held liable, and the question as to whether the victims actions are 'daft' is a question of fact for the jury: *Marjoram* (2000).
❖ It is important to note that a victim's wilful neglect or deliberate aggravation of wounds that have been caused by the defendant are unlikely to break the chain of causation: *Dear* (1996).
❖ Where D inflicts harm, physical or psychological, on a victim and the victim goes on to commit suicide, D may be held liable for V's death: *Dhaliwal* (2006).

## Problem areas: drug cases

❖ Cases involving the consumption of drugs are particularly problematic. They involve unlawful activity by the drug dealer (the sale of a controlled substance) and aggravating factors on behalf of the victim (the consumption of the drug). Where the victim dies as the result of the consumption of drugs provided by D, liability may arise under the *Miller* principle as extended in *Evans* (2009) where D fails to summon help.
❖ Where D injects the controlled substance into V and V dies, D may be held liable for the death of V: *Cato* (1976).
❖ A drug dealer does not cause a victim to take controlled substances even if the consumption of the substance is foreseeable: *Dalby* (1982).

❖  Where D hands the drugs and or other drug paraphernalia to V, who then voluntarily consumes the drugs and dies, D is not liable for the death of V: *Kennedy* (2007).

Consider the example below:

**Example**: Refath attacks Phil and as a result of this attack Phil suffers post-traumatic stress disorder (PTSD). Phil commits suicide.

What principles of law and which cases do you feel would be relevant to establishing causation in this case?

## Aim Higher

Remember that few scenarios are clear-cut, it is essential that you debate the issues in your paper. As has been mentioned, you are constructing liability; you are not there to deliver a verdict – that is the role of the jury/magistrates. Your role is to consider:

❖  which offences D may be liable for;
❖  whether liability can be constructed from those offences;
❖  what defences if any D may avail himself of;
❖  if there are alternative or lesser charges.

From this we can conclude that intervening acts are an important element within the chain of causation, and therefore in demonstrating the *actus reus*. Any intervening acts must originate from the three sources above, and be significant within the chain.

## A summary of the points that we have considered in this section

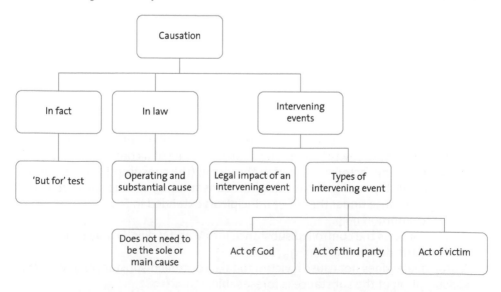

# Coincidence of *actus reus* and *mens rea*

In order for liability to exist there must be coincidence of *actus reus* and *mens rea*. We will now consider this requirement in more detail.

This rule requires that the defendant must have had the requisite *mens rea* for the offence at the time the *actus reus* of the offence was committed – some textbooks refer to this as contemporaneity of *actus reus* and *mens rea*. Therefore, let us imagine that Zena plans to murder Bernie on Saturday morning whilst he is asleep. On Friday evening Zena reverses out of the drive and accidently runs Bernie over, and Bernie dies in hospital the next day. Zena cannot be convicted of Bernie's murder because there is no coincidence of *actus reus* and *mens rea*.

| *Actus reus* | AR and MR must coincide in time for liability to exist | *Mens rea* |
|:---:|:---:|:---:|

Now consider the following leading case in this area. This case involves a defendant committing the *actus reus* of an offence before forming the *mens rea* for the offence. It explains how the courts have developed mechanisms to deal with such situations to ensure that justice is served.

---

### Case precedent – *Fagan v MPC* [1969] 1 QB 439

**Facts:** D accidentally drove onto a police officer's foot. When he realised what he had done, he refused to move the car, despite the repeated request of the police officer.

**Principle:** Coincidence of *actus reus* and *mens rea*

**Application:** The court agreed that the *actus reus* and *mens rea* must coincide but one could occur before the other. In this case, the *actus reus* took place before the *mens rea* materialised (when D knew that he was actually on the police officer's foot).

---

The prosecution must also establish that the *actus reus* and *mens rea* coincide. If the prosecution is unable to establish these factors beyond a reasonable doubt the defendant is entitled to an acuital.

In the next case the defendants form the *mens rea* for the offence before they commit the *actus reus* of the offence.

---

### Case precedent – *Thabo Meli and Others* (1954)

**Facts:** The Ds in this case had agreed to kill V. They took V off to a secluded location and beat him. Thinking that they had killed the V, the Ds threw V's body off a cliff. In reality V was still alive, but died some time later from exposure.

**Principle:** Coincidence of *actus reus* and *mens rea*

**Application:** In this case the *mens rea* was in existence before the Ds actually committed the *actus reus* of the offence (the death of V). The court held that it was impossible to divide up what was essentially a series of acts.

The two cases above describe the different situations in which coincidence of *actus reus* and *mens rea* can present difficulty for the courts. As a general rule if you are facing a problem question in which there is an issue with coincidence of *actus reus* and *mens rea* you should consider the following:

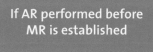

| If AR performed before MR is established | • Apply *Fagan* |

| If MR is established before AR is committed | • Apply *Thabo Meli* <br> • Followed in *Church* (1965) and *LeBrun* (1991) |

## Key Points Checklist

| | |
|---|:---:|
| ❖ The physical element of a crime is called the **actus reus** | ✔ |
| ❖ If the **actus reus** cannot be proved, then the defendant cannot be convicted | ✔ |
| ❖ **Mens rea** describes the mental state of the defendant | ✔ |
| ❖ If a defendant is to be convicted of a criminal offence then the **actus reus** and **mens rea** MUST coincide | ✔ |

A useful technique that will help you prepare for the examination is to work through scenarios in your course textbook identifying the *actus reus* and *mens rea* of each offence. This will help you to identify both elements clearly within a problem question.

We are now moving on to consider the second element of criminal liability, which is *mens rea*.

## Mens rea

*Mens rea* (Latin for guilty mind) must coincide with the *actus reus* of an offence in order for D to be liable for a criminal offence. Like the term *actus reus* you must be careful when dealing with *mens rea* as the term is frequently misunderstood as motive or premeditation, neither of which are relevant to a consideration of *mens rea*.

In this section we will consider:

It is important to note that you must have a sound understanding of *actus reus* (AR) and *mens rea* (MR) in order to answer any problem question in criminal law. These are the buliding blocks of criminal liability – this is not a area of criminal law that you can afford to have a poor understanding of. A detailed understanding of AR and MR are essential to your success in your criminal law assessments.

As you are working your way through this textbook you will need to refer back to this section on *mens rea* frequently as the concepts we discuss in this section permeate all criminal offences.

## Types of *mens rea*
In this chapter we will consider the following types of mens rea:

❖ intention
❖ recklessness

It is important to note that these are not the only forms of *mens rea*. Other forms of *mens rea* include:

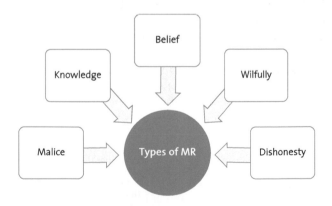

Intention will now be examined in each of these areas, in detail.

# Intention

The primary meaning of intention is an aim, purpose or desire to bring about a particular consequence. What is significant in relation to the concept of intention in criminal law is that its meaning has been found by the courts to be a little wider than simply 'aim, purpose or desire'.

Thus a person who embarks on a particular course of conduct in the knowledge that certain consequences are 'virtually certain' to occur is also deemed to have intended the consequences, irrespective as to whether it was their primary aim, purpose or desire.

Thus intention encapsulates two different forms of intention:

❖ direct intention; and
❖ oblique intention, sometimes referred to as an indirect intention.

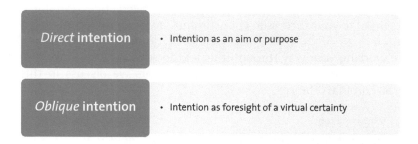

Look at the example below, and consider whether Jodie possesses direct intention or oblique intention.

**Example**: Jodie owns a taxi firm and is struggling with money, she decides that she can solve her money problems if she makes a claim on her insurance for one of the cars. She decides to cut the brakes on a car with the aim that the car will be badly damaged in an accident. Jodie does not care whether the driver and other people are in the taxi when it crashes. Does Jodie have the *mens rea* for murder?

We could say that Jodie does not aim to hurt people in this case. That is not her purpose. She may in fact hope that everyone is able to jump to safetly! However, she does have foresight of a virtual certainty that the driver/customers/pedestrians may be seriously injured in the process if she cuts the brakes of the car.

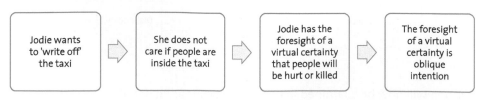

We are now going to consider some of the key cases that have refined the meaning of intention – specifically oblique intention. These cases exclusively involve homicide: murder cases to be more specific. We would recommend that you look at the chapter on murder (Chapter 5) in more detail once you have completed this section on intention.

# Refining the meaning of oblique intention

Our starting position is to recognise that there is no statutory definition of intention and that the courts have remained remarkably reluctant to supply students of law and practitioners with a nice, neat definition of the concept! It is also worth noting that the judiciary have tended to consider what does not constitute intention – as opposed to what does constitute intention!

The current approach to the meaning of intention has evolved through a series of cases in which the central argument has always concerned the degree of foresight of probability.

Each case will now be briefly considered, including its importance.

| Case law | Circumstances |
|---|---|
| *Hyam* [1974] 2 All ER 41 | D had caused the death of two of V's children when setting fire to V's house, an action which she insisted was intended merely to frighten V. The House of Lords held that murder could be committed by a person who foresaw the high degree of probability of death or serious injury. |
| *Moloney* [1985] AC 905 | D shot and killed his stepfather, V. The House of Lords held that the judge had misdirected the jury that intention included foresight of probability. The jury should have been directed that a consequence is intended where it is the natural consequence of D's actions. |
| *Hancock and Shankland* [1986] AC 455 | Two miners, who were taking part in a national strike, sought to prevent another miner from going to work. They pushed concrete objects from a motorway bridge into the path of a convoy of vehicles taking the miner to work. One of the objects smashed through the windscreen of the taxi and killed the driver. The court held that the greater the degree of probability, the greater the degree of foresight. |
| *Nedrick* [1986] 3 ALL ER 1 | The defendant had a grudge against Y and set fire to her house in the early hours of the morning. Y's child, V, died in the fire. The defendant said that his only aim was to wake Y up and frighten her. The court held that a virtually certain consequence was sufficient in order for a jury to find that D intended the result. |
| *Woollin* [1999] 1 AC 82 HL | In this case the D was frustrated by his baby's continual crying and threw the child against the wall. The child died of head injuries. The court affirmed the decision in *Nedrick* and held that a jury was entitled to infer intention of the basis that the consequences of D's actions were virtually certain. |

The case of *Woollin* is therefore the leading case in relation to intention now.

These cases can be summarised in the following timeline:

| *Hyam* [1974] 2 All ER 41 | *Moloney* [1985] AC 905 | *Hancock and Shankland* [1986] AC 455 | *Nedrick* [1986] 3 All ER 1 | *Woollin* [1999] 1 AC 82 |

From these cases we can identify intention as having developed from:

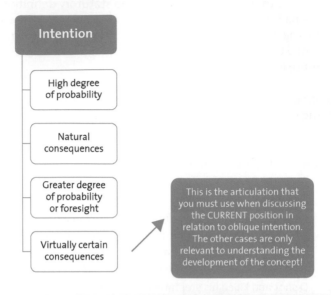

Intention

- High degree of probability
- Natural consequences
- Greater degree of probability or foresight
- Virtually certain consequences

This is the articulation that you must use when discussing the CURRENT position in relation to oblique intention. The other cases are only relevant to understanding the development of the concept!

---

**Case precedent – *R v Woollin* [1998] 3 WLR 382**

**Facts:** D threw his baby in exasperation when it wouldn't stop crying. The baby died from head injuries. It was accepted that the defendant did not intend to cause harm to the child.

**Principle:** Oblique intention

**Application:** His conviction for murder was upheld by the Court of Appeal, and his appeal was allowed by the House of Lords. It was found that the appropriate test for oblique intention was that formulated in *Nedrick*, and that this should have been applied to this case.

---

A jury may find that a defendant intended an outcome if it was a **virtually certain consequence** of his actions and he realised this was the case.

## Aim Higher

It is important to note that foresight of a virtual certainty is evidence of intention upon which a jury MAY infer intention. A judge should not equate foresight of a virtual certainty with intention. They are not one and the same.

In *Matthews and Alleyne* [2003] EWCA Crim 192, the Court of Appeal found that foresight of virtual certainty is evidence of intention, in which a jury may infer intention. They are under no obligation to do so.

So we can see the continued further refinement of the meaning of oblique intention here. This is a useful case to use in an assignment relating to intention and the evolution of law.

In the next section we are going to consider recklessness. Given that the meaning of intention clearly includes foresight of a virtual certainty a good starting position for understanding recklessness is to view it as a situation in which D has foresight of harm that falls bellow 'virtual certainty'.

# Recklessness

The term recklessness refers to the situation in which a defendant takes a risk which is unjustifiable.

Historically the courts have accepted two species of recklessness:

1. Subjective recklessness
2. Objective recklessness

What is interesting about recklessness is that the courts appear to have gone full circle in terms of which form of recklessness should be applicable in English criminal law.

## The recklessness full circle

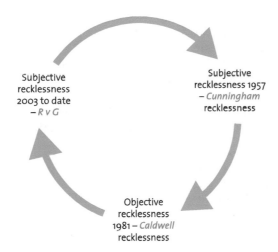

Subjective
recklessness
2003 to date
– *R v G*

Subjective
recklessness 1957
– *Cunningham*
recklessness

Objective
recklessness
1981 – *Caldwell*
recklessness

The two tests which are used to determine subjective and objective recklessness are:

| Subjective test | Objective test |
| --- | --- |
| • Proof that D is aware of, or foresees the risk of harm | • Proof that the reasonable man would have foreseen the risk of harm |
| • The taking of the risk is not justifiable | • The taking of the risk is not justifiable |

The leading case law with regard to the subjective test for recklessness is the case of *Cunningham*.

**Case precedent – *Cunningham* [1957] 2 All ER 412**

**Facts:** Cunningham stole his mother-in-law's gas meter from the basement of the house because it contained cash. However, the gas was still turned on, and she was badly hurt as a result of inhaling the gas. He was charged with maliciously administering a noxious substance so as to endanger life. The *mens rea* for this offence is recklessness.

**Principle:** Subjective recklessness.

**Application:** If D had foreseen the risk of harm caused by ripping out the gas meter and gone on to take the risk nonetheless then D was subjectively reckless if the taking of the risk was unjustifiable.

In 1981 the House of Lords introduced an objective form of recklessness in the case of *Caldwell*. It was held that a defendant need not subjectively recognise the risk of harm in order to be reckless. If the reasonably prudent bystander would have foreseen the risk of harm then this was sufficient to establish liability.

The difficulty with this objective test was that it operated particularly harshly in relation to individuals who were unable through age or infirmity to recognise the risk of potential harm. An illustration of the harsh operation of the test can be seen in the case of *Elliot v C (a minor)* (1983).

In *G and another* (2003) the House of Lords overruled *Caldwell* and restored the subjective test for recklessness. You can see the timeline of cases in the diagram below:

| Cunningham (1957) 2 QB 396 | Caldwell [1981] 2 WLR 509 | Lawrence [1981] AC 510 | R v G & R [2003] 3 WLR |

In *R v G and another* (2003) their Lordships agreed that 'reckless' in criminal damage bears the subjective meaning defined by the Law Commission in its Report, *A Criminal Code for England and Wales Volume 1: Report and Draft Criminal Code Bill* (Law Comm. No 177, 1989). That definition was:

*A person acts recklessly within the meaning of section 1 of the Criminal Damage Act 1971 with respect to –*

*(i) a circumstance when he is aware of a risk that it exists or will exist;*

*(ii) a result when he is aware of a risk that it will occur;*

*and it is, in the circumstances known to him, unreasonable to take the risk.*

# Transferred malice

In circumstances where a defendant has the *mens rea* to commit a particular crime but the actual victim differs from the intended victim the defendant does not escape liability. The doctrine of transferred malice operates to ensure that a defendant cannot escape liability on the basis that the actual victim differs from the intended victim: *Latimer* (1886).

**Example**: Sue hates Yusuf and decides to kill him. She tries to shoot Yusuf, but misses and shoots Ralph. Is Sue liable for the death of Ralph?

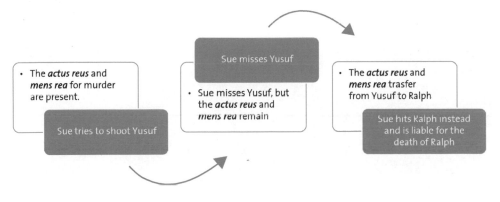

- The *actus reus* and *mens rea* for murder are present.

Sue tries to shoot Yusuf

Sue misses Yusuf

- Sue misses Yusuf, but the *actus reus* and *mens rea* remain

- The *actus reus* and *mens rea* trasfer from Yusuf to Ralph

Sue hits Ralph instead and is liable for the death of Ralph

## Case precedent – *Latimer* [1886] 17 QBD 359

**Facts:** D aimed a blow at another person's head. The blow missed the intended victim and hit another person instead.

**Principle:** Transferred malice

**Application:** The *mens rea* of this offence remains the same, transferring from the intended victim to the other person. Therefore the *mens rea* remains as recklessness.

It is important to remember that the *mens rea* transfers exactly in the doctrine of transferred malice. The importance of this can be seen in the case of *Pembliton* (1874). In this case D threw a stone at V, but missed and the stone broke a window instead.

The *mens rea* was intention or recklessness but for an offence against a person, not against property.

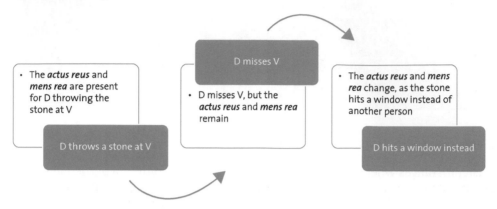

In *Pembliton* (1874) the jury found that the defendant's intention was to hit a person not property and therefore D was not liable.

Look at this case again – what would have happened if a piece of stone flew off and injured B (not the intended victim)? In this case, it *would* constitute transferred malice, as the *actus reus* and *mens rea* are the same, but is transferred from V to B.

## Common Pitfall

When applying transferred malice be careful to ensure that the *mens rea* transfers completely and in the same form.

For example, the *mens rea* cannot transfer if the subsequent offence is different from the intended offence.

In the next section we will consider offences for which *mens rea* is not required in respect to at least one aspect of the *actus reus*. These offences are called strict liability offences.

# Strict liability

What is key about these strict liability offences is that the defendnt can be convicted even where he or she was unaware of the circumstances. It is important to note that these offences are controversial in nature. As they run counter to the general principle pervading the criminal law that it is the defendant's culpability that justifies the imposition of a criminal sanction.

Strict liability offences are normally created by statutes and it is fair to say that they relate to criminal offences which are less serious in nature than the majority of offences that we are considering together in this book. Strict liability offences are most commonly used for regulatory offences, or in relation to health and safety.

In order to be convicted of a strict liability offence the defendant need not have intended, or known about the circumstances or consequence of the act. This means that if the person has committed the act, then they are legally responsible, whatever the circumstances – whatever their mental state. The defendant can then be convicted without the need for the prosecution to demonstrate intention, knowledge, recklessness or negligence.

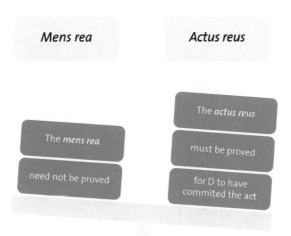

## Up for Debate

Strict liability offences are controversial, not least because they are inconsistent with the general ethos of culpability. You will find that there are many articles that focus on this critical debate. Given the nature of strict liability offences and that their focus tends to be regulatory in nature it is more likely that an examiner will set an essay question on this topic. This means that you will need to demonstrate critical understanding of the arguments for and against the use of strict liability offences. Irrespective of your position one thing is for certain: the government are increasing creating strict liability offences. For example HMRC (Her Majesty's Revenue and Customs) in 2014 announced its intention to introduce a strict liability offence of failing to disclose offshore taxable income.

**Example:** Tony sells cigarettes to Laura, who is 14 years old (under the legal age to buy cigarettes). Strict liability would apply in the following way:

In another example, Zena is late for an appointment and speeds in her car along the motorway. Strict liability would apply in the following way:

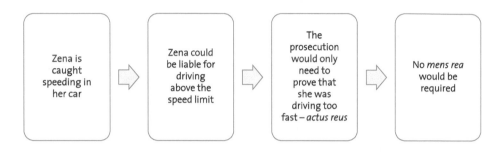

There are a number of useful cases which can be applied when assessing whether an act is classified as strict liability. For example:

| Case precedent – *Alphacell v Woodward* [1972] AC 824 |
|---|

**Facts:** D's factory waste pipe became blocked, and pollutants from the factory entered the local river, polluting the water.

**Principle:** Strict liability offences do not require proof of *mens rea* or negligence.

**Application:** D was liable under strict liability because the waste from the factory was the pollutant, despite D not being negligent.

The case of *Gammon v AG* (1985) laid down a set of useful criteria regarding whether or not an offence should be deemed strict. These criteria include:

1. The crime is regulatory as opposed to a true crime; or
2. The crime is one of social concern; or
3. The wording of the Act indicates strict liability; or
4. The offence carries a small penalty.

Strict liability is also often criticised for producing unfair and harsh outcomes. This was highlighted in the case of *Pharmaceutical Society of Great Britain v Storkwain*

(1986). In this case pharmacist provided drugs to a person who had forged the prescription. The pharmacist did not know that the prescription was forged, but was on the basis prosecuted strict liability for providing the drugs to the person. Only the act of providing the drugs had to be established.

## Aim Higher

Strict liability offences can be justified as they provide a greater level of protection and safety to the public; and because the *mens rea* does not need to be proved, a conviction may be more likely.

## A summary of the points we have covered in this section is:

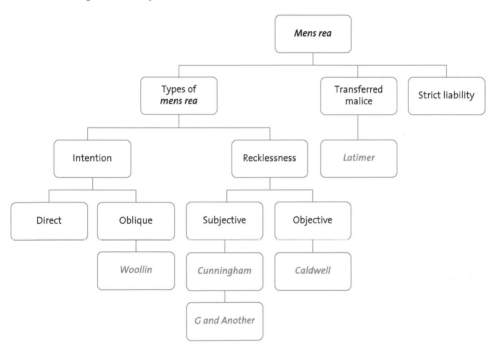

# Absence of defence

Chapter 1. That being the formula for constructing criminal liability involves: *actus reus + mens rea +* the absence of a defence + criminal liability. Therefore is D commits and criminal offence and is able to demonstrate the existence of a valid defence then D will not be held criminally liable.

On the other hand if the D has the committed the *actus reus* of an offence with the requisite *mens rea* but fails to put forward a defence they will held liable for their conduct.

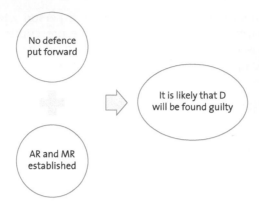

General defences are considered in much more detail later on in this book in Chapter 10 and Chapter 11.

# Putting it into practice

To aid your understanding of *mens rea*, and intention in particular, plan how you would answer the following question. Remember to include case law to illustrate your answer.

'Intention must always be proven in the case of serious offences.'

## Suggested solution

You should always adopt a structured response to an essay question rather than writing down everything that you know in no particular order!

1.  Introduction
2.  Main body
3.  Conclusion

This question is asking you to consider two separate issues:

1.  What is intention – what does it mean?
2.  Whether anything less than intention can suffice in the case of serious criminal offences.

In relation to part 1, you will need to explain the following:

❖   that there is no statutory definition of intention;
❖   intention means – aim, purpose desire;
❖   it also has a broader meaning – explain the difference between direct and oblique intention;
❖   you should provide an explanation of the historical development of the concept of oblique intention;
❖   you must explain the leading case of *Woollin* and recent refinements such as the case of *Matthews* and *Alleyne*.

In relation to part 2 you will need to consider:

❖ any historic blurring between the test for oblique intention and recklessness;
❖ where intention ends and recklessness begins;
❖ what is meant by the term recklessness: subjective and objective recklessness;
❖ whether intention should include foresight of a virtual certainty;
❖ the most serious criminal offences require proof of intention – however, there are still some very serious offences that can be committed where there is proof of recklessness – subjective reckless manslaughter, for example.

# Table of key cases referred to in this chapter

| Key case | Brief facts | Principle |
|---|---|---|
| *Fagan v MPC* [1968] 3 All ER 442 | D omitted to act by driving off the policeman's foot | Omissions |
| *DPP v Santana-Bermudez* [2003] EWHC 2908 (Admin) | D created danger by failing to tell the policeman about the needle in his pocket | Omissions |
| *Pittwood* [1902] TLR 37 | Omission under D's duty to act, under his employment contract | Omissions |
| *R v Quick & Paddison* [1973] 3 AFR 397 | Automatism is a possible defence for actions | Voluntariness |
| *Pagett* [1983] 76 Cr App R 279 | D caused the death of V, even though D did not directly kill V himself | Legal causation |
| *R v Jordan* [1956] 40 CR App R 152 | D stabbed V, but V died from poor treatment at the hospital, rather than the injuries | Legal causation |
| *R v Cheshire* [1991] 3 All ER 670 | D shot V. V died of complications from the gunshot wound. | Legal causation |
| *Blaue* [1975] 1WLR 1411 | D stabbed V, V refused treatment on religious grounds. D liable for the death of V | Thin skull rule |
| *Hyam* [1974] 2 ALL ER 41 | D set fire to a house, causing the death of two children | Intention |
| *Moloney* [1985] AC 905 | D shot his father, but was unaware that the gun was pointing at him | Intention |
| *Hancock and Shankland* [1986] AC 455 | Two miners threw a concrete brick from a bridge. Their intention was to stop the car, not cause injury. | Intention |

| Key case | Brief facts | Principle |
|---|---|---|
| *Nedrick* [1986] 3 ALL ER 1 | D set fire to V's house, killing V. Intention was present. | Intention |
| *Woollin* [1998] 3 WLR 382 | D threw his crying baby, who died. However, D did not intend to harm the child. | Intention |
| *Cunningham* [1957] 2 QB 396 | D took a gas meter off the wall, poisoning his mother-in-law | Subjective recklessness |
| *Caldwell* [1981] 2 WLR 509 | House of Lords refined the meaning of recklessness into objective recklessness | *Caldwell* (objective) recklessness |
| *Lawrence* [1981] AC 510 | House of Lords refined the meaning of recklessness into objective recklessness | *Caldwell* (objective) recklessness |
| *R v R & G* [2003] 3 WLR | Two boys started a fire in a bin, which spread to a shop | Subjective recklessness |
| *Latimer* [1886] 17 QBD 359 | D tried to hit A, missed and hit B instead | Transferred malice |
| *Pembliton* [1874] LR CCR 119 | D threw a stone at V, missed and hit a window instead | Transferred malice |
| *Alphacell v Woodward* [1972] AC 824 | Pollutants from D's factory entered a river course | Strict liability |
| *Sweet v Parsley* [1969] AC 132 | Landlady not convicted because she did not intend her house to be used for drug taking | Strict liability |
| *Gammon v AG* [1985] AC 1 | Identified criteria for determining strict liability | Strict liability |
| *Pharmaceutical Society of GB v Storkwain* [1986] 2 ALL ER 265 | When strict liability can lead to an injustice | Strict liability |

---

@ **Visit the book's companion website to test your knowledge**

❖ Resources include a subject map, revision tip podcasts, downloadable diagrams, MCQ quizzes for each chapter, and a flashcard glossary

❖ www.routledge.com/cw/optimizelawrevision

# 3

# Non-fatal Offences Against the Person

## Understand the law

- Can you define each of the offences in this chapter?
- Which offences in this chapter are common law offences, and which are statutory offences outlined in the OAPA 1861?

## Remember the details

- Can you remember the *actus reus* and *mens rea* of each offence?
- Can you define each element of the *actus reus* and *mens rea* using case law examples?

## Reflect critically on areas of debate

- Do you understand how consent may operate as a defence to an offence in this chapter?
- Can you define intention and recklessness accurately and critically discuss them in relation to case law examples?

## Contextualise

- Can you relate these offences to other areas of criminal law such as sexual offences and homicide?

## Apply your skills and knowledge

- Can you complete the example essay and problem questions provided in each section of this chapter using case law and statutes to support your answer?

# Chapter Map

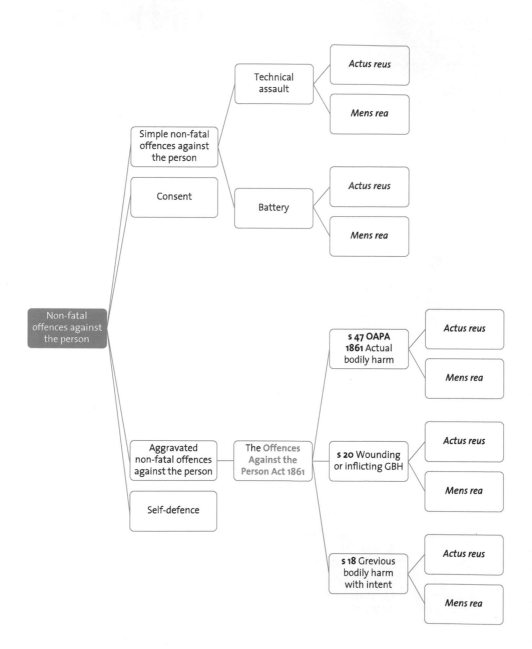

# Elements Chart

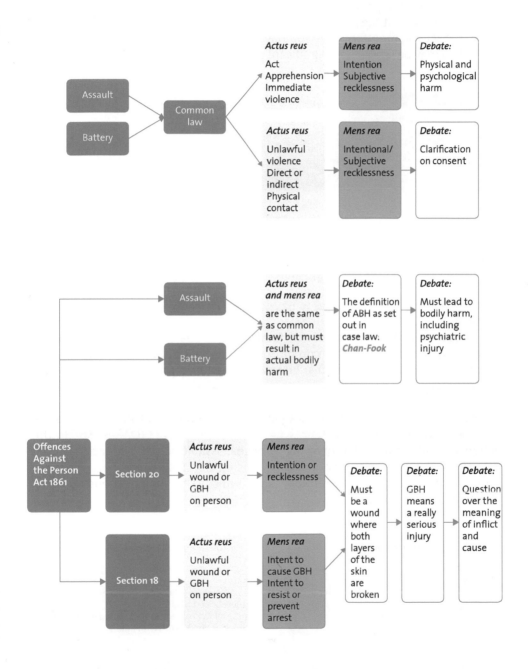

# Introduction

In this chapter we are going to consider non-fatal offences against the person. This is a popular examination topic in its own right, but issues in relation to non-fatal offences against the person can overlap with sexual offences, property offences and homicide against the person. This is another area of the criminal law syllabus in which is it vitally important that you have a solid understanding of because this area of law may be related to a significant proportion of your studies.

## Aim Higher

As you progress through this chapter, think about how these non-fatal offences relate to other criminal offences, such as homicide, sexual offences or property offences. This will help your understanding of these and other offences, and how they interact.

In this chapter we will start by considering the least serious offences against the person and at the end we will consider the most serious offences against the person. A traditional classification for non-fatal offences against the person is to classify them as 'simple offences' and 'aggravated offences'.

## Simple non-fatal offences and aggravated offences against the person

We will start our consideration of non-fatal offences against the person by considering offences created under the common law. These non-fatal offences against the person are common law offences; however, they are charged under s 39 of the Criminal Justice Act (CJA) 1988.

The more serious non-fatal offences against the person are statutory offences and they are provided for in the Offences Against the Person Act (OAPA) 1861. In this section we will consider the following offences: assault occasioning actual bodily harm (ABH) (s 47), malicious wounding or causing GBH (s 20) and finally malicious wounding or causing GBH with intent (s 18), which is the most serious non-fatal offence against the person.

| Common law | Offences Against the Person Act 1861 |
|---|---|
| • Technical assault<br>• Battery<br>• Charged under s 39 Criminal Justice Act 1988 | • s 47 OAPA 1861 Assault occasioning actual bodily harm<br>• s 20 OAPA 1861 Malicious wounding or causing grievous bodily harm<br>• s 18 OAPA 1861 Malicious wounding or causing grievous bodily harm with intent |

We will look at each of the offences in turn. As you read through this chapter, it is important to be clear about the differences between the simple common law offences and the statutory aggravated offences created by the OAPA 1861.

# Simple non-fatal offences against the person

## Introduction

Before we start this section we need to issue you with words of warnings: criminal law students and the media often use the term 'assault' rather loosely, and it is important that you use language with precision. The term assault is an umbrella term, and it is frequently used to describe:

❖ a technical assault or 'psychic assault'
❖ a battery.

We would encourage you to identify the specific offences – and rather than using the term 'assault', demonstrate to the examiner that you are aware that there are two distinct offences that fall under this umbrella term.

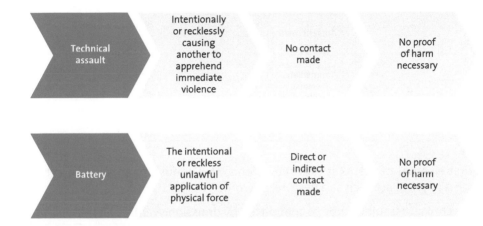

## Section 39 Criminal Justice Act 1988

Although the offences of technical assault and battery are common law offences they are charged under s 39 of the CJA 1988. Section 39 provides that these offences are summary offences and upon conviction a person is liable for a level 5 fine and a maximum term of imprisonment of six months.

## Technical assault

This offence is a common law offence and as such, the definition of the offence is not located in the statute books. The case of *Collins v Wilcock* (1984) 3 All ER 374 provides a definition for the two offences:

> The law draws a distinction ... between an assault and battery. **An assault is an act which causes another person to apprehend the infliction of immediate unlawful force on his person**; a battery is the actual infliction of unlawful force on another person.

We will now identify the elements of the *actus reus* (AR) and *mens rea* (MR) for the offence of technical assault.

You must remember that it is vital that you split the definition of each offence into the AR and MR and that you deal with each of these elements individually.

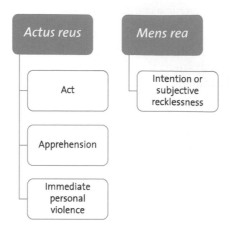

## D does an Act

The first element of the AR is that the defendant (D) must do an act. The act can include a physical act such as a gesture, or words.

❖ A technical assault cannot be committed by omission: *Fagan v Metropolitan Police Commissioner* (1968). We considered this case in Chapter 2 on General Principles of Criminal Law. In this case D's refusal to move his car off the police officer's foot was considered a continuing act.

## Up for Debate

In order for the offence of technical assault to be made out the D must have done an act. This means an act, rather than an omission: *Fagan v MPC* (1969). However, in *DPP v Santana-Bermudez* (2003), the Divisional Court stated:

> 'where someone (by act or word or a combination of the two) creates a danger and thereby exposes another to a reasonably foreseeable risk of injury which materialises, there is an evidential basis for the actus reus of an assault occasioning actual bodily harm.'

Thus there are situations in which a failure to act will be deemed sufficient – primarily where the D creates a dangerous situation.

❖ An act can also refer to other types of action. This means that the threat does not need to be a purely physical act. It can be committed by words.

---

#### Case precedent – *Constanza* [1997] Crim LR 576

**Facts:** D sent two threatening letters, made numerous silent phone calls, wrote offensive words on Vs front door and regularly followed her home. This led to V suffering clinical depression.

**Principle:** The Court of Appeal held that letters and words could amount to an act for the purposes of a technical assault.

**Application:** Use this case to illustrate that words alone, written or verbal, are sufficient to constitute an act for the purposes of a technical assault.

---

It is important to note that words can also negate a technical assault which may otherwise occur. For example in *Tuberville v Savage* (1669) it was held that words can also indicate that an act will not occur.

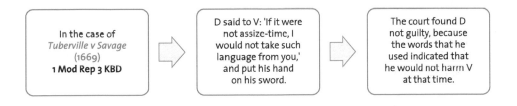

The *actus reus* of the technical assault also requires that V **apprehend immediate unlawful force**.

## D causes V to apprehend immediate unlawful force

As in any area of law, whenever you identify what the law is, you need to make sure you break it down into its constituent parts and define it. In this case, the act of common law assault is when V:

But what do each of these mean? Some elements seem obvious, but others need further clarification (such as 'immediate'). The only way that some words can be fully understood is through examining the refinement of the terms through case law.

## Aim Higher

You will gain extra marks by using case law to provide authority for your articulation of the law. Using case law demonstrates your level of knowledge to the examiner, and strengthens the point you are making.

The case precedents in this textbook are not the ONLY precedents to illustrate points of law though, and it is possible to have different cases illustrating the same point of law!

Distinguishing apprehension from fear

For the *actus reus* of assault, the requirement is that V must **apprehend** immediate personal violence.

## Common Pitfalls

Be careful here, as there is a common mistake that is made by many – this is not about being in fear; instead V must '*apprehend*' the violence immediately.

When looking at a problem question, you must be clear that V has actually **apprehended** the violence.

**Example:** If D swings a baseball bat towards V, then V will probably see it as it is being swung and apprehend immediate unlawful personal violence. Apprehension is not necessarily the same thing as fear, though!

The apprehension of violence does not need to be apprehension of significant violence: it can be trivial but it does need to be unwanted, and therefore unlawful.

In this example, Nigel shouting at Moe and saying that he wants to fight him is the act that leads Moe to apprehend the violence. Moe rolling up his sleeves and walking towards Nigel further evidences this.

However, if we manipulate the facts of the example and Nigel now sees Moe whilst Nigel is a passenger on a train that is moving, it is obvious that Moe cannot use force against Nigel in this situation. Therefore there is no apprehension of immediate unlawful force and there is no technical assault.

### Immediate

The apprehension must be of immediate unlawful force. The immediacy of the force is important, because it is directly related to V apprehending and/or experiencing the force. If the violence is not immediate, then the *actus reus* cannot be made out.

The term immediate does not mean instantaneous; it means imminent: *Smith v Chief Superintendent of Woking Police Station* (1983).

The next question considers how immediate the threat of violence must be. Let us work through an example, which you can then reapply to a problem question.

Sally tells her neighbour, Holly, that if she does not keep her garden tidy, she is going to give her 'a slap' in a fortnight. Has Sally committed a technical assault?

There are various issues arising here:

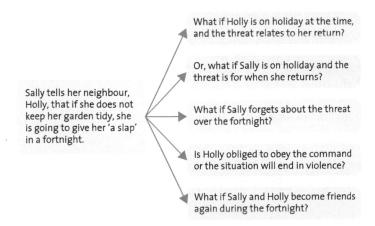

We can see from this diagram that there are many variables, all arising from the lack of immediacy. From these, we can see that immediacy is missing from this scenario.

This is a useful way to analyse a scenario within a problem question or exam, by determining how 'immediate' the unlawful violence would be, and if the period is short enough or imminent enough for apprehension to occur.

### Unlawful force
The force which D is threatening must be unlawful. This simply means that the offence of technical assault will not be made out where the threatened force is lawful. We will consider the concept of when force is lawful or unlawful in more detail later in this chapter.

We are now going to move on to consider the *mens rea* for the offence of technical assault.

## Intention or subjective recklessness
We considered the concepts of intention and subjective recklessness in Chapter 2. Technical assault is a crime of basic intent. This means that intention or proof of recklessness will suffice.

**Intention:** This is where it is D's aim, purpose or desire to bring about a particular consequence. A jury or magistrates are also entitled to infer intention on the basis that D foresaw the consequences of his actions as virtually certain.

**Subjective recklessness:** The test for subjective recklessness was articulated in the case of *Cunningham*. It provides that D is reckless where he foresees the risk of harm and goes on to take that risk. The risk is an unjustifiable risk.

Another relevant case regarding recklessness is *R v Spratt* (1991). In this case, D was shooting an air rifle at a target, but shot a young girl, who he did not know was there. The Court found D not guilty, because he did not act intentionally or recklessly.

**Example:** Roger and Jane have an argument and Roger walks up and down the road looking for Jane, intending to frighten her into agreeing with his viewpoint by pointing a gun at her.

We can see from this example that the aim, purpose or desire of Roger's actions is to frighten Jane.

If this was a problem question, think about how you would establish that Roger has committed the offence of technical assault.

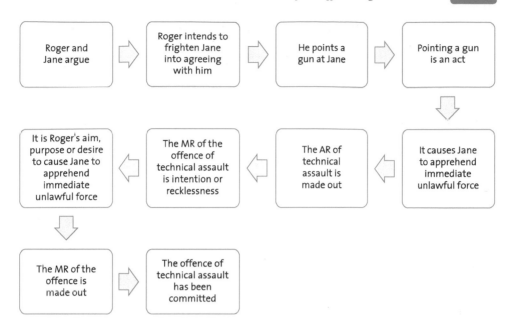

We are now going to consider the second simple non-fatal offence against the person: Battery.

## Battery

As you will recall from the introduction to simple non-fatal offences against the person, this offence is a common law offence. As such the definition of the offence is located in the decisions of the courts and not in the statute books.

We return again to the case of *Collins v Wilcock* (1984), which provides a definition for the two offences:

> The law draws a distinction ... between an assault and battery. An assault is an act which causes another person to apprehend the infliction of immediate unlawful force on his person; **a battery is the actual infliction of unlawful force on another person.**

Thus the offence of battery requires the infliction of unlawful force on another person. As with technical assault, make sure that you discuss and define the meaning of the words. For example, a discussion of 'infliction' would be essential when considering the offence and liability.

Reminder – the *actus reus* and *mens rea* for common law battery are:

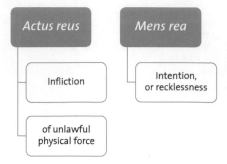

## Infliction

The *actus reus* requires the infliction of physical force. We must therefore understand what is meant by the term infliction.

❖ The slightest application of physical force may amount to an infliction.
❖ This includes the touching of a victim's clothing: *Thomas* (1985).
❖ The application of force will often involve direct contact and touching between D and V. However, this is not a requirement because the contact can also be indirect. For example:

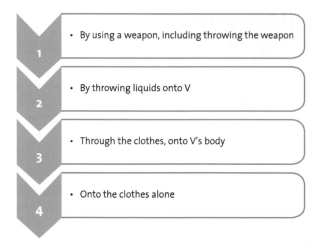

The courts have also taken a view, as with technical assault, that the infliction must require some positive action and not an omission. This was highlighted in the case of *Innes v Wylie* (1844), where a policeman blocked the path of a defendant. The judge held that battery should be a positive act, rather than inaction. Therefore the defendant must have done some act in order for it to be constituted as a battery.

## Aim Higher

Contrast the cases of *Santana-Bermudez* (2004) and *Miller* (1983) to consider omissions within these cases.

Both cases are particularly important in relation to omissions, and are extremely useful cases when answering a problem question on battery.

**Example:** Nora pokes Shaun with a sharp pencil. From the discussion above, would you argue that this is direct or indirect force? Why is this? Which cases can you use to support your argument?

❖ There is no requirement that the touching is hostile: *Wilson v Pringle* (1986).
❖ A battery may include a continuing act as per the case of *Fagan*.
❖ The application of physical force need not be a direct application of force; it can be achieved indirectly: *DPP v K* (1990).

---

**Case precedent – *DPP v K* [1997] 1 ALL ER 331**

**Facts:** A young boy put acid from the school science lab into a hand drier in the toilet block. The acid caused harm to another child when he operated the drier.

**Principle:** D was found guilty, and the judge noted that for battery, force need not be directly applied.

**Application:** The application of force need not be direct.

---

The second element of the AR is that the infliction of physical force must be unlawful

## The physical force must be unlawful
In order to construct liability for battery the prosecution must be able to establish that the application of physical force was *unlawful*. So, there is no battery where:

---

V expressly or impliedly consents to the touching and has the capacity to consent

| Consent can be provided throughout everyday life | For example shaking hands, moving past someone or giving someone a hug |

D has an excuse for inflicting physical force, or genuinely believes that he has a lawful justification

| For example he acts in self-defence or to prevent a crime from taking place | Action is a parent reasonably chastising a child |

This can of course provide problems for the court in terms of when such actions can be classed as unlawful, for example everyday actions where people touch another, such as walking down a busy street or shaking hands with a client.

When answering a problem question on simple offences against the person check the type of unlawful touching which has occurred, and if it can actually constitute everyday activity. If so, it is unlikely that this would constitute unlawful personal violence.

Other factors that you might want to take into consideration include the proximity of the touching and the degree of physical force used. For example:

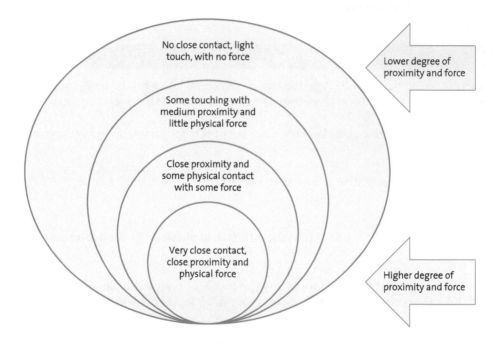

The higher the degree of proximity and the greater the degree of force the more likely it will be unlawful.

As with common law assault, the rule on omissions is the same in relation to battery as it is for technical assault. The offence cannot be committed by omission. It is possible for psychiatric injury to constitute a battery.

**Case precedent – *R v Ireland* [1997] 3 WLR 534**

**Facts:** D made a number of silent phone calls to women, who suffered psychological injuries as a result. The issue here was whether silent phone calls can constitute a technical assault and whether the psychological injury caused can constitute a battery.

**Principle:** Words alone and silent phone calls can amount to a technical assault; psychological injury caused by this can amount to a battery and potentially an aggravated offence.

**Application:** Use this case to illustrate that the application of force can take many forms.

## Intention or recklessness

For the *mens rea* of battery D must intend to apply unlawful force onto V, even if it does not lead to harm or injury. Intention and subjective recklessness are also considered above in relation to technical assault

For example:

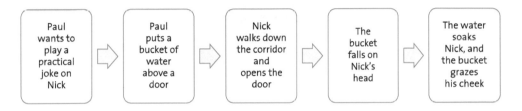

In this example, the water soaks Nick, and the bucket grazes his cheek. Paul has shown intention as it is his aim, purpose or desire that Nick gets covered in water. He is reckless as to whether force will be applied in other ways (through the bucket hitting Nick).

A useful case to help explain recklessness in relation to battery is *R v Venna* (1975). In this case, D resisted arrest by a policeman, and in so doing broke a bone in the policeman's hand. D argued that he did not intend to harm the policeman. The Court found D guilty as he was subjectively reckles as to whether the police officer would be injured.

## Activity 1

**Using case law to support your answer, attempt the following questions.**

(1)  Annie throws a rock at Brian, which misses him. Just after it happens, Brian is told that Annie threw the rock at him. Does this constitute an assault?

(2)  Nigel and Daphne have an argument at work. Later that evening Nigel phones Daphne and threatens to hit her. Does this constitute assault?

Using the discussion above, consider the circumstances of each question, and identify if an assault has occurred in each question.

A summary of the points we have covered in this section is:

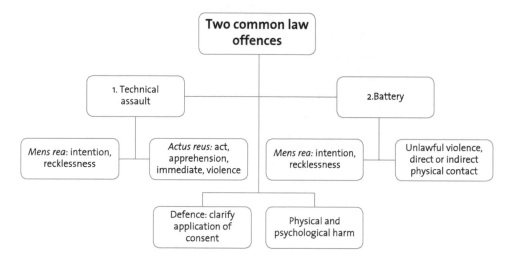

In the next section of this chapter we are going to consider aggravated offences against the person.

# Aggravated offences against the person

## Introduction

There are three aggravated offences against the person created under the **Offences Against the Person Act (OAPA) 1861**.

1. Assault occasioning actual bodily harm: s 47.
2. Maliciously wounding or inflicting grievous bodily harm: s 20.
3. Maliciously wounding or inflicting grievous bodily harm with intent: s 18.

In relation to aggravated offences it might help you to remember that the lower the section number the more serious the offence is! These offences are aggravated offences because, unlike technical assault and battery, these offences require proof of some degree of harm.

## Section 47: Assault occasioning actual bodily harm
Section 47 provides:

> Whosoever shall be convicted upon an indictment of any assault occasioning actual bodily harm shall be liable to be kept in penal servitude.

As with our discussion of all other substantive offences we must first break down the elements of the offence created by s 47.

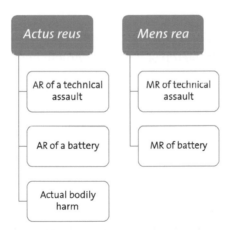

One of the most important points for you to remember (this is something that is very often overlooked) is that in order to establish liability for the s 47 offence you must be able to establish the AR and MR, or technical assault or battery AND actual bodily harm.

### *Actus reus of technical assault or battery*
We have covered these issues in detail earlier in this chapter. You should remind yourself of the constituent elements of both a technical assault and a battery.

## Occasioning actual bodily harm

You must additionally be able to demonstrate that the technical assault or battery has 'occasioned' or caused actual bodily harm.

It is important to understand the meaning of the words **actual bodily harm**, to ensure that you do not confuse this offence with the offences of battery or wounding. In this section, we will use the case of *Chan-Fook* (1994) as a basis.

In *Chan-Fook* the words actual bodily harm were defined by the judge, and are now understood as:

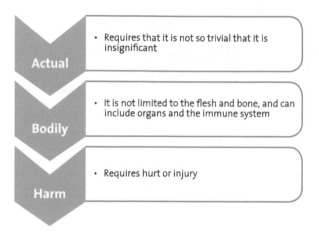

**Actual**
- Requires that it is not so trivial that it is insignificant

**Bodily**
- It is not limited to the flesh and bone, and can include organs and the immune system

**Harm**
- Requires hurt or injury

These meanings were tested in the case of *DPP v Smith* (2006), when D cut off V's ponytail and some hair off the top of her head without her consent. V became very distressed as a result. However, D was acquitted because the judge ruled that hair was above the body and consists of dead follicles. But on appeal, D was found guilty. Sir Igor Judge stated:

> In my judgment, whether it is alive beneath the surface of the skin or dead tissue above the surface of the skin, the hair is an attribute and part of the human body. It is intrinsic to each individual and to the identity of each individual. Although it is not essential to my decision, I note that an individual's hair is relevant to his or her autonomy. Some regard it as their crowning glory. Admirers may so regard it in the object of their affections. **Even if, medically and scientifically speaking, the hair above the surface of the scalp is no more than dead tissue, it remains part of the body and is attached to it.** While it is so attached, in my judgment it falls within the meaning of 'bodily' in the phrase 'actual bodily harm'. It is concerned with the body of the individual victim.
>
> In my judgment, the respondent's actions in cutting off a substantial part of the victim's hair in the course of an assault on her – like putting paint on it or some unpleasant substance which marked or damaged it without causing injury elsewhere – is capable of amounting to an assault which occasions actual bodily harm. The justices were wrong in law.
>
> *(DPP v Smith [2006] EWHC 94 Para 18)*

This case is important because it identifies that hair is considered part of the body, and its unlawful cutting is an offence. The case is summarised below, and is a useful case to remember and apply in an exam:

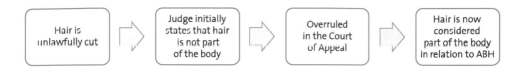

Going back to the case of *Chan-Fook* (1994), this case also highlighted that *bodily* is not limited to 'skin, flesh and bones' since the body includes organs, the nervous system and the brain, and also *psychiatric* injury.

However, 'bodily' does not include:

❖ emotions such as fear, distress or panic;
❖ states of mind which are not evidence of an identifiable clinical condition.

This definition was tested in the case of *R v D* (2006), when clarification was provided by the courts on the nature of psychiatric injury, as in the case precedent below:

### Case precedent – *R v D* [2006] EWCA Crim 1139

D's wife committed suicide, and D was charged with manslaughter and GBH. The judge ruled that the case should not proceed, as there was not a reasonable chance of conviction. The Court sought to provide a distinction between a medically diagnosed *psychological* condition and a medically diagnosed *psychiatric* condition. The court stated:

> 'The problem which we have to address is whether psychological injury, not amounting to recognisable psychiatric illness, falls within the ambit of bodily harm for the purposes of the 1861 Act. The Chan-Fook case drew a clear distinction between such identifiable injury and other states of mind. It did so consistently with authority in the civil law. The line identified in Chan-Fook was applied by the House of Lords to the criminal law, and has been consistently applied in claims for damages for personal injury' (Para 31).

Thus following *Chan-Fook* (1994), when V claims psychiatric injury as part of the harm suffered, it is essential to gain expert advice to substantiate that the injury has taken place, and is as a result of D. The *Chan-Fook* case is key in determining the meaning of ABH, and a number of cases have subsequently refined the meaning of ABH. These are described in the case law timeline below.

This timeline is really useful to remember because it tells you the three key cases regarding the definition of ABH, which you can then apply to a problem question or scenario, when discussing the relevant offence.

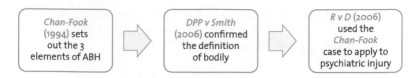

We are now going to consider the *mens rea* for the **s 47** offence.

## Intention or recklessness as to the technical assault or battery

We have already considered the meaning of both intention and recklessness in the context of technical assault and battery. We will not repeat these principles here. What is key, however, is that it is not necessary for the defendant to have had foresight that ABH would be caused: *Savage* (1992).

### Activity 2
**Look at the scenario below, and then answer the following question:**

Ali is out walking in the park with his dog. Bee and his wife Cea walk over to pat the dog. Ali, thinking Bee may be coming to attack him, instructs the dog to attack Bee. The dog bites Bee's hand, and Cea, witnessing the incident from a few yards away, becomes scared and runs off. Cea is now suffering from anxiety (due to the incident) and goes to see her doctor.

Which offences if any have been committed here?

Faced with this scenario, it is important to first break down the information, and then consider each of the non-fatal offences (NFOs) in turn.

### Aim Higher

It is not uncommon for a question on non-fatal offences against the person to include a number of different potential offences. The best strategy when you have multiple events and/or multiple parties is to deal with the parties or events in the order in which they appear in the question.

Let's try breaking this scenario down into manageable components. This can be shown diagrammatically, which is a useful way to plan your answers when dealing with a scenario or problem question within an exam:

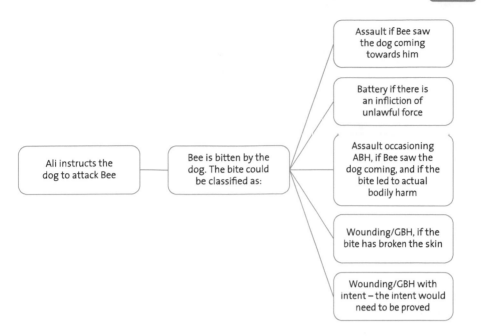

Ali instructs the dog to attack Bee → Bee is bitten by the dog. The bite could be classified as:

- Assault if Bee saw the dog coming towards him
- Battery if there is an infliction of unlawful force
- Assault occasioning ABH, if Bee saw the dog coming, and if the bite led to actual bodily harm
- Wounding/GBH, if the bite has broken the skin
- Wounding/GBH with intent – the intent would need to be proved

## Aim Higher

The examiner will be looking for a good level of detail in relation to your knowledge and application of law. You will always attract more marks where your analysis is supported by reference to authority.

Authority includes:

1. relevant cases
2. relevant statutes
3. academic opinion.

# Malicious wounding and causing grievous bodily harm

## Introduction

The **Offences Against the Person Act (OAPA) 1861** contains two offences which, on the face of it, appear very similar. They both involve the concept of grievous bodily harm. However, one offence is much more serious and this is the s 18 offence because it is committed with intent to commit grievous bodily harm.

We can see below the scale of seriousness between the two offences, and why s 18 is more serious:

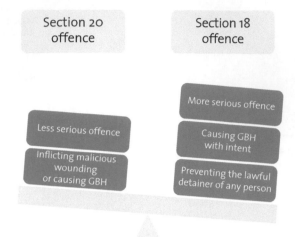

The table below outlines the two different offences. It is important to understand the full differences between them.

| Section 20 | Section 18 |
| --- | --- |
| The less serious offence, which is malicious wounding (infliction) or causing grievous bodily harm (GBH) (**Offences Against the Person Act 1861** s 20). | The second and more serious offence is causing grievous bodily harm with intent to cause grievous bodily harm or with intent to resist or prevent the lawful apprehension or detainer of any person (**Offences Against the Person Act 1861** s 18). |

### Common Pitfalls

Remember that wounding and GBH relates to **s 20** of the **OAPA 1861**, and that wounding and GBH **with intent** refers to **s 18** of the **OAPA 1861**. But, that they are separate offences.

## Section 20: wounding or inflicting GBH
Section 20 of the **OAPA 1861** provides:

Whosoever shall unlawfully and maliciously wound or inflict any grievous bodily harm upon any other person, either with or without any weapon or instrument, shall be guilty of a misdemeanour, and being convicted thereof shall be liable ... to be kept in penal servitude ...

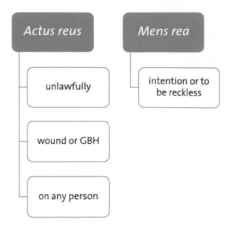

As is now our tradition we will now consider each of the elements of the s 20 offence in detail.

## Actus reus – the meaning of unlawful
An act will not be considered unlawful where it was:

| To prevent another crime | Reasonable chastisement | In self-defence |
| --- | --- | --- |
| • The act may be justified if it was taken to prevent a more serious crime | • For example, a parent using reasonable chastisement on a child | • The act may be justified if D can show that he acted in self-defence |

## Distinguishing between a wound and GBH
For both the s 20 and s 18 offences, there must be a wound or GBH arising from D's actions.

**A wound** occurs where both layers of the skin (the dermis and the epidermis) are broken.

---

**Case Quote**

For example in the case of *C (A Minor) v Eisenhower* [1983] 3 WLR 537, when an air gun pellet caused a bruise and weeping to the eye, Robert Goff LJ stated that:

> '*In my judgment, having regard to the cases, there is a continuous stream of authority – to which I myself can find no exception at all – which does establish that a wound is, as I have stated, a break in the continuity of the whole skin.*'

The outcome of the case was, therefore, that D was found not guilty, because the wound did not break both layers of the skin.

**Grevious bodily harm (GBH)** is defined as 'a really serious injury', such as a broken bone, severe bruising, missing teeth etc. This meaning was tested in the case of *Bollom* (2003).

---

**Case Quote**

In *R v Bollom* [2003] 2 Cr App R6, the defendant injured his partner's young toddler, causing bruising and grazes. He was found guilty of GBH, but appealed on the basis that the injuries were not severe enough to constitute GBH. The Court of Appeal found that the phrase should be given its ordinary and natural meaning of 'really serious bodily harm'. Thus, in the Court's view:

*'The ambit of grievous bodily harm is therefore potentially wide, as is demonstrated by the inclusion, for instance, of psychiatric injury . . . The prosecution do not have to prove that the harm was life- threatening, danger ous or permanent: R v Ashman (1858) . . . Moreover, there is no requirement in law that the victim should require treatment or that the harm should extend beyond soft tissue damage . . . or the harm would have lasting consequences.'*

---

The victim in *Bollom* was a young child. This prompted the court to further remark that, when assessing the severity and impact of injuries, other considerations such as age and health should be included.

## Examples of wounds and GBH

**Wound:** Cuts, puncture wounds including those caused by a broken bone piercing through the skin

**GBH:** Broken bones, internal injuries, pscyhiatric injury

---

**Aim Higher**

More detail on the type of injuries that will constitute:

1.  battery
2.  ABH

3.  GBH
4.  wounding

can be found in the CPS Charging Standards on the CPS website: www.cps.gov.uk/
legal/l_to_o/offences_against_the_person/

Demonstrating an understanding of how the CPS views the severity of different injuries for charging purposes will enhance the quality of an answer on offences against the person (OAP) and attract more marks from the examiner.

It is important to note that GBH can also include psychiatric injury, although this must also be sufficiently serious to be classed as GBH: *Burstow* (1997).

In *Burstow*:

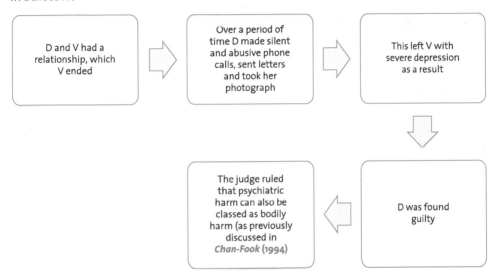

## Key Points: Offences Against the Person Act

| Offence | The injury | Examples/case law |
|---|---|---|
| Assault | There is no physical injury, but there is apprehension of violence | *Constanza* (1997) *Tuberville v Savage* (1669) *Fagan v MPC* (1969) *Cunningham* (1957) |
| Battery | A trivial injury, such as a poke or push | *R v Ireland* (1997) *DPP v K* (1990) *R v Venna* (1975) |
| ABH | Is more than trivial, and requires hurt or injury, such as a graze or bruise | *Chan-Fook* (1994) *DPP v Smith* (2006) *R v D* (2006) |

| Offence | The injury | Examples/case law |
|---------|-----------|-------------------|
| A wound | Occurs when both layers of the skin are broken – the dermis and the epidermis | *C v Eisenhower* (1983) *R v Belfon* (1976) *Savage and Parmenter* (1991) |
| GBH | Is a really serious injury, such as missing teeth or severe bruising | *Burstow* (1997) *Bollom* (2003) |

## Aim Higher

A really useful exercise when revising for a criminal law assessment is to create your own case tables. Putting examples and case law into columns can serve as a really useful quick reference resource – particularly in the last moments before you go into the examination room!

## On any person

The *actus reus* here is very straight forward, and ensures that the offence is committed against **another person**.

## Mens rea

The s 20 offence can be committed by proving that D acted intentionally or recklessly. We have considered the *mens rea* of intent and recklessness already within this chapter, and again the same principles apply here.

The defendant need not have foreseen the severity of the harm caused, but should have some foresight of harm: *Mowatt* (1968).

It is worth noting that the wording of s 20 includes the term 'maliciously'. This simply means with intention or subjective recklessness.

## Section 18: grievous bodily harm

Section 18 of the **OAPA** provides:

Whosoever shall unlawfully and maliciously by any means whatsoever wound or cause any grievous bodily harm to any person ... with intent ... to do some ... grievous bodily harm to any person, or with intent to resist or prevent the lawful apprehension or detainer of any person, shall be guilty of felony, and being convicted thereof shall be liable ... to be kept in penal servitude for life ...

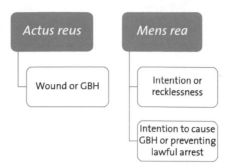

We will now consider the individual elements – although, as you will see, many of the principles that we have discussed in relation to s 20 of the OAPA are applicable here also.

## D must cause a wound or cause GBH
The first point worth noting is that s 20 uses the word 'inflict' and s 18 uses the word 'cause'. The following cases confirm that *cause* and *inflict* have the same meaning:

## D must have acted recklessly or acted with intention
The same principles in relation to intention and recklessness apply here as applied in relation to our earlier discussion of these *mens rea* elements.

However there is an important difference between the s20 and s18 offences and that is the issue of ulterior.

* The s 20 offence requires intention or recklessness as to some level of harm.
* The s 18 offence requires ulterior intention to be proved – that is in relation to an intention to cause GBH or intention to resist/prevent a lawful arrest.

We will now consider the last element of the *mens rea* for this offence.

## Ulterior intent to cause GBH or to prevent/resist a lawful arrest
In order for these criteria to be made out, D must have:

1. acted with the intent to cause GBH; or
2. intention to prevent or resist a lawful arrest.

If the ulterior intent cannot be satisfied then the s 20 offence will be applicable. A useful case to remember is *R v Belfon* (1976), which is explained below.

| Case precedent – *R v Belfon* [1976] 1 WLR 741 |
| --- |

**Facts:** D pushed a girl to the ground, and then attacked a passer-by who tried to help her. D caused very serious injuries to these people.

**Principle:** D was cleared of the s 18 offence, because it could not be shown that he had the full intent of causing GBH, and instead he was convicted of the s 20 offence.

**Application:** If the ulterior intent cannot be established and all that is in existence is an intention to cause general harm then s 20 is the appropriate offence.

## Transmission of diseases

The transmission of diseases such as sexually transmitted infections, sometimes referred to as biological injury, has become increasingly important in recent years, as the implications of sexually transmitted infections (STIs) become more apparent. The transmission of an STI can constitute a s 20 offence, where it can be demonstrated that D was reckless or acted with intention to cause some harm to V.

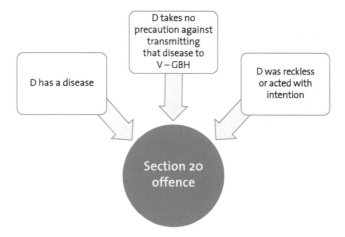

## What is intention to resist or prevent the lawful detention of any person?

A quite specific part of the *mens rea* is related to resisting or preventing the lawful detention of any person. So, for example, if D is arrested by a policeman and resists the arrest by using force, then D may have committed an offence. This can be D resisting his own arrest, or D may prevent the lawful arrest of another person.

## Aim Higher

The Law Commission is undertaking a consultation process in relation to reforming the law in relation to non-fatal offences against the person. The Act is regarded by many as being archaic and outdated. The first stage is a scoping paper, which is expected to lead to a series of recommendations, and the restructuring of the offences within the Act.

http://lawcommission.justice.gov.uk/areas/offences-against-the-person.htm

Look at the Law Commission's website to find an update on this exercise, and think about the potential impact on non-fatal offences from such an exercise.

Activity 3

Roger and Tariq are in a cafe, eating their lunch. Simon sees them through the window, and storms into the café, shouting, 'I've been looking for you, I'm going to give you a good hiding,' at Tariq. He pulls Tariq up from the chair and punches him three times in the face, breaking his nose, cutting his lip and knocking out two teeth.

Now answer these two questions, giving reasons for your answers:

1. Was the injury to Tariq a wound or GBH?
2. Was this a s 18 or a s 20 offence?

## Aim Higher

When you are writing coursework, it is important that you fully reference your work. This includes the sources that you have used – both text and internet sources – and quotations/paraphrasing. Referencing is important for all your coursework, including problem questions and scenarios, and an assessor will check your work to ensure that it is fully and properly referenced.

A summary of the points we have covered in this section is:

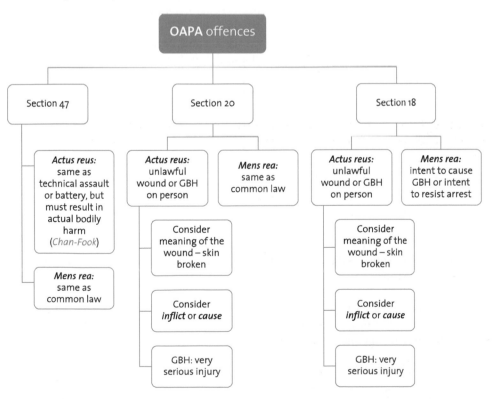

# Potential defences to non-fatal offences against the person

In this last section we are going to consider two potential defences to a non-fatal offence against the person. These defences are:

1. Consent
2. Self-defence.

You will need to understand the operation of both of these defences in relation to an allegation that the defendant has committed a non-fatal offence against the person. Once again a complete understanding of this topic necessitates understanding as to when a valid defence will negate liability.

## Consent

Consent is an important element of non-fatal offences, as it can negate the unlawfulness of the defendant's actions. Thus there are circumstances in which consent will operate as a defence to such an allegation. There will always be circumstances in which individuals will need to be able to consent to varying levels of physical harm. For example:

* tattooing
* contact sports
* surgical operations.

All of these activities and many more involve the defendant suffering a varying level of harm (in some cases a potentially very serious level of harm). However, these activities are considered 'lawful' activities and as such, irrespective of the severity of the harm inflicted, consent will operate as a valid defence. The law does not, however, deem all activities that an individual can consent to lawful and we will now consider two key cases that underscore the importance of the activity being deemed 'lawful' if the defence is to succeed.

---

### Case precedent – *Brown* [1993] 2 All ER 75

**Facts:** D undertook sadomasochistic practices at home, in private with the consent of others. The actions included acts of extreme violence, often to V's genitals, to gain pleasure. Brown was charged with assault and ABH, and found guilty. The trial and appeal judges upheld the conviction, dismissing the defence that V consented.

**Principle:** Sadomasochistic activity was not a lawful activity and as such consent was no defence. The court held that consent could only be a defence to activity that did not cause bodily harm.

**Application:** This case can be applied to demonstrate that not all consensual activities are lawful ones. It can also be used to illustrate the distinction between offences that cause bodily harm and those that do not.

In the case of *Wilson* (1996) the Court of Appeal held that the case of *Brown* did not apply where a husband branded his name on his wife with a red-hot knife. This created some blurring of the boundaries of the law and some argued that this meant that sadomasochistic activity between a husband and wife would not give rise to prosecution. This question was put to rest in the case of *Emmett* (1999).

## Key principles in relation to valid consent

❖ The victim must understand what s/he is consenting to: *Burrell v Harmer* (1967).
❖ We are all deemed to consent to low-level contacts with other people that come about as part of our everyday lives – for example as a result of standing on a crowded underground train or bus: *Wilson v Pringle* (1986).
❖ In the context of a contact sport it is presumed that the participants consent to a normal degree of contact and contact that is clumsy or misjudged. However, where a player deliberately inflicts harm they will not be able to argue the defence of consent: *Barnes* (2005).

### Aim Higher

An excellent example of this principle was seen very recently in the 2014 football World Cup in Brazil, where in the midst of a match one player was alleged to have bitten a player on the opposing team. Whilst all participants in the match would be deemed to have consented to a certain level of contact, even those tackles that are the result of a late decision or poor judgement, it is impossible to argue that football players consent to being bitten while on the pitch. Thus were this incident to have occurred in England the player in question would not have been able to argue consent as a defence and could have been charged with a criminal offence – some might argue 'and quite rightly so'!

### Aim Higher

Defences against offences, including non-fatal offences, are a basis for academic debate across many areas, particularly consent.

A useful article for further reading on consent in particular is Elliot and de Than, 'The case for a rational reconstruction of consent in criminal law', *Modern Law Review* (2007), pages 229–49.

We are now going to consider self-defence.

## Self-defence

Self-defence is a justificatory defence in which D uses force against V in order to protect:

* himself;
* another; OR
* property.

Additionally, D can use reasonable force when attempting to prevent the commission of a crime: s 3(1) **Criminal Law Act 1967**.

The ingredients of the defence are as follows:

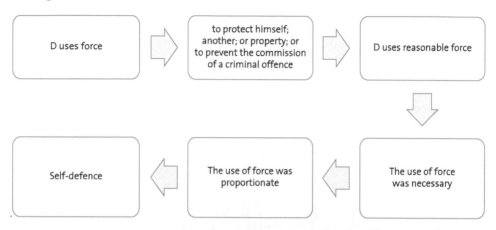

## In what circumstances can force be used?

Self-defence originated as a common law defence, but it has been put on a statutory footing under the **Criminal Justice and Immigration Act 2008**. Section 76 leaves the common law framework of the defence intact. It provides that self-defence and use of reasonable force are defences in the following circumstances:

* to protect oneself;
* to protect another;
* to protect property;
* to prevent the commission of a criminal offence;
* to assist in the apprehension of a person at large.

## The use of force must be reasonable

There are two separate components to this requirement. The first is that the use of force must be necessary; the second is that the use of force must be proportionate. If D fails to meet one of these criteria, the defence fails. We will now consider each of these elements.

### The use of force was necessary (necessity test)

This is evaluated from the defendant's perspective – it is therefore a subjective test. Thus when attempting to apply this test you must ask yourself: did D believe that the use of force was necessary in the circumstances? If the answer is yes then you can proceed to the next question (the proportionality test). If the answer is no, i.e. the defendant did not believe that the use of force was necessary, then the defence fails. It does not matter that a reasonable man would have felt the use of force necessary, as the test is a subjective one.

In the event that the defendant makes a mistake and believes mistakenly that the use of force is necessary, the defence does not automatically fail. The question is: did the defendant honestly believe that force was necessary? If the answer to this question is yes, the defence may still succeed: *Williams* (1987). There is an important limitation to a mistaken belief that the use of force was necessary, and that is where the defendant has voluntarily become intoxicated. In these circumstances, where the mistake is induced by the consumption of drugs or alcohol, the defence will fail: *O'Grady* (1987). There are clearly good policy reasons for this limitation.

### The use of force was proportionate (proportionality test)

If it is established that the use of force was necessary, the next test that must be passed is that the degree of force used was in the circumstances proportionate. If the use of force was excessive, the defence will fail. In relation to the proportionality of the force used the following observations can be made:

* ❖ The test is an objective one. In the circumstances as D believed them to be, was the degree of force used reasonable?
* ❖ The defendant should do no more than is necessary to address the gravity of the threat.
* ❖ The defendant can use a pre-emptive strike: *Beckford* (1988).
* ❖ It is important to consider whether the defendant's actions are in response to the perceived threat, or whether they may be motivated by revenge.

> ## Aim Higher
>
> In the case of *Bird* **(1985)** a failure to retreat was held to be evidence that the defendant wanted to engage in confrontation. Although this is not an established principle of law it is worth considering the point at which the force was used. If force is used against an attacker who is unconscious on the floor this force would be unreasonable and would be evidence of revenge, not reasonable force.

# Putting it into practice

## Feedback on Activity 1

1. If Brian had no knowledge that a rock was being thrown at him by Annie, then he does not 'apprehend immediate unlawful personal violence'.
2. Yes, based on the case law of *Ireland* and the use of silent phone calls – please note though that it would depend on the proximity between D and V and whether it could be immediate.

## Feedback on Activity 2

The issues are that the dog could be classified as a weapon. If Bee sees the dog coming it could be assault (apprehension of immediate unlawful personal violence), battery, and could also be actual bodily harm (it could be more – but ABH is sufficient here). For Cea, if there was psychiatric injury we would need to find the assault or battery that would cause that (which is unlikely here as it does not say that she is apprehending immediate unlawful personal violence).

## Feedback on Activity 3

1. GBH is defined as 'really serious injury', which includes a broken nose and knocked-out teeth. This was confirmed in *Bollom* (2003) and *Wilson* (1984). This differentiates the injury from ABH or wounding, as it is very serious.
2. Section 20 requires some intention or recklessness, whereas s 18 requires intent to be proved. The main issue here is the level of intent, as indicated by the words spoken by Simon before the offence. For s 18 it would need to be proved that Simon intended to cause harm – it was his overriding purpose – and that Simon knew the consequences of his actions and the harm/injury caused. From this, we can tell whether it was a s 18 or a s 20 offence.

In both questions, you need to make reference to the *actus reus* and *mens rea* as the guides for liability of an offence – work through each step and apply it to the question.

# Table of key cases referred to in this chapter

| Case name | Area of law | Principle |
|---|---|---|
| *Bollom* [2003] 2 CR App R 6 | Type of injury and GBH | GBH is defined by the judge as 'really serious harm' |
| *Brown* [1993] 2 All ER 75 | Consent | Under the legal concept of assault and battery, the victim does not consent |
| *Burstow* [1997] 1 Cr App R 144 | No difference between inflicting and causing GBH | The judge ruled that psychiatric harm can be classed as bodily harm |
| *Chan-Fook* [1994] 1 WLR 689 | Elements of ABH | The judge defined the words 'actual bodily harm' |
| *Clarence* [1888] 22 QBD 23 | Defined the term *inflict* | Passing on a sexual disease was not 'inflicted' |
| *Constanza* [1997] Crim LR 576 | Clarification of immediate personal violence | V apprehends injury at some time, not excluding the immediate future |
| *Cunningham* [1957] 2 All ER 412 | Precedent on recklessness | D's actions were reckless, and he understood the consequences |

| *R v D* [2006] EWCA Crim 1139 | Clarification of psychiatric injury | Distinction between psychological and psychiatric condition |
|---|---|---|
| *Dica* [2004] 3 All ER 593 | Infliction and cause have the same meaning | Consent was irrelevant, as the women became infected as a result of D's actions |
| *Donovan* [1934] 25 Cr App R 1 | Consent | V consented to the harmful activity |
| *DPP v K* [1990] 1 All ER 331 | The use of force within battery | For battery, force need not be directly applied |
| *DPP v Smith* [2006] EWHC 94 | Definition of bodily | Hair is now regarded as part of the body in regard to 'bodily' |
| *Eisenhower* [1983] 3 WLR 537 | Definition of a wound | The judge defined the wound as a break in the continuity of the whole skin |
| *Fagan v MPC* [1969] 1 QB 439 | Act of assault precedent | An act rather than an omission is required |
| *Haystead v Chief Constable of Derbyshire* [2000] 3 All ER 890 | Common law offences v OAPA 1861 | The judge defined that assault and battery are common law offences |
| *Ireland* [1997] 3 WLR 543 | Act of assault | Silent phone calls constitute common law assault |
| *Konzani* [2005] All ER D 292 | Transmitted diseases | D found guilty, although the Judge agreed that D 'honestly believed' that there was consent |
| *Miller* [1954] 2 QB 282 | Definition of injury | Definition of ABH from D's actions |
| *Mowatt* [1968] 1 QB 421 | Use of the word malicious | D's actions were malicious, and this can be seen from the actions themselves |
| *Parmenter* [1991] 2 WLR 408 | Recklessness | Provides a link between the act and its consequences |
| *Savage* [1991] 94 Cr App R 193 | Recklessness | Provides a link between the act and its consequences |
| *Spratt* [1991] 1 WLR 1073 | Recklessness | D was not guilty, because it was not his intention to act recklessly |

| Case name | Area of law | Principle |
|---|---|---|
| *Tuberville v Savage* [1669] 1 Mod Rep 3 KBD | Use of words in assault | Words indicated that D would not harm V |
| *Venna* [1975] 3 All ER 788 | Recklessness | The recklessness of Ds actions caused the injury to the policeman |
| *Wilson* [1996] Crim LR 573 | Consent | Issues regarding V giving explicit consent, by an adult in their own home |

@ **Visit the book's companion website to test your knowledge**

❖ Resources include a subject map, revision tip podcasts, downloadable diagrams, MCQ quizzes for each chapter, and a flashcard glossary

❖ www.routledge.com/cw/optimizelawrevision

# 4

# Sexual Offences

## Understand the law

- Can you distinguish between the following offences: rape, assault by penetration, sexual assault?

## Remember the details

- Can you remember the *actus reus* and *mens rea* for each offence?
- Can you support each element of the *actus reus* and *mens rea* by reference to relevant case law and statutory provisions?

## Reflect critically on areas of debate

- Do you understand the distinction between conclusive and evidential presumptions?
- Are you able to articulate the definition for consent under the Sexual Offences Act (SOA) 2003?

## Contextualise

- Can you relate the offences to other areas of the law, such as non-fatal offences?

## Apply your skills and knowledge

- Can you complete the activities in this chapter, using relevant authority to support your answers?

# Chapter Map

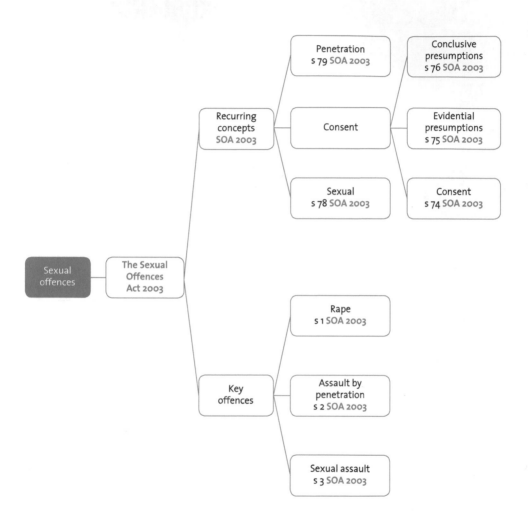

# Introduction

In this chapter we are going to consider sexual offences. Sexual offences is a topic that does not appear on all criminal law courses, so you must check the syllabus for your course before revising this topic. If sexual offences are included in your course it is important to check which specific offences are covered, as there can be some variation. The key offences are:

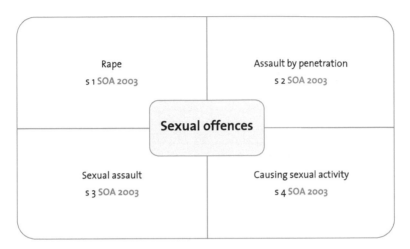

In this chapter we will focus on:

* ❖ rape
* ❖ assault by penetration
* ❖ sexual assault.

This is an area of law that was significantly reformed by the Sexual Offences Act (SOA) 2003. This Act brought together a number of statutory and common law provisions. The SOA 2003 simplified the law, abolishing some offences and introducing a number of others. As we progress through this chapter you will notice that many of the key authorities in this area of law were decided before the SOA 2003 was introduced. Do not let this concern you; it is not unusual for case law to remain 'good law' after significant statutory reform.

We will not consider in any detail offences against young children or people who suffer from a mental disorder, and will not cover preparatory offences (which are offences with the intent of committing a sexual offence, such as grooming).

# Recurring concepts in the Sexual Offences Act 2003

There are a number of recurring concepts in the SOA 2003 and before we consider the key offences we are going to examine these concepts, as an understanding of these concepts is critical to understanding the ingredients of the key offences under the SOA 2003. These recurring concepts are:

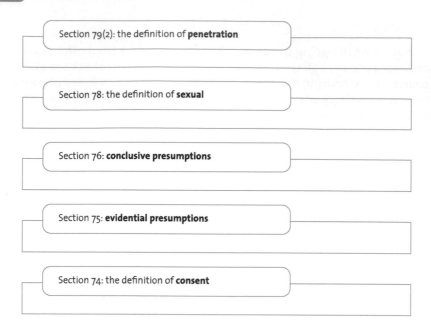

Section 79(2): the definition of **penetration**

Section 78: the definition of **sexual**

Section 76: **conclusive presumptions**

Section 75: **evidential presumptions**

Section 74: the definition of **consent**

We will now examine each of these terms in detail. You will need to be comfortable with these recurring concepts if you are planning on answering a question on sexual offences.

## Penetration

Section 79(2) stipulates that penetration is a continuing act from entry to withdrawal. This gives statutory effect to the decision in *Kaitamaki* (1984). Consensual penetration can become unlawful if consent is withdrawn at any point: *Cooper and Schaub* (1994). The slightest penetration will suffice: s 79(9) SOA 2003.

## Sexual

Several offences under the SOA 2003 require 'sexual activity'. The term *sexual* is defined in s 78 of the SOA 2003. Section 78 of the SOA 2003 stipulates that an act is sexual if a reasonable person would consider that:

a) Whatever the circumstances or any person's purpose in relation to it, it is because of its nature sexual, or

b) Because of its nature it may be sexual and because of the circumstances or the purpose of any person in relation to it (or both) it is sexual.

From this section of the SOA 2003, it is apparent that an act can be sexual in nature based on the **circumstances** and/or the **nature and purpose** of the act. Therefore s 78 SOA 2003 provides that:

| s 78(a) | The act is inherently sexual | Sexual intercourse, oral sex, masturbation | A reasonable person would regard the action as sexual |
|---------|------------------------------|-------------------------------------------|---------------------------------------------------------|
| s 78(b) | The act is potentially sexual | Touching, kissing, penetration | It may be sexual, depending on the circumstances and the nature and purpose of D's motives |

In *H* (2005) the court laid down a two-stage test to s 78(b) SOA 2003.

1. The jury must be satisfied that the act is capable of being sexual; and then
2. Would a reasonable person considering the context and the surrounding circumstances and the purpose of D regard the act as actually sexual?

The following cases illustrate forms of behaviour that have been deemed sexual by the courts:

❖ touching the breasts of a victim – *Burns* (2006);
❖ kissing a victim – *W* (2005);
❖ stroking the legs of another is capable of being deemed sexual – *Price* (2004).

## Aim Higher

Sexual offences can sit in parallel with other offences, such as non-fatal offences. Where the defendant's actions are not sexual but are not consensual it is possible to construct liability for another non-fatal offence against the person.

When planning your answer to a problem question on sexual offences, work through the *actus reus* and *mens rea* for the possible sexual offences, and then consider whether D may be liable for alternative offences.

Thinking through and mapping out your answer first will really help you do this. Demonstrating the ability to identify alternative/parallel offences will enable the examiner to award more marks.

## Consent

In the following sections we are going to consider conclusive and evidential presumptions that relate to consent to sexual activity. We will also consider the general definition of consent. Before we do this it is important to explain these terms.

| Conclusive presumptions | A conclusive presumption cannot be rebutted |
|-------------------------|---------------------------------------------|
| Evidential presumptions | The defence can rebut an evidential presumption |

## Aim Higher

When working your way through a question on sexual offences make sure that you deal with the issue of consent in the following order:

1.   Is there a conclusive presumption (s 76)?
2.   Is there an evidential presumption (s 75)?
3.   The general definition of consent (s 74)?

If you find that there is a conclusive presumption (s 76) there is no need to go on to consider s 75 or s 74. If you find that there is an evidential presumption it may not be necessary to go on to consider the general definition of consent.

## Conclusive presumptions
Section 76 of the SOA 2003 provides that:

(1)   If in proceedings for an offence to which this section applies it is proved that the defendant did the relevant act and that any of the circumstances specified in subsection (2) existed, it is to be conclusively presumed—
   (a)   that the complainant **did not consent** to the relevant act, **and**
   (b)   that the defendant **did not believe** that the complainant consented to the relevant act.
(2)   The circumstances are that—
   (a)   the defendant intentionally **deceived** the complainant as to the nature or purpose of the relevant act;
   (b)   the defendant intentionally **induced** the complainant to consent to the relevant act by impersonating a person known personally to the complainant.

## Up for Debate

Do you feel that these conclusive presumptions encapsulate the most serious situations in which consent is not present? It is interesting that deceit and inducement are high-lighted as conclusive presumptions, whereas violence and being unlawfully detained are rebuttable presumptions.

We will now examine s 76(2)(a) and (b) in more detail.

## Deceit
Section 76(2)(a) deals with fraud and deceit. Where a defendant deceives the victim as to the nature of the act that is being performed there will be a conclusive presumption that the victim did not consent **and** that the defendant did not believe that the victim was consenting. Examples of conduct that would fall within the remit of s 76(2)(a) include:

| Williams (1923) | The defendant had sex with the victim telling her that the act would improve her breathing |
| Flattery (1877) | The defendant had sex with the victim telling her that the act was a medical procedure that would improve her illness |

The following are examples of conduct that will not trigger s 76(2)(a):

| *Linekar* (1995) | The defendant had sex with the victim promising to pay her money. He left without paying. |
|---|---|
| *Jheeta* (2007) *B* (2013) | The deceit must be in relation to the nature not the quality of the act |

The nature or purpose of the relevant act is key, and V should be aware of and consent to the act proposed by D, for deceit to be established. This was seen in the case of *R v Jheeta* (2007), where D sent threatening text messages to V and pretended to be a police officer in order to enable him to continue a sexual relationship with V.

### Example

D pretends to be a doctor undertaking a survey on breast cancer. On this basis three women allow D to undertake a breast examination, including touching of their breasts. Would you consider this deceit as to the nature of the part of D?

This is based on the facts of a real case, *R v Tabassum* (2000), in which D pretended to be a doctor. On appeal, the Judge ruled that the women gave their consent to touching for medical purposes only, and that D had deceived the women as to this purpose.

### Induced

Section 76(2)(b) deals with inducement in a very specific form. This is where the defendant impersonates a person known personally to the complainant in order to induce the victim into sexual activity. In these circumstances there will be a conclusive presumption that the victim did not consent **and** that the defendant did not believe that the victim was consenting.

An example of inducement through impersonation can be seen in the following case:

### Case precedent – *R v Elkekkay* [1995] Crim LR 163 (CA)

**Facts:** D is in a flat with a couple. V goes to bed and her boyfriend falls asleep on the sofa. D climbs into V's bed while she is asleep and, believing D is her boyfriend, V speaks to D and begins to have sexual intercourse with D. When V realises D is not her boyfriend, she screams and manages to escape.

**Principle:** Inducement

**Application:** D is convicted of rape, as it is demonstrated that he impersonated V's boyfriend.

The key to the operation of s 76(2)(b) is that the impersonation must be of someone known personally to the victim. Thus impersonating a film star or other celebrity not known personally to the victim will not trigger s 76(2)(b).

## Evidential presumptions

Evidential presumptions are rebuttable presumptions. This means that they are accepted as being true, unless the defence is able to rebut them by adducing evidence to the contrary. Section 75 of the SOA 2003 provides that a presumption against valid consent will arise in the following situations.

(1) If in proceedings for an offence to which this section applies it is proved—

   (a) that the defendant did the relevant act,
   (b) that any of the circumstances specified in subsection (2) existed, and
   (c) that the defendant knew that those circumstances existed, the complainant is to be taken not to have consented to the relevant act unless sufficient evidence is adduced to raise an issue as to whether he consented, and the defendant is to be taken not to have reasonably believed that the complainant consented unless sufficient evidence is adduced to raise an issue as to whether he reasonably believed it.

(2) The circumstances are that—

   (a) any person was, at the time of the relevant act or immediately before it began, **using violence against the complainant** or causing the complainant to fear that immediate violence would be used against him;
   (b) any person was, at the time of the relevant act or immediately before it began, **causing the complainant to fear that violence was being used**, or that immediate violence would be used, against another person;
   (c) the complainant was, and the defendant was not, **unlawfully detained** at the time of the relevant act;
   (d) the complainant was **asleep or otherwise unconscious** at the time of the relevant act;
   (e) because of the complainant's **physical disability**, the complainant would not have been able at the time of the relevant act to communicate to the defendant whether the complainant consented;
   (f) any person had administered to or caused to be taken by the complainant, without the complainant's consent, **a substance** which, having regard to when it was administered or taken, was capable of causing or enabling the complainant to be stupefied or overpowered at the time of the relevant act.

(3) In subsection (2)(a) and (b),

   the reference to the time **immediately before the relevant act** began is, in the case of an act which is one of a continuous series of sexual activities, a reference to the time immediately before the first sexual activity began.

## Common Pitfalls

Be careful if one of the characteristics above is raised as part of the offence for rebuttable presumption. This is because there must be proof that D did the act and that D knew that there was the existence of any of the points set out below.

You cannot simply assume this without proof.

This is particularly important if you are answering a question on rebuttable presumptions. You would need to demonstrate in your argument that D was aware of one or more of the points below in s 75.

It is important to note that the prosecution does not have to prove that the victim did not consent. It is for the defence to rebut the evidential presumption that there was no valid consent by adducing sufficient credible evidence to the contrary: *Larter and Castleton* (1995). If the defendant fails to do so, it will be presumed that the victim did not consent and that the defendant had no reasonable belief in the victim's consent: *Ciccarelli* (2012).

Use the steps below to work through whether an evidential presumption could apply:

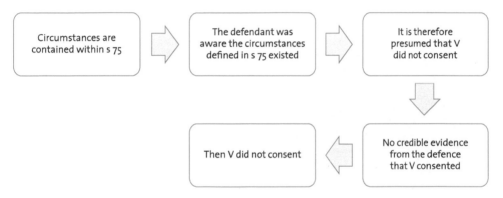

Circumstances are contained within s 75 → The defendant was aware the circumstances defined in s 75 existed → It is therefore presumed that V did not consent ↓ No credible evidence from the defence that V consented ← Then V did not consent

## The definition of consent

In the vast majority of cases the issue of consent does not hinge on the existence of conclusive or evidential presumptions. Thus the jury will determine consent on the basis of s 74 of the **Sexual Offences Act (SOA) 2003**, which provides a general definition of consent. Section 74 provides that:

A person consents if he agrees by choice, and has the freedom and capacity to make that choice.

❖ A failure to resist does not equate to consent: *Olugboja* (1982).
❖ Submission is not the same thing as consent: *Doyle* (2010).
❖ For consent to be valid it must be given by free choice: *Jheeta* (2007).

## A reasonable belief in consent

Prior to the **Sexual Offences Act 2003**, where a defendant had an honest but mistaken belief that the victim consented he could escape liability. This was the case even if the honest mistaken belief was entirely unreasonable.

**Case precedent – *DPP v Morgan* [1976] AC 182**

**Facts:** The case surrounded three appellants who were convicted of rape. They had been drinking with an RAF officer who invited them back to his house to have sexual intercourse with his wife. The appellants highlighted that he had told them that his wife would be consenting, but would protest for enhancement. V did not consent, and sustained physical injuries.

**Principle:** Honest belief of consent

**Application:** The Judge directed the jury that the defendants' belief in consent had to be reasonably held and they were found guilty. They appealed, contending there was no requirement that the belief needed to be reasonably held. On appeal the court agreed that there was no requirement that the belief was reasonable, only honest.

The **Sexual Offences Act 2003** changed this position. The belief in consent must now be a reasonable one.

**Aim Higher**

The new legislation altered the law contained in the **SOA 1956**, which provided the accused with a defence where he was found to have an 'honest belief' that V was consenting.

If you are going to use the case of Moran in relation to consent you must remember to explain that it is no longer good law!

There are a number of factors that may impact on a victim's ability to provide valid consent. In addition to those considered in s 76 and s 75 of the **SOA 2003** these include:

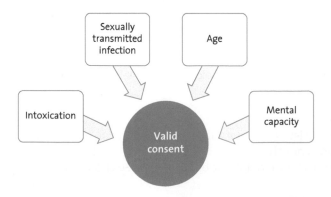

## Consent and intoxication

Section 75(2)(f) of the **SOA 2003** considers the issue of intoxication in the context of substances administered without the victim's consent. This of course could include drugs and/or alcohol. What happens when the victim has become voluntarily intoxicated?

The issue of intoxication and consent has given rise to much debate over the years. Following the leading case of *Bree* (2007), a drunken consent is valid consent. However, in circumstances where the victim has temporarily lost the capacity to choose whether or not to engage in sexual activity the victim does not consent.

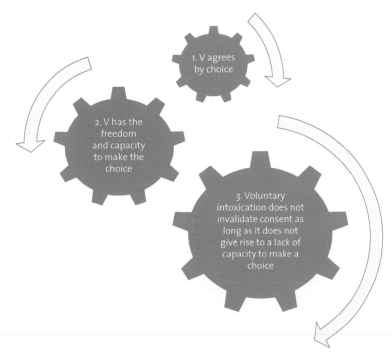

## Consent and capacity

Only a person who has the capacity to consent to sexual activity can give valid consent. Unfortunately the SOA 2003 does not provide a definition of the term capacity. The following points should be borne in mind when dealing with the issue of capacity in relation to consent:

❖ The victim must have sufficient knowledge and understanding in order to provide valid consent: *Howard* (1965).
❖ Issues in relation to capacity can arise in relation to the victim's age, intoxication, physical and/or mental disability.

## Informed consent: failure to disclose sexually transmitted infections

Where a defendant has sexual intercourse with an individual and fails to disclose a sexually transmitted infection the failure to disclose does not vitiate the victim's consent: *Dica* (2004).

In *B* (2007) the court held that a defendant's failure to disclose that he was HIV positive did not trigger s 76(a) SOA 2003 where there was no deceit. In *McNally*

(2013) the court left the question unanswered as to whether a defendant who gives a positive assurance that they are not HIV positive when in fact they are HIV positive could potentially vitiate consent.

In *Assange v Swedish Prosecution Authority* (2011) it was suggested that a failure to disclose HIV status is not relevant to the issue of consent under s 74 **SOA 2003**.

You will find the following flowchart of use when dealing with issues in relation to consent.

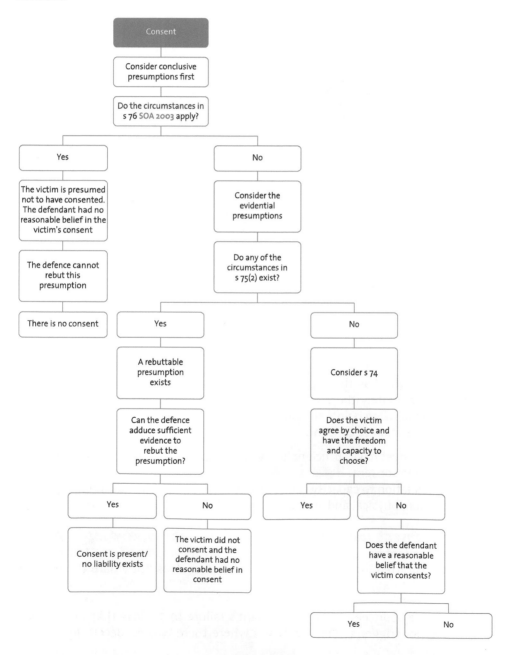

# The Key Offences

In the next section of this chapter we will consider the main sexual offences contained in the Sexual Offences Act (SOA) 2003. Each will be considered in turn, focusing on how the different offences are defined and the key elements of each offence.

## Rape
By s 1 of the SOA 2003, the *actus reus* of rape is committed where:

> (1) A person (A) commits an offence if —
>
> (a) he intentionally penetrates the vagina, anus or mouth of another person (B) with his penis,
> (b) B does not consent to the penetration, and
> (c) A does not reasonably believe that B consents.

This can be split into the following *actus reus* and *mens rea* elements:

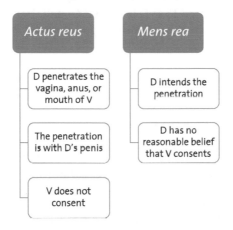

### Actus reus: *D penetrates the vagina, anus or mouth of V*
This is an important element, as it recognises that penetration must occur for the offence to be constituted.

Penetration may involve the slightest penetration of the vulva, thus full penetration is not required. It is also important to note that ejaculation does not need to occur for the act to be deemed penetration. This supports the earlier discussion regarding rape as a continuing act.

### 2 Actus reus: *the penetration is with D's penis*
This element identifies that D must be male (with his penis), although V can be either male or female.

It is useful to note that this is the only offence requiring penetration specifically with the penis. This is not a requirement of other offences in this chapter.

## Actus reus: *V does not consent*

We have already discussed the basis of consent above. However, with rape, it is also important to consider the age of V. This is because age can determine whether D is liable for the offence of rape, of for another offence regarding children.

If you are answering a problem question, the age of V may be noted, and this could lead you to a different offence for discussion.

### Common Pitfalls

When you are looking at sexual offences, it is important to consider the age of V.

Under s 5 of the **SOA 2003**, rape is committed where V is below the age of 13 regardless of any consent from V. This affects the *actus reus* for consent, as set out above.

## Mens rea: *D intended the penetration*

Here it must be demonstrated that D intended to penetrate V with his penis. It is vital that penetration takes place with the penis, and the penetration must be intentional.

For example, if D accidentally penetrates the anus instead of the vagina during consensual sexual intercourse, would this constitute intent? This is more likely to be considered a mistake, particularly if D is inexperienced. Therefore, it is for the prosecution to prove that D intended the penetration.

## Mens rea: *D has no reasonable belief that V consents*

An important element of the *mens rea* for rape is that the D must have a reasonable belief in the V's consent.

The law in relation to the marital rape was overturned in 1992 when a landmark case found that a woman does not automatically give consent to her husband, thereby ending the husband's immunity from rape.

### Case precedent – *R v R* [1992] 1 AC 599

**Facts:** D and V were married, but were living separately. V was living at her parents' house. D entered V's parents' house and raped V.

**Principle:** End of husband's immunity from rape

**Application:** D was found guilty of rape, because V did not consent. From this point, a wife is not assumed to automatically consent to sexual activity with her husband, and can withdraw consent from her husband.

# Assault by penetration

By s 2 of the SOA 2003, the *offence* of assault by penetration is committed where:

(1) A person (A) commits an offence if—

    (a) He intentionally penetrates the vagina or anus of another person (B) with a part of his body or anything else,

    (b) The penetration is sexual,

    (c) B does not consent to the penetration, and

    (d) A does not reasonably believe that B consents.

(2) Whether a belief is reasonable is to be determined having regard to all the circumstances, including any steps A has taken to ascertain whether B consents.

This can be split into the following *actus reus* and *mens rea* elements:

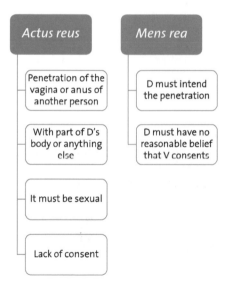

## Actus reus: *penetration of the vagina or anus of another person*

This offence is similar to rape (as set out above), but there are some important differences:

❖ penetration does not need to have taken place with the penis (considered below);

❖ penetration of the mouth is not included in this offence.

The reason why this offence was included in the SOA 2003 was due to concerns that the gravity of penetration with another object was not fully captured by the offence of sexual assault (discussed below). Hence, the offence of assault by penetration was created, providing a maximum sentence of life imprisonment.

> ## Common Pitfalls
>
> This offence does not extend to penetration of the mouth, as it was felt that penetration of the mouth **was** already fully considered within the offences of rape and sexual assault.
>
> When answering a problem question, do ensure that you are clear about the facts of the offence, as this can lead you to determine whether D is liable for the offence of rape or for assault by penetration.

## Actus reus: *with part of D's body or anything else*
Another difference from the offence of rape is that penetration does not have to be by the penis. This means penetration could be by another part of the body, such as fingers, or with an object.

The significance of this element is that D is not, therefore, automatically male – D may be male or female, as can V.

| Rape | Assault by penetration |
|---|---|
| D is always male as penetration must be with his penis | D can be male or female, as penetration can be by part of the body or something else |

## Actus reus: *it must be sexual*
This element is another difference from the offence of rape – assault by penetration is sexual, whereas rape is not required to be sexual. This gives the offence a broader scope than rape, and widens liability for the offence.

We have briefly considered the meaning of *sexual* already, and will consider this in more depth in the next section. But it is useful to note that there are grey areas between sexual and non-sexual penetration, and you should begin to explore these as part of a discussion on sexual offences.

## V does not consent
We have considered the issue of consent earlier in this chapter.

## Mens rea: *D must intend the penetration*
This intention is the same as that for the offence of rape, as is the nature of the intention.

## Mens rea: *D has no reasonable belief that V consents*
Reasonable belief is also the same as for the offence of rape, and is considered in more detail in the next section.

S 5 of the SOA 2003 and above, s 6 cover the situation where V is below the age of 13. It provides that the offence of assault by penetration is committed whether or not V consents.

### Example

Rachel and Steve are having consensual intercourse when Steve asks Rachel if he can penetrate her vagina with his hand. She says no and tries to move away, but Steve does so anyway.

In this example, the offence of assault by penetration would be applicable – think through the *actus reus* and *mens rea* for this offence, and use the diagram below to check through your working.

How would the diagram be different if Steve did not hear what Rachel said?

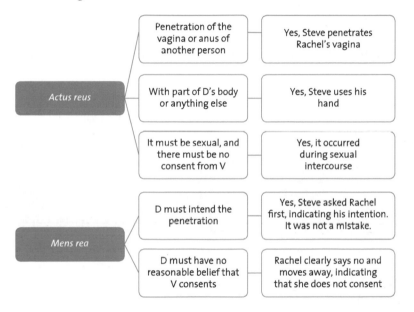

# Sexual assault: section 3

Section 3 of the SOA 2003 covers sexual assault, and provides:

(1) A person (A) commits an offence if—

    (a) He intentionally touches another person (B),
    (b) The touching is sexual,
    (c) B does not consent to the touching, and
    (d) A does not reasonably believe that B consents.

(2) Whether a belief is reasonable is to be determined having regard to all the circumstances, including any steps A has taken to ascertain whether B consents.

This can be split into the following *actus reus* and *mens rea* elements:

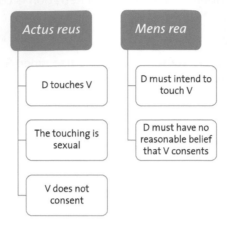

As with the offence of assault by penetration, in sexual assault both D and V can be either male or female.

> ## Common Pitfalls
>
> If you have read the chapter on non-fatal offences, compare the *actus reus* and *mens rea* for sexual assault with the *actus reus* and *mens rea* for assault. You will see that the *actus reus* and *mens rea* for sexual assault are much broader, and involve touching, whereas assault refers to the immediate apprehension of violence.
>
> Do be careful not to confuse the two offences when answering a problem question, as the two offences are quite different.

### Actus reus: *D touches V*
Touching can include:

* touching through clothing;
* touching any part of the body;
* with anything else.

To help your understanding of the concept of touching, look at the chapter on non-fatal offences to find further definitions of touching, and what can and cannot be regarded as touching in terms of these offences.

### Actus reus: *the touching is sexual*
For sexual assault, it needs to be demonstrated that the touching is of a sexual nature, relating to the intention of D and the circumstances of the offence.

In many cases this touching can be very obvious, but it is not always clear. The case below refined the definition of touching in sexual assault.

---

**Case precedent – *R v H* [2005] 2 All ER 859**

**Facts:** D approached V, whom he did not know, and tried to pull her towards him using her tracksuit trouser pockets on each side and asked if she wanted to have sexual intercourse.

**Principle:** Touching through the clothes

**Application:** It was held that touching through the clothes was enough to commit a sexual offence, even though the touching itself may not constitute a sexual offence but the intention and the circumstances were sexual in nature.

---

This case identifies that touching through clothes is part of the *actus reus* (above), but the influence of the sexual intention and circumstances constitute the difference between sexual assault and common law assault.

When you are working through a problem question which involves touching, work through these steps to decide if this touching is of a sexual nature and would constitute sexual assault.

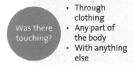  

If the answer to the questions above is yes, then liability for sexual assault may be present. If the answer to these questions is no, then the touching is not sexual and as such liability for sexual assault cannot exist. However, D may have committed another offence; assault and battery, for example.

## Actus reus: *V does not consent*
As with the other sexual offences, the consent of V is required as this constitutes an important element of the *actus reus*.

## Mens rea: *D must intend to touch V*
As noted above, D must intend to touch V. This is important to the *mens rea*, because it differentiates between intentional touching and a mistake. For example:

❖ not intentionally touching V;
❖ brushing past a person;
❖ shaking their hand.

Again, further information on touching is set out in the chapter on non-fatal offences, and sets out the nature of touching another person.

### Mens rea: *D has no reasonable belief that V consents*

We have already touched upon reasonable belief of consent, and this is an important element of sexual assault.

This is particularly relevant here, as consent is not always sought in advance, such as when giving a person a hug or putting your arm around a person.

### Up for Debate

The **SOA 2003** was written following concern that the **SOA 1956** was outdated and needed reform, and to respond to changing attitudes in society. There was also concern that the **SOA 1956** did not provide sufficient definition of consent.

Now you have considered liability for the main sexual offences in the **SOA 2003,** do you think that these concerns have been addressed?

There is clearly a view that the range of offences has been widened, and it affords greater protection to children in particular. Given that the legislation is still relatively new, this additional protection will be tested through the courts over the coming years.

# Putting it into practice

## Question 1

Mike and Alison meet at a party. They have been drinking heavily and return to Mike's flat together, where consensual intercourse takes place. Mike wakes up in the middle of the night and decides to have intercourse with Alison again, even though she is asleep. Alison wakes up to find Mike on top of her, penetrating her. She protests and tries to push him off, but her speech is slurred and Mike cannot make out what she is saying. He continues to penetrate her, and is subsequently charged with rape.

Consider Mike's criminal liability (if any).

## Suggested solution

The defence cannot argue that Alison was consenting to sex, since it is well established that a person who is asleep or unconscious cannot consent to intercourse (*R v Fletcher* (1859)). The defence will therefore have to argue that (i) Mike genuinely believed Alison was consenting and (ii) he had reasonable grounds for doing so (s 1(1)(c) **SOA 2003**). Thus, even if the jury are convinced that Mike's belief in consent was genuine, they must also conclude he had reasonable grounds for holding it.

On this point, s 75(2)(d) provides a presumption that D did not hold a reasonable belief since 'the complainant was asleep or otherwise unconscious at the time of the relevant act'. The defence will thus be under an obligation to adduce sufficient evidence of reasonable grounds. Mike may try to argue that the fact Alison had sex with him some hours earlier suggested in his mind that she would consent to having sex again. On the other hand, however, the fact that Alison was making muffled protests at the time may tend to suggest that Mike should have been aware that she was not consenting, and he should have ceased penetration at that point. There may also be an issue here with regard to intoxication. However, even if Mike is drunk, intoxication is no defence to a charge of rape (*R v Woods* (1981) 74 Cr App R 312).

## Question 2

Gordon and Eliza meet in a pub, and are drunk. They return to Gordon's house and have sexual intercourse. The next morning Eliza cannot remember if she consented to the intercourse.

Given s 74 of the SOA 2003, do you think Eliza had the freedom and capacity to consent, or could any form of consent be classed as full consent?

Make sure you evidence your thoughts and ideas, to build a strong argument.

Work through s 74 of the SOA 2003, and apply the definitions to the example. You will probably focus on the freedom and capacity to consent, i.e. if Eliza was drunk, did she have the full capacity to make this decision? Or, did Gordon pressure her, but she cannot remember?

These types of situation can be difficult to judge, so you must go back to the legislation and case law, work through each methodically, and use the findings to draw a conclusion. Sometimes, particularly with these types of offence, they are not the answer you wish to hear – but it is still essential.

# Key Points Checklist

| | |
|---|---|
| The law in relation to sexual offences was reformed by the **Sexual Offences Act 2003** – this is the key legislative provision that you must be familiar with in relation to this topic. The key offences are: Rape, s 1 SOA 2003; Assault by Penetration, s 2 SOA 2003; Sexual Assault, s 3 SOA 2003. | ✔ |
| The *actus reus* of rape is: penetration; of the anus, vagina or mouth; with the defendant's penis; lack of consent on the victim's behalf. The *mens rea* of rape is: intentional penetration of the anus, vagina or mouth with the penis; D does not reasonably believe that V consents. | ✔ |

| | |
|---|---|
| The **actus reus** of assault by penetration is: penetration of the anus or vagina; with any part of the D's body or any object; lack of consent on the victim's behalf; the penetration must be sexual. The **mens rea** of the offence is: intentional penetration of the anus or vagina; D does not reasonably believe that V consents. | ✔ |
| The **actus reus** of sexual assault is: D touches V; the touching is sexual; V does not consent. The **mens rea** of the offence is: D intends to touch V; D does not reasonably believe that V consents. | ✔ |
| The SOA 2003 provides a definition for consent: s 74 SOA 2003. It also creates a number of conclusive and evidential presumptions regarding the existence of consent. | ✔ |
| Consent is a feature of the **actus reus** and the **mens rea** of these three offences and you must therefore address consent in relation to BOTH aspects. | ✔ |

# Table of key cases referred to in this chapter

| Key case | Brief facts | Principle |
|---|---|---|
| *Katamaki v R* [1985] **AC 147** | Not withdrawing when there is no consent | Rape is a continuing act |
| *R v Lineker* [1995] **2 Cr App R49** | Non-payment to a prostitute | The form of consent from V |
| *DPP v Morgan* [1976] **AC 182** | Three defendants having intercourse with another's wife on his instructions, in the belief she was willing | Honestly held belief in relation to consent |
| *R v R* [1992] **IAC 599** | Husband and wife were separated when he raped her | Removal of the marital exemption |
| *R v H* [2005] **2 All ER 859** | D touched V through her clothes and requested sexual intercourse | Refines the definition of touching |
| *R v Doyle* [2010] **EWCA Crim (CA)** | V submits to intercourse as she is not able to withdraw consent | Submission to sexual intercourse is not consent |
| *R v Bree* [2007] **EWCA Crim 804** | D and V had been drinking and were both intoxicated when sexual intercourse occurred | Consent while intoxicated |
| *R v Malone* [1998] **2 Cr App R 447** | V did not make D aware of her lack of consent | Evidential presumptions – circumstances |
| *R v Hysa* [2007] **EWCA Crim 2056** | V could not recall the events due to intoxication | Evidential presumptions – capacity to consent |

| *R v Jheeta* [2007] **EWCA Crim 1699** | D sent threatening text messages, and pretended to be a policeman | Conclusive presumptions – deceit |
|---|---|---|
| *R v Tabassum* [2000] **2 Cr App R 328 (CA)** | D pretended to be a doctor and V let him touch her breasts on this basis | Impact of deceit on consent |
| *R v Elkekkuy* [1995] **Crim LR 163 (CA)** | D pretended to be V's boyfriend | Conclusive presumptions – inducement |

---

@ Visit the book's companion website to test your knowledge

❖ Resources include a subject map, revision tip podcasts, downloadable diagrams, MCQ quizzes for each chapter, and a flashcard glossary

❖ www.routledge.com/cw/optimizelawrevision

# 5

# Homicide – Including Murder and Manslaughter

**Understand the law**

- Can you identify the difference between murder, voluntary manslaughter and involuntary manslaughter?

**Remember the details**

- Can you remember the definition for each offence?
- Can you remember the *actus reus* and *mens rea* for each offence?

**Reflect critically on areas of debate**

- Can you reflect critically on the proposed reforms to the law in relation to homicide?

**Contextualise**

- Can you relate the offences to other areas of the law, such as non-fatal offences against the person?
- Can you relate this area of law to general defences such as self-defence?

**Apply your skills and knowledge**

- Can you complete the activities in this chapter, using relevant authorities to support your answers?

# Chapter Map

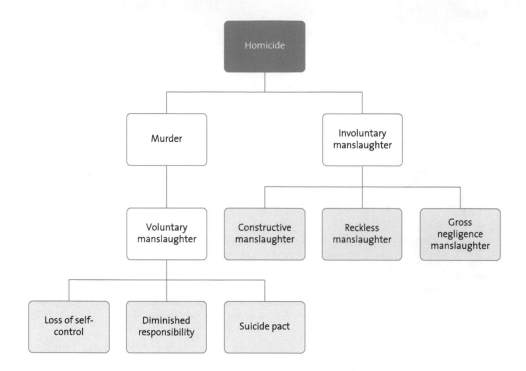

# Liability Chart

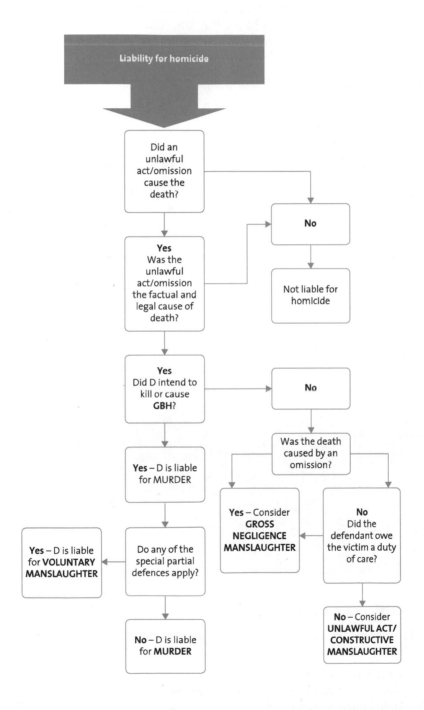

**Liability for homicide**

Did an unlawful act/omission cause the death?

**Yes** Was the unlawful act/omission the factual and legal cause of death?

**No**

Not liable for homicide

**Yes** Did D intend to kill or cause **GBH**?

**No**

Was the death caused by an omission?

**Yes** – D is liable for MURDER

**Yes** – Consider **GROSS NEGLIGENCE MANSLAUGHTER**

**No** Did the defendant owe the victim a duty of care?

**Yes** – D is liable for **VOLUNTARY MANSLAUGHTER**

Do any of the special partial defences apply?

**No** – Consider **UNLAWFUL ACT/ CONSTRUCTIVE MANSLAUGHTER**

**No** – D is liable for **MURDER**

# Introduction

In this chapter we will consider homicide. Homicide is an umbrella term for unlawful killings. Most criminal law courses consider a discrete number of homicide offences including murder, voluntary manslaughter and involuntary manslaughter. It is important that you are able to identify the common and unique elements of each of these offences. Homicide is a very popular topic with examiners and as such it frequently features in multiple formats in examination papers.

> ## Common Pitfall
>
> The term homicide is used as an overarching term under which a number of specific offences are grouped. We do not charge suspects with homicide or convict defendants of homicide. Be careful not to make this novice error in your assessments!

The offences that we will consider in this chapter are common law offences. Therefore the definitions of the separate offences are not found in statutes or Acts of Parliament. They are located in the decisions of the superior courts of England and Wales. A common mistake that students make when discussing homicide is to attribute the definitions of these offences to the Homicide Act 1957 (and sometimes to other statutory modifications).

# Chapter summary

Homicide ⟩ Murder ⟩ Voluntary manslaughter ⟩ Involuntary manslaughter ⟩ Reform

> ## Common Pitfall
>
> Problem questions on homicide are particularly popular with examiners and, in such a question, the distinction between the different offences of murder and manslaughter can be unclear. This is quite deliberate on the part of examiners, who typically want to provide you with the opportunity to show your knowledge of the case law and apply the legal principles of the different offences.
>
> Remember that you cannot construct criminal liability without working your way through the *actus reus* and *mens rea* for each potential offence.

# The common elements of homicide offences

The offences that we will consider in this chapter share some common elements. These elements are:

1. There must be a killing.
2. The killing must be of a human being/person.
3. The killing must be unlawful.

**Aim Higher**

As you progress through this chapter, you will see reference to a number of legal principles which also apply to non-fatal offences.

These principles can apply to both homicide and non-fatal offences, and are therefore crucial important for you to fully understand. As you work through these principles, check that you understand how they can apply to both types of offence, and this will help your understanding.

We will start our examination of these offences by considering the most serious of the homicide offences: murder.

# Murder

The traditional definition of murder was drawn from the seventeenth-century writings of the then Chief Justice, Sir Edward Coke (1552–1634). This definition remains the core or the basis of the modern definition of murder. You will find that many textbooks on criminal law break this original definition into individual components.

*Murder is when a man of sound memory, and at the age of discretion, unlawfully killeth within any country of the realm any reasonable creature in rerum natura under the King's peace, with malice aforethought, either expressed by the party or implied by law [so as the party wounded, or hurt, died of the wound or hurt within a year and a day at the same].*

*(Coke 3 Inst 47)*

Not all of this definition remains good law: for example, the requirement that the victim must die within a year and a day was reformed by the Law Reform (Year and a Day Rule) Act 1996. As such, students are generally to be encouraged to use the more modern and user-friendly definition of the offence!

## Definition

Murder is the unlawful killing of another human being with malice aforethought (this simply means intention to kill or cause grievous bodily harm).

As is always the case when dealing with a criminal offence, you must break the definition down into the constituent elements. The key elements of the offence of murder are:

1. There must be a killing.
2. The killing must be of a human being (a person).
3. The killing must be unlawful.
4. The killing must be committed with malice aforethought (intention to kill or cause GBH).

We now need to divide the different components into the distinct elements that represent the *actus reus* and *mens rea* of the offence of murder.

You can see that we have done this for you here:

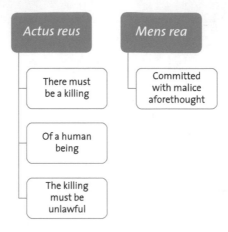

## Actus reus

We will now explore the elements that constitute the *actus reus* of murder. If you are answering a question on murder you must methodically work your way through each element.

### There must be a killing

The defendant must have caused an acceleration of the victim's death. There are two aspects here to consider: the first is that the victim must be dead and the second is that the defendant's acts or omissions must be the cause of the victim's death.

#### Death

Although it may seem rather obvious that the victim must be dead it is important to understand the point at which life ceases to exist in law. The common law position is that a person who has suffered brain death is legally dead. The legal consequence of this is that a person who is brain dead in law cannot be killed, whether by a medical practitioner or by anyone else.

In circumstances where the victim is not brain dead but is being sustained by life support, the victim is considered alive. Therefore, if life support is removed it results in the death of the victim. There are circumstances in which life support can be removed lawfully from a person who is not brain dead. Doctors may, for example, remove life support from a patient where it is no longer in the patient's best interests.

#### Causation

The defendant's acts or omissions must be the cause of the victim's death. Murder is a result crime and as such it must be established that the defendant is the factual and legal cause of death. We have considered causation in Chapter 2.

The act or omission must cause the death of the victim. It is not sufficient that the act causes significant injury.

For example, Billy, intending to kill or cause GBH, hits Simon on the head with a baseball bat, causing a significant head injury to Simon. Simon is in a coma and being kept alive on a life-support machine.

If Simon is not brain dead, then Billy cannot be liable for murder because in law Simon is still alive and as such there has been no killing. Billy may be liable for a non-fatal offence against the person instead.

However, if Simon's life support is withdrawn and as a result of the withdrawal of life support, Simon subsequently dies, then Billy could be held liable for murder.

It can help to remember the steps below:

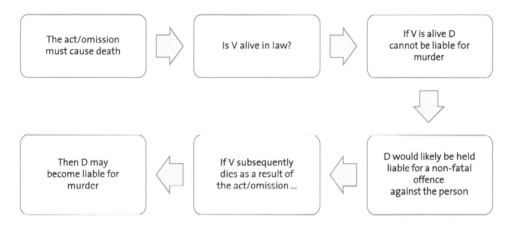

## The killing must be of a human being

In Coke's definition of murder a human being is *'any reasonable creature in rerum natura'*. *In rerum natura* means 'in the nature of things' or 'in existence'. For our purposes it is a person. Although this may seem rather obvious, there is an important point that must be understood in relation to this element of the offence.

Crucially at what point does an unborn child/foetus become a human being; or, put another way, at what point does an unborn child acquire the status of a person?

In order to be considered a 'person or human being' the child/foetus must be wholly expelled from the mother. Complete expulsion means that no part of the child remains in the birth canal. It does not, however, require the umbilical cord to have been cut: *Poulton* (1832). Therefore an unborn child is not a person: *AG Ref No 3 1994* (1998).

The final element of the *actus reus* is that the killing must be unlawful.

## The killing must be unlawful

One interpretation of this requirement is that it simply means that a killing will not be deemed unlawful where it is justified or excused. This could mean that the defendant has used reasonable force in self-defence, for example. In the case of *Re A (children)* (2000) the Court of Appeal held that an operation which separated conjoined twins would not be an unlawful killing where it was carried out to save the life of one twin, even though separation would inevitably result in the death of the weaker twin.

---

**Case precedent – *A (Children) (Conjoined Twins: Medical Treatment)* [2001] 2 WLR 480**

**Facts:** This case involved conjoined twins. Doctors advised that in order to preserve the life of one twin, the babies needed to be separated. If the twins were not separated both twins would certainly die. However, the separation of the twins would lead to the death of the weaker twin. The doctors sought permission from the courts to separate the twins in the absence of parental consent. They also sought a ruling from the court as to whether the operation would be lawful given that it was virtually certain that the weaker twin would die as a result of the separation.

**Principle:** Unlawful killing and necessity

**Application:** The courts allowed the operation to take place. The separation was lawful despite the virtually certain death of the weaker twin on the basis of necessity.

---

In the next section we will consider the impact that consent has on whether a killing is deemed unlawful.

### Consent

It is clear that an individual can consent to certain harmful activity, activity that would in the absence of consent render the activity unlawful and potentially criminal. Good examples of this are contact sports, surgery, body piercing and tattooing. In the context of homicide a victim's consent does not generally affect the unlawfulness of criminal homicide. In other words a victim cannot consent to being murdered!

Whilst an individual has the right to refuse medical treatment, they cannot request that a doctor 'actively kill them'. The outcomes may in this illustration be the same (the patient dies), but individuals do not have the right to implicate another in a positive act that will end their life. This was made clear in the case of *Purdy* (2009) (Art 8(1) **European Convention on Human Rights**).

We have now considered the *actus reus* elements of the offence of murder. In order to establish liability for the offence we must now deal with the *mens rea* for the offence.

## Mens rea

There is one *mens rea* element for the offence of murder. In Coke's definition of murder the *mens rea* for the offence is termed 'malice aforethought', and you need to be careful with this term as it is potentially misleading. Malice aforethought simply means intention to kill or cause grievous bodily harm: *Cunningham* (1982).

> *Murder is, of course, killing with malice aforethought, but 'malice afore-thought' is a term of art. It has always been defined in English law as either an express intention to kill, as could be inferred when a person, having uttered threats against another, produced a lethal weapon and used it on a victim or implied where, by a voluntary act, the accused intended to cause grievous bodily harm to the victim and the victim died as a result.*
>
> *(per Lord Hailsham in Cunningham (1982),*
> *citing Lord Goddard CJ in Vickers (1957))*

### Common Pitfall

Be careful with the term malice aforethought. The term malice aforethought is not the same as premeditation, or motive. It has nothing to do with malice or wickedness either. The term refers to an intention to kill or cause grievous bodily harm.

## Key point

It is very important to remember that the *mens rea* is what differentiates the offence of murder from manslaughter. Remember that the *actus reus* elements are the same for these different homicide offences.

We have discussed intention earlier in Chapter 2 and you will recall that intention can take two forms: either direct intention or oblique intention.

| Direct intention | • When it is D's aim or purpose to achieve a result.<br>• Therefore D wanted to kill V – it was D's aim to kill V. |
|---|---|
| Oblique intention | • When it is not D's aim but it is virtually certain to happen as a consequence.<br>• Therefore D may not wish to kill V or to cause GBH, but it is virtually certain to happen as a result. |

The *mens rea* for murder is present where there is intent to kill, or intention to cause grievous bodily harm (really serious harm). The leading case is the case of *Woollin*. It is important to note the significance of the decision in *Matthews and Alleyne* as this case established the principle that whilst foresight of a virtual certainty may be evidence of intention the jury is not bound to infer that this is the case. The jury *may* conclude that it is evidence of intention.

---

**Up for Debate**

There have been a number of calls for reform of the offence of murder, most recently in 2005 when different degrees of murder were proposed (first and second degree murder and manslaughter).

However, given the political importance of the offence of murder and politicians' commitment to a mandatory life sentence for the offence, these reforms have stalled.

Reform of the law in relation to homicide remains topical and it would be sensible to familiarise yourself with the key reforms. Showing an understanding of areas of law that have been identified as in need of reform is a good way to attract extra marks in an assessment.

---

A summary of the points we have covered in this section is:

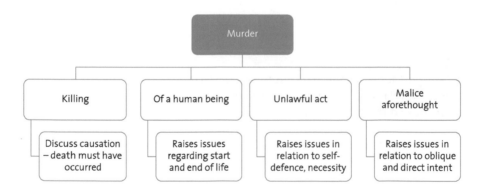

## Voluntary manslaughter

### Introduction

In this section we are going to consider manslaughter. Like homicide, manslaughter is a generic term. There are two forms of manslaughter: voluntary manslaughter and involuntary manslaughter. Voluntary manslaughter is closely related to murder, in so far as the *actus reus* and *mens rea* for murder are present. However, in the case of voluntary manslaughter there are 'special circumstances' in existence that enable the defendant to avail themselves of one of three special partial defences.

The diagram below illustrates the relationship between the different offences.

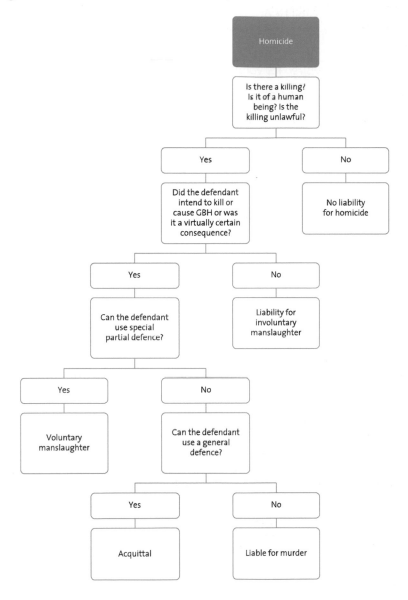

Voluntary manslaughter has exactly the same *mens rea* and *actus reus* as the offence of murder; however, there are circumstances that exist that enable the defendant to run a special partial defence. In successfully running one of these special partial defences the charge of murder is reduced to voluntary manslaughter. This is significant because the only sentence that can be handed down in a murder trial is a mandatory life sentence. In reducing the charge to voluntary manslaughter the judge has discretion in sentencing, although it is important to note that the maximum sentence that can be passed in the case of voluntary manslaughter is a life sentence.

The special partial defences are:

❖ diminished responsibility; or
❖ loss of self-control (previously referred to as provocation); or
❖ suicide pact.

The *actus reus* and *mens rea* for voluntary manslaughter are:

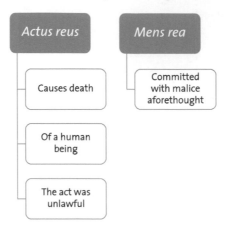

As you can see, the *actus reus* and *mens rea* are identical to those of murder.

## Actus reus

The *actus reus* of this offence is the unlawful killing of a human being.

## Mens rea

The *mens rea* for the offence of voluntary manslaughter is malice aforethought or intention to kill or cause GBH. It is important to remember that a finding of voluntary manslaughter cannot be made if the *mens rea* for murder is absent. If intention to kill or cause GBH is missing, or if there is a reasonable doubt that it may not be present, you should move on to consider involuntary manslaughter as a lesser or alternative charge.

## Special partial defences

What distinguishes voluntary manslaughter from murder is the existence of special circumstances. These special circumstances allow the defendant to run a special partial defence applicable **ONLY** to a murder charge.

### Common Pitfall

Remember that these special partial defences are applicable ONLY to a charge of MURDER. It is not uncommon for students to assume that diminished responsibility and loss of control are general defences applicable to any charge. This is a fundamental mistake. These defences cannot be utilised in the case of a non-fatal offence against the person.

Do not use these defences for any offence other than murder!

We will now consider each of the special partial defences which, if established, reduce the offence from murder to voluntary manslaughter.

## Diminished responsibility

Diminished responsibility is a statutory defence, found in s 2 of the Homicide Act 1957 as amended by s 52 of the Coroners and Justice Act 2009. The substance of this defence is that at the time of the killing the defendant was suffering from a recognised mental abnormality.

The statutory definition of diminished responsibility was originally laid down in s 2(1) of the Homicide Act 1957, which stated:

> Where a person kills or is a party to the killing of another, he shall not be convicted of murder if he was suffering from such abnormality of mind (whether arising from a condition of arrested or retarded development of mind or any inherent causes or induced by disease or injury) as substantially impaired his mental responsibility for his acts and omissions in doing or being a party to the killing.

In 2009 the provisions in s 2(1) of the Homicide Act were amended by the Coroners and Justice Act (CJA).

| | |
|---|---|
| **Homicide Act 1957** set out the law on diminished responsibility | **Coroners and Justice Act 2009** amended the Homicide Act 1957 |

Section 2 of the Homicide Act 1957 is amended by s 52 of the CJA 2009. The key provision that you should use when considering this partial defence states:

> (1) A person (D) who kills or is a party to the killing of another is not to be convicted of murder if D was suffering from an abnormality of mental functioning which:
>
> (a) arose from a recognised medical condition;
> (b) substantially impaired D's ability to do one or more of the things mentioned in subsection (1A); and
> (c) provides an explanation for D's acts and omissions in doing or being a party to the killing.

In the same way that we break down a criminal offence into constituent elements you should break down a defence into the different ingredients or elements of the defence. You must remember to consider ALL of the different ingredients.

The ingredients of this defence can be identified as follows:

1. D must be suffering from an abnormality of mind.
2. The abnormality of the mind must arise from a recognised medical condition.
3. The abnormality must have impaired D's ability.
4. The abnormality provides an explanation for D's acts or omissions.

We will now consider each of these elements in further detail.

## Aim Higher

As you read through the rest of this section, think about how this differs from the **Homicide Act 1957**, and why these changes were made.

This will help you to consider the circumstances of a problem question, but will also help you to discuss the differences in more depth, if you are answering an essay question on reform of homicide or on defences. Given the relatively recent change, this is quite a useful example to cite.

### The defendant must be suffering from an abnormality of mental functioning

In the case of *Byrne* (1960), Lord Parker described abnormality of mind as

> a state of mind so different from that of ordinary human beings that the reasonable man would term it abnormal.

The abnormality of mental functioning does not need to be permanent, nor does it need to have existed since birth.

### The abnormality must be a recognised medical condition

There are a number of pre-CJA 2009 cases which illustrate a range of conditions that would fall within the definition of an 'abnormality of mental functioning'. The table below illustrates a range of conditions caught by the definition.

| Issue/behaviours | Case |
|---|---|
| Battered woman's syndrome | *Hobson* [1997] Crim LR 759 – V stabbed and killed her abusive husband. Psychiatric reports found she was suffering from battered woman's syndrome. |
| Paranoid psychosis | *Sanderson* (1993) CR App R 325 – D beat and killed his girlfriend. Psychiatric reports found that D suffered from paranoid psychosis due to a traumatic upbringing. |
| Depression | *Gittens* (1984) 79 Cr App R 272 – D was suffering from depression and killed his wife when released from hospital. |

It is worth noting that in the case of *Dowds* (2012) it was held that the presence of a recognised medical condition is a 'necessary, but not necessarily a sufficient, condition to raise diminished responsibility as a defence'.

The table above only provides a snapshot of conditions. Other conditions that are likely to be captured by the term 'recognised medical condition' include:

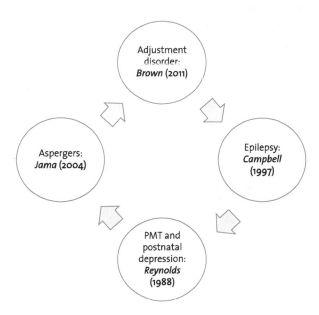

Medical evidence is vital to the success of the defence of diminished responsibility. In *Dix* (1982) it was held that medical evidence was 'a practical necessity'. It is important to note that once medical evidence has been presented it is up to the jury as to whether they accept the evidence. It is important to remember that when you are answering a problem question your role is to construct criminal liability; you are not the jury and therefore you must note when issues are a matter of fact for the jury.

The defendant bears the burden of proof when advancing the defence of diminished responsibility. However, the defence only need establish the existence of diminished responsibility on the balance of probabilities: *Dunbar* (1958).

---

### Case precedent – *Campbell* [1986] 84 Cr App R 255

**Facts:** D killed V when giving her a lift, after she refused his advances. D was convicted and won an appeal after determining that he suffered from epilepsy and put forward the defence of diminished responsibility due to frontal lobe damage. This information was not available at the time of the trial.

**Principle:** Diminished responsibility

**Application:** It is important to note here that if the issue of diminished responsibility emerges through the evidence, then the judge must point this out to D's counsel.

## Substantially impaired D's ability to do one or more of the things mentioned in subsection (1A)

It must be demonstrated that the recognised medical condition substantially impaired the defendant's ability to do one or more of the following:

(a)  to understand the nature of their own conduct;
(b)  to form a rational judgement; and
(c)  to exercise self-control.

The question as to whether the defendant's ability was substantially impaired is a question for the jury: *Khan* (2010).

### Aim Higher

If you decide to answer a question on diminished responsibility in an exam you need to work through each of the ingredients outlined in this section – you need to remember to then apply the law to the facts of the question!

In short, you must determine whether the illness described in the question is likely to be considered a recognised medical condition, and whether the illness has impaired D's ability. Keep focused on these points, and this will help you reach a conclusion.

## The abnormality of mental functioning MUST provide an explanation for D's acts and omissions in doing or being a party to the killing

The abnormality of the mental functioning must be a cause of or a significant contributory factor towards D causing or carrying out the conduct. This is essentially a causal connection between the abnormality of mental functioning and the defendant's action or omission.

**Note the emphasis on 'cause' here – it demonstrates the direct relationships required to prove this defence.**

The interpretation by the courts has been that diminished responsibility must be an inside cause, without an external influence. For example, intoxication is classed as an external influence and is not therefore considered as diminished responsibility.

However, if long-term alcoholism or addiction has caused long-term internal damage, then this could be taken into consideration.

### Case precedent – *Dowds* [2012] EWCA Crim 281

**Facts:** D and V were frequent binge drinkers and D killed V after one such binge. The Court of Appeal rejected the argument that binge drinking is a recognised medical condition.

**Principle:** Diminished responsibility

**Application:** Voluntary intoxication does not give rise to diminished responsibility.

## Diminished responsibility and intoxication

Provided that the defendant is not so intoxicated that they are unable to form the *mens rea* for murder they will not be able to avail themselves of diminished responsibility, as voluntary intoxication cannot itself provide an 'abnormality of mental functioning': *Fenton* (1975). The case of *Dowds* (2012) above illustrates this point.

We need, however, to consider the situation in which the defendant is voluntarily intoxicated and also happens to be suffering from another 'abnormality of mental functioning'. In this situation the trial judge should instruct the jury to ignore the effects of intoxication: *Gittens* (1984). The question that should be put to the jury is whether or not the defendant would still have had an 'abnormaility of mind' had he not been drinking: *Dietschmann* (2003).

We can see the timeline of these key cases regarding the relationship between diminished responsibility and intoxication as:

| Fenton (1975) | Dietschmann (2003) | Dowds (2012) |

It is important to note that the law differs where the defendant's abnormality of mind is the product of long-term drug or alcohol abuse. This is often referred to as Alcohol Dependency Syndrome (ADS). In *Tandy* (1989) it was held that alcoholism was not on its own sufficient for a plea of diminished responsibility. More recently, in the case of *Woods* (2008) a more lenient approach to ADS has been adopted and it now seems clear that there are certain circumstances in which ADS may give rise to a valid claim of diminished responsibility. These circumstances were later clarified in the case of *Stewart* (2010).

When considering a problem question, work through the following steps to determine whether D is suffering from diminished responsibility:

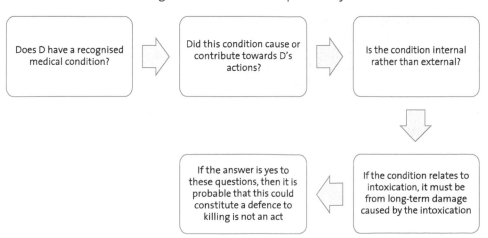

We are now moving on to consider the second special partial defence and that is the defence of loss of self-control. This defence was previously called provocation.

## Loss of self-control

Where diminished responsibility considers the internal working of the defendant's mind at the time of the killing, loss of self-control considers the external factors leading up to the killing.

---

### Common Pitfall

Many students make the mistake of discussing provocation in relation to non-fatal offences.

Loss of self-control, like diminished responsibility, is a defence only to MURDER, and you should not therefore discuss this defence in relation to any other offences that have been committed. Countless papers submitted by students have discussed provocation/loss of self-control where the victim has been assaulted following a disagreement. This is incorrect, and you will lose time and possibly marks with this approach in an exam.

---

The defence of provocation was contained within the Homicide Act 1957. The Coroners and Justice Act (CJA) 2009 abolished the partial defence of provocation, replacing it with the partial defence of loss of self-control.

| Provocation within the **Homicide Act 1957** | **CJA 2009** changed this defence | Now called loss of self-control |
|---|---|---|

Before considering the law as it currently stands it is helpful to take a brief overview of the law of provocation before it was reformed. If you answer an essay question on reform of this area of law you will certainly need to understand the position prior to reform. It is also worth noting that the defence of provocation is still applicable in cases where the offence was committed prior to October 2010.

### Provocation

Section 3 of the Homicide Act 1957 states:

> Where on a charge of murder there is evidence on which the jury can find that the person charged was provoked (whether by things done or by things said or by both together) to lose his self-control, the question whether the provocation was enough to make a reasonable man do as he did shall be left to be determined by the jury; and in determining that question the jury shall take into account everything both done and said according to the effect which, in their opinion, it would have on a reasonable man.

If we deconstruct the definition outlined above we can see that the defence of provocation consists of the following elements:

1.  Provocative conduct (things done or said or both).
2.  This caused the D to lose their self-control.
3.  The reasonable man would have done as D did.

## Loss of control

Section 56 of the Coroners and Justice Act 2009 abolished the defence of provocation, and replaced it with a new defence called 'loss of control'.

Section 54 defines the loss of self-control as follows:

(1)

   (a) D's acts and omissions in doing or being a party to the killing resulted from D's loss of self-control,
   (b) The loss of self-control had a qualifying trigger, and
   (c) A person of D's sex and age, with a normal degree of tolerance and self-restraint and in the circumstances of D, might have reacted in the same or in a similar way to D.

(2) For the purposes of subsection (1)(a), it does not matter whether or not the loss of control was sudden.

(3) In subsection (1)(c) the reference to 'the circumstances of D' is a reference to all of D's circumstances other than those whose only relevance to D's conduct is that they bear on D's general capacity for tolerance or self-restraint.

(4) Subsection (1) does not apply if, in doing or being a party to a killing, D acted in a considered desire for revenge.

We now need to break the defence down into the constituent elements. If you answer a question on loss of self-control you must establish each of these three elements. If you fail to do so the defence will fail.

1.  There must be a qualifying trigger.
2.  The qualifying trigger must result in the defendant losing self-control.
3.  A person of D's sex and age, with a normal degree of tolerance and self-restraint, would have acted as the defendant did.

We will now look at each of these elements in turn.

## Qualifying trigger

The meaning of a qualifying trigger is highlighted in s 55:

> From this it is important to note that the loss of self-control must have a **qualifying trigger**. This is a fundamental difference from the law on provocation (above).

(3) This subsection applies if D's loss of self-control was attributable to D's fear of serious violence from V against D or another identified person.

(4) This subsection applies if D's loss of control was attributable to a thing or things done or said (or both) which –

    (a) constituted circumstance of an extremely grave character, and
    (b) caused D to have a justifiable sense of being seriously wronged.

(5) This subsection applies if D's loss of self-control was attributable to a combination of the matters mentioned in subsections (3) and (4).

(6) In determining whether a loss of self-control had a qualifying trigger –

    (a) D's fear of serious violence is to be disregarded to the extent that it was caused by a thing which D incited to be done or said for the purposes of providing an excuse to use violence.
    (b) A sense of being wronged by a thing done or said is not justifiable if D incited the thing to be done or said for the purpose of providing an excuse to use violence.
    (c) The fact that a thing done or said constituted sexual infidelity is to be disregarded.

We can summarise these points as follows:

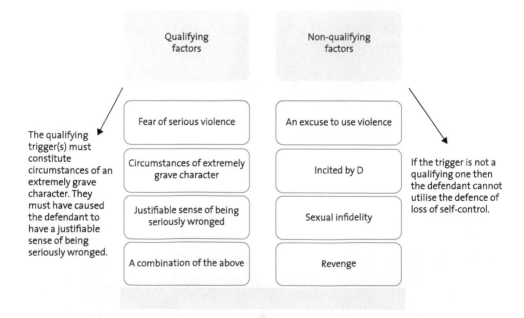

The qualifying trigger(s) must constitute circumstances of an extremely grave character. They must have caused the defendant to have a justifiable sense of being seriously wronged.

**Qualifying factors**

- Fear of serious violence
- Circumstances of extremely grave character
- Justifiable sense of being seriously wronged
- A combination of the above

**Non-qualifying factors**

- An excuse to use violence
- Incited by D
- Sexual infidelity
- Revenge

If the trigger is not a qualifying one then the defendant cannot utilise the defence of loss of self-control.

What we can see from the above diagram is that there is clear guidance as to what will and what will not constitute a 'qualifying trigger'. The defendant's response must be the result of one or both of the qualifying triggers. The qualifying triggers can be further subdivided into:

| Trigger 1:<br>Fear | Trigger 2:<br>Anger | Trigger 3:<br>Both together |
|---|---|---|

### Fear

In order to be operative the defendant must fear violence from the victim and not from another person. The fear must also be directed at an 'identified person'.

### Anger

The second trigger can be the result of words said, acts done, or both together. However, the 2009 Act requires that the trigger must give rise to:

❖ circumstances of an extremely grave character; and
❖ a justifiable sense of being seriously wronged.

It is clear that these additional requirements render the defence of loss of self-control much narrower than its predecessor of provocation: *Clinton* (2012). The case of *Zebedee* (2012) illustrates that the practical impact of these additional requirements is to ensure that trivial acts or words of provocation cannot give rise to a legitimate claim of loss of self-control.

It is also clear from the diagram on page 122 that certain circumstances/situations can never give rise to a qualifying trigger regardless as to whether the circumstances are of an extremely grave in character and led to the defendant feeling a justifiable sense of being wronged.

### Limitations

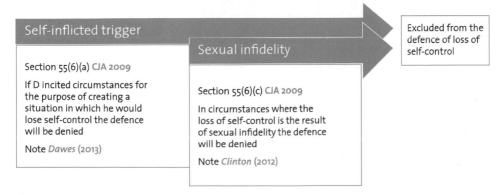

In relation to s 55(6)(C) of the CJA 2009 it is worth noting that in the case of *Clinton* (2012) this provision was interpreted in such a way as to allow evidence in relation to sexual infidelity to be considered in relation to loss of self-control.

## D must have suffered a loss of self-control

Once it has been established that the circumstances arose as a result of a qualifying trigger, it must also be established that D suffered a loss of self-control as a result of the qualifying trigger. This is akin to the old subjective test in provocation.

The loss of self-control need not be 'sudden': s 54(2). This is another significant change, as the previous guidance on provocation stipulated that the loss of self-control had to be a 'sudden and temporary' loss of self-control.

### Up for Debate

The law on provocation was reformed because it was widely recognised that it failed to operate adequately in relation to people who kill in response to a 'fear of serious violence', in cases where there was a backdrop of continuing domestic violence.

As a relatively recent change in the law, it will be interesting to see how effective the new provisions will be in addressing cases where domestic violence is alleged.

## A person of D's sex and age, with a normal degree of tolerance and self-restraint, would have acted as the defendant did

The third and final ingredient for this defence is that a person of the defendant's age and sex, with a normal degree of tolerance and self-restraint, would have acted as the defendant did. This is akin to the objective test in the now-abolished defence of provocation.

A normal person is therefore of the same sex and age as the defendant, which confirms the position under the common law prior to the CJA 2009: *DPP v Camplin* (1978). A normal person has a 'normal degree of tolerance and self-restraint'. What this means in practice is that the following characteristics cannot be attributed to the 'normal person', for the purposes of this test.

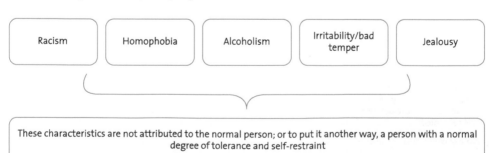

| Racism | Homophobia | Alcoholism | Irritability/bad temper | Jealousy |

These characteristics are not attributed to the normal person; or to put it another way, a person with a normal degree of tolerance and self-restraint

## Outcome of loss of self-control

The outcome of a successful plea of loss of control is the same as it was for the defence of provocation. The defendant is not acquitted but convicted of the lesser offence of voluntary manslaughter.

## Burden and standard of proof

One area that students typically neglect in relation to all defences, is the burden and standard of proof. With respect to the defence of loss of self-control the defence bears the evidential burden:

> Section 54(5). On a charge of murder if sufficient evidence is adduced to raise an issue with respect to the defence under subsection (1), the jury must assume that the defence is satisfied unless the prosecution proves beyond reasonable doubt that it is not.

This means that once the defence has raised evidence in relation to the defence of provocation/loss of control, the legal burden then rests with the prosecution, who must prove beyond all reasonable doubt that the defendant did not suffer a loss of control.

### Example

Tom and Ed have a long-running feud. They meet in the street and Tom says, 'I am going to kill you right now, because of what you have done.' Tom reaches into his bag. Ed fears that Tom is taking out a weapon. Ed grabs a glass bottle lying on the ground and stabs Tom 60 times in the face and Tom dies as a result.

Could loss of control be used as a defence for Ed? Work through the following steps to come to a conclusion:

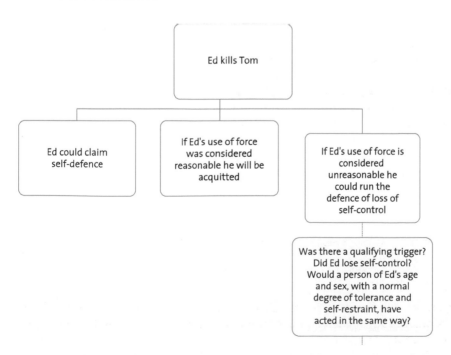

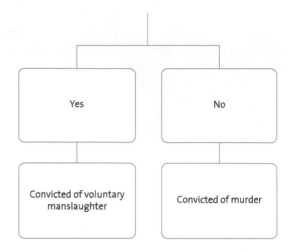

The final special partial defence that we will consider is suicide pact.

## Suicide pact

Suicide pact is the third defence which can alter the offence of murder to voluntary manslaughter. It is contained within s 4(1) of the Homicide Act 1957.

> A suicide pact is defined as a common agreement between two or more persons having for its object the death of all of them.

The defence operates in the following way.

If D and V have entered into a suicide pact and D survives, then D can put forward this defence to reduce the offence from murder to voluntary manslaughter. It is important to note that the defence bears the burden of proof.

Remember that it is not an offence for a person to commit suicide, but it is an offence for someone to assist in the suicide, such as enabling V to take pills for an overdose.

## Common Pitfall

Be careful not to confuse a suicide pact with assisting a suicide, which is a completely different offence. For the offence of voluntary manslaughter, there must be a **suicide pact** in place, rather than a pact to assist a death.

## Example

Sue and Julie make a pact to commit suicide using a shotgun. Sue tries to shoot herself but cannot pull the trigger. Julie shoots Sue and then turns the shotgun on herself. She pulls the trigger but her injury is not fatal and she survives. Julie is charged with Sue's murder.

In this example, it would be for Julie's defence to prove that there was a suicide pact, and the circumstances of this pact. If the jury were convinced that a suicide pact was operative at the time of Sue's death then Julie would be convicted of voluntary manslaughter.

A summary of the points we have covered in this section:

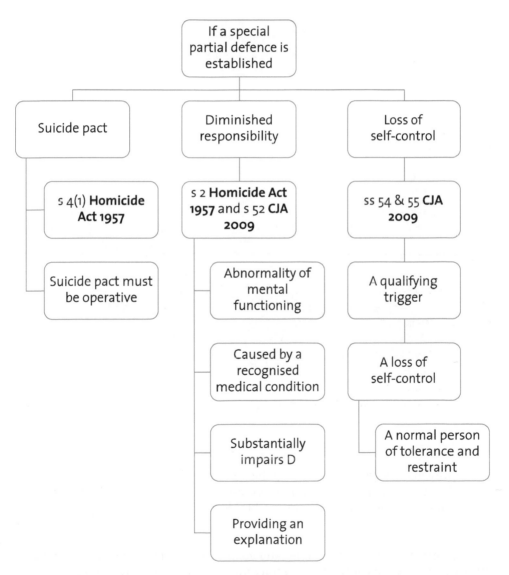

## Aim Higher

There are two common types of assessment question in criminal law. These are the essay question and the problem question. The different types of question assess different skills; they therefore require very different approaches.

When initially faced with a problem question many students feel a little overwhelmed and anxious. Problem questions are typically quite long and involve several parties and more than one potential offence. The good news is that, although they can be daunting at first, most students with a little guidance prefer answering problem questions.

The most important thing to remember when answering problem questions is: STRUCTURE, STRUCTURE, STRUCTURE! Your job when answering a criminal law problem question is to identify potential liability and construct liability. You cannot do this if you adopt a haphazard approach. If you use the following structure or method you will demonstrate logical thought and progression in your answer. You will also tick off the key elements required to construct liability.

### Answer Structure

1. **Identify and define the offence** – remember to give a source – is it a common law offence or a statutory offence? What is the maximum penalty upon conviction for this offence?
2. **Define the offence** – provide an accurate legal definition – make sure you provide an authority/source for the definition.
3. *Actus reus* – outline the *actus reus* of the offence – if you are dealing with a result crime make sure that you discuss causation.
4. *Mens rea* – explain the *mens rea* for the offence – ensure that you provide relevant authority.
5. **Defences** – consider the existence of relevant defences – make sure that you work your way through the ingredients of each potential defence. Consider the impact of a successful use of specific defences; for example, will running this specific defence result in an acquittal or a special verdict?
6. **Alternate or lesser offences** – consider alternate or lesser offences that may be relevant.
7. **Reform** – a good way to pick up extra marks in a problem question is to note where a particular area of law has been subject to proposals for reform.

# Involuntary manslaughter

Involuntary manslaughter is a less culpable form of homicide. It extends to a killing in which D's *mens rea* is less than that required for murder, i.e. there is no malice aforethought (no intent to kill or cause GBH). We will investigate this further later on in this section.

The key differences between murder and voluntary manslaughter (which we have already considered above) and involuntary murder can be summarised as:

| Murder | • An unlawful killing of a human being + intention to cause death <u>OR</u> GBH (malice aforethought) = murder |
| --- | --- |
| Voluntary manslaughter | • An unlawful killing of a human being + loss of self-control <u>OR</u> diminished responsibility <u>OR</u> killing in a suicide pact = voluntary manslaughter |
| Involuntary manslaughter | • An unlawful killing of a human being + no intention to cause death (or GBH) + unlawful and dangerous act <u>OR</u> gross negligence <u>OR</u> + recklessness = involuntary manslaughter |

As highlighted above, involuntary manslaughter is a form of homicide where the defendant is held responsible for causing the victim's death, even though the defendant did not intend to kill or cause the victim GBH. In this situation the defendant has committed the *actus reus* of homicide but lacks the *mens rea* for a conviction of murder/voluntary manslaughter.

There are three different types of involuntary manslaughter. A defendant can be held liable:

❖ by committing an unlawful and dangerous act (**unlawful act or constructive** manslaughter);
❖ where the defendant owes the victim a duty of care and breaches the duty of care with gross negligence (**gross negligence** manslaughter);
❖ in the course of any conduct, being subjectively reckless as to serious injury (**subjective recklessness** manslaughter).

We will now consider the first two types of voluntary manslaughter, as they are the most likely forms of manslaughter to arise in an exam. You will need to be aware of the key differences, in order to construct liability for the correct offence.

## Aim Higher

Involuntary manslaughter is a step between homicide which is intended and accidental homicide; that is, the death is not intended but is the result of an act or conduct. It therefore has a potentially wide span, and circumstances are extremely important here.

Be careful not to confuse involuntary manslaughter with tort or accidental death when considering the circumstances of a death.

## Unlawful act (or constructive) manslaughter

Involuntary manslaughter by an unlawful act is also known as *constructive manslaughter*. The Homicide Act 1957 changed the name and meaning of constructive manslaughter, and it is now more widely referred to as unlawful act manslaughter.

In this instance, the death must have occurred from an unlawful act (discussed below), and there must be a risk of some personal injury (not to the extent of GBH, otherwise this would then constitute murder).

There are three *actus reus* elements to unlawful act manslaughter – note that the *mens rea* is the same as for the unlawful act itself.

The *actus reus* and *mens rea* for unlawful act manslaughter are:

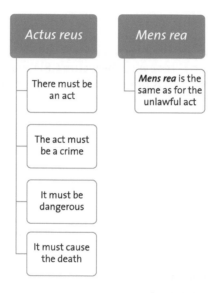

We will now consider these individual elements in more detail.

### There must be an act
Unlawful act manslaughter cannot be committed by omission, it requires a positive act: *Lowe* (1973).

### The act must be unlawful
The defendant must commit an unlawful act and that act must constitute a criminal offence. A civil wrong will be insufficient grounds on which to construct liability for unlawful act manslaughter: *Lamb* (1967). The unlawful act does not need not be directed at the victim. See *R v Mitchell* (1983).

## Common Pitfall

Be careful here, because although the courts insist on using the term 'unlawful act' they actually mean a criminal offence.

**Case precedent – *R v Franklin* [1883] 15 Cox CC 163**

**Facts:** D threw an item into the sea, hitting and killing a swimmer. It was argued that the act was a civil act, rather than an unlawful act.

**Principle:** Unlawful act

**Application:** This case confirms that the defendant must commit an unlawful act – a criminal offence in the case of unlawful act manslaughter.

The diagram bellow illustrates some of the base level crimes on which the courts have constructed liability for constructive manslaughter.

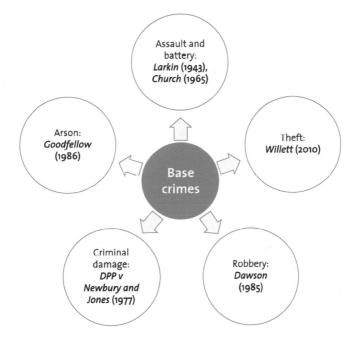

In the case of *Meeking* (2012) a conviction for unlawful act manslaughter was upheld where the base level crime was contrary to s 22A(1)(b) of the **Road Traffic Act 1988**.

## *The act must be dangerous*

The third element of unlawful act manslaughter is that the act must be a dangerous one. In *Church* (1965) it was held that:

> the unlawful act must be such as all reasonable and sober people would inevitably recognise must subject the other person to, at least, the risk of some harm therefrom, albeit not serious harm.

The test used to determine whether an act is an objective test: *Ball* (1989). If the defendant has knowledge of the victim or acquires knowledge of the victim whilst committing the crime this knowledge can be ascribed to the 'reasonable man' when applying the objective test: *Watson* (1989).

In *Bristow* (2013) it was held that a burglary, although not normally considered a dangerous crime, could be committed in a dangerous manner. In this case the defendant used a vehicle to commit the offence. A resident at the property was run over and killed in the commission of the offence and the court upheld a conviction for unlawful act manslaughter.

## The unlawful act must cause the death of the victim

The defendant's unlawful act must be the cause of the victim's death: *Mitchell* (1983). We discuss the rules of causation in detail in Chapter 2. If you are answering a problem question you must be satisfied that the defendant's actions are a factual and legal cause of death.

### Aim Higher

The chapter on the general principles of criminal liability (Chapter 2) considers causation in more detail, and it is recommended that you review this in the context of homicide, so that you are able to apply the same principles to a problem question on homicide.

## The mens rea *requirement for unlawful act manslaughter*

The *mens rea* for unlawful act manslaughter is the same as that required for the unlawful act itself (the base level offence). There is no separate *mens rea* required.

This is an important point to note and you should remember to pull this out and explain the rationale within an answer, so it is clear for the examiner.

| Base level offence | *Mens rea* for base level offence | *Mens rea* for constructive manslaughter |
|---|---|---|
| Criminal damage | Intention or recklessness | Intention or recklessness |
| Assault | Intention or recklessness | Intention or recklessness |
| Theft | Intention and dishonesty | Intention and dishonesty |

## Example

Look at this example, and then use the chart below to consider whether this is a case of unlawful act manslaughter:

Chris is short of money, so decides to rob a post office. Chris enters with a gun, and threatens Jill, the postmistress, telling her to hand over the money, or she will be shot. Jill is very frightened and hands the money to Chris. Jill then collapses and dies from a heart attack.

| Is there an act? | Is the act a crime? | Are the *actus reus* and *mens rea* of robbery present? | Is the act dangerous? | Was the death caused by the unlawful act? | Is *mens rea* present? |
|---|---|---|---|---|---|
| Did John commit a positive act? | Is robbery a crime? | Are the *actus reus* and *mens rea* elements for robbery present in this case? | The unlawful act must be dangerous | Is John the legal and factual cause of Jill's death? | The *mens rea* is the same as for robbery |
| Yes, John committed an act not an omission | Yes robbery is a crime: s 8 **Theft Act 1968** | Yes, the AR and MR of the offence are present | Yes, robbery is a dangerous act: *Dawson* **(1985)** | Apply tests for factual and legal causation | There is no additional MR requirement |

## Summary

Use this checklist to ensure that you understand the requirements for the unlawful act manslaughter.

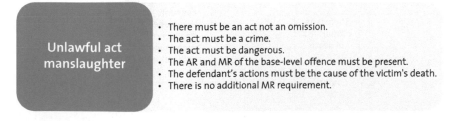

Unlawful act manslaughter

- There must be an act not an omission.
- The act must be a crime.
- The act must be dangerous.
- The AR and MR of the base-level offence must be present.
- The defendant's actions must be the cause of the victim's death.
- There is no additional MR requirement.

## Gross negligence manslaughter

Gross negligence manslaughter is the second type of manslaughter and occurs when D acts unlawfully, but in such a way that D's actions render the defendant criminally negligent.

Therefore the act is not unlawful, but there is a high degree of negligence (gross).

## Common Pitfall

Be careful here not to confuse gross negligence manslaughter with tort. You will see similarities in language and principles being discussed, but remember that gross negligence manslaughter is a criminal offence, and negligence is a tort civil wrong.

## Introduction

Like the other offences in this chapter gross negligence manslaughter is a common law offence. The leading case is that of *Adomako* (1995). This case laid down the basic elements of the offence. These can be articulated as follows:

1. The defendant must owe the victim a duty of care.
2. The defendant must breach that duty of care.
3. There must be an obvious risk of death.
4. The breach of duty of care must be the cause of the victim's death.
5. The breach must amount to gross negligence and be so serious as to justify the imposition of criminal sanction.

We will look at each of these elements in turn. It is important to remember that each of these elements must exist if liability for gross negligence manslaughter is to be established.

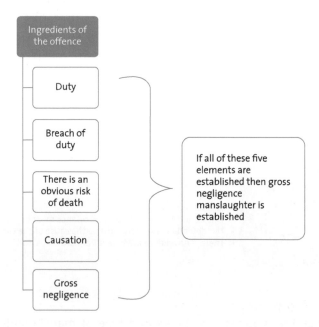

If all of these five elements are established then gross negligence manslaughter is established.

## The defendant must owe the victim a duty of care

As with the tort of negligence, there must be a duty of care on the part of D towards V. In Chapter 2 we considered a number of situations in which the criminal law will find the existence of a duty of care. In reality the finding of a duty of care is not limited to these situations. In *Adomako* it was held that the finding of a duty of care is to be determined according to the 'ordinary principles of the law of negligence'.

In the case of *Donoghue v Stephenson* (1932) It was held that In ascertaining whether a duty of care exists:

> You must take reasonable care to avoid acts or omissions which you reasonably foresee would be likely to injure your neighbour. Who then is my neighbour? The answer seems to be – persons who are so closely and directly affected by my act (or omission) that I ought reasonably to have them in my contemplation as being so affected when I am directing my mind to the acts or omissions.

Therefore, the existence of a duty of care is critical to the construction of liability for this offence. The following circumstances, in addition to those established in Chapter 2 have been held by the courts to give rise to a duty of care in relation to gross negligence manslaughter:

- ❖ By a lorry driver who conceals immigrants in a lorry: *Wacker* (2003).
- ❖ By firefighters to civilians, even where they have ignored requests to move away: *Winter* (2011).
- ❖ By a ship's master to crew: *Litchfield* (1998).
- ❖ By a drug dealer who fails to take adequate steps to summon medical attention for a person to whom they have supplied drugs: *Evans* (2009).

The question as to whether a duty of care exists is a matter of law for the judge to determine: *Evans* (2009).

Therefore:

If a duty of care cannot be established

D cannot be liable for gross negligence manslaughter

## Breach of the duty of care

The next element that must be established beyond a reasonable doubt is that the defendant breached the duty of care owed to the victim. This is judged objectively against the standard of the reasonably competent person performing the activity in question: *Andrews v DPP* (1937).

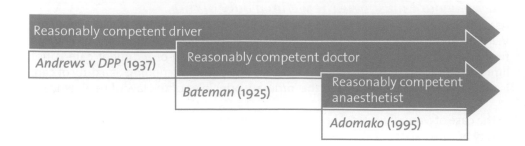

Reasonably competent driver

*Andrews v DPP* (1937)

Reasonably competent doctor

*Bateman* (1925)

Reasonably competent anaesthetist

*Adomako* (1995)

Therefore if the defendant's acts or omissions fall below the standard expected of the reasonably competent person performing that particular activity there is a breach of duty.

## There must be an obvious risk of death

In the case of *Singh* (1999) it was established that 'a reasonably prudent person would have foreseen a serious and obvious risk not merely of injury, even serious injury, but of death'. The case of *Misra* (2005) confirmed this requirement. It is not necessary for the prosecution to prove that the defendant actually foresaw the risk of death, only that the act or omission created an 'obvious' risk of death: *Mark* (2004).

## The breach of duty must be the cause of the victim's death

It is essential that the breach of duty is the cause of the victim's death. The normal rules of causation apply here. Thus the defendant's actions or omissions must be the factual and legal cause of the victim's death. If a causal link cannot be established then D is not liable.

## The jury must be satisfied that the breach of duty is serious enough to constitute gross negligence and as such it should be regarded a crime

Negligence is rarely sufficient fault for criminal liability, so the degree of negligence must be exceptional. It must constitute gross negligence. This is a question for the jury: *Adomako* (1994).

In *Bateman* (1925) it was held that:

> the facts must be such that, in the opinion of the jury, the negligence of the accused went beyond a mere matter of compensation between subjects and showed such disregard for the life and safety of others as to amount to a crime against the state and conduct deserving of punishment.

A key precedent often referred to as the test of gross (a high degree of) negligence is set out below:

---

### Case precedent – *R v Adomako* [1995] 1 AC 171 (HL)

**Facts:** D was an anaesthetist. During an operation, D did not notice that a breathing tube was not attached properly and the patient died as a result.

**Principle:** The defendant's conduct fell so far below the standard of care expected of a reasonably competent doctor that it was sufficient to be regarded as grossly negligent and as such criminal.

**Application:** This case offers a means by which to identify and define negligence. In problem questions, consider how the situation compares with the facts in *Cunningham* to help decide whether a party has been reckless.

Another useful example of grossly negligent conduct is the case of *Reid* (1992), where a diver jumped from a springboard into a pool without considering the danger of hitting anyone who might have been swimming in the pool at the time. D killed another swimmer. It is clear that a very high degree of negligence is required in order to constitute gross negligence: *Andrews v DPP* (1937). It is, however, important to note that the test for gross negligence is rather elastic in nature.

Unlike unlawful act or constructive manslaughter, gross negligence manslaughter can be committed by omission, as well as by a positive act.

## Up for Debate

It is for a jury to decide whether the level of negligence is sufficient to be classed as gross negligence, and therefore a criminal act (i.e. what constitutes gross negligence).

There are differing views on whether this uncertainty is actually useful. For example, would it be more useful to be set out clearly, or are the grey areas more useful in terms of evolving law and the range of different circumstances which are covered by this offence?

### Mens rea

In *AG's Reference (Number 2 of 1999)* (2000) it was held that proof of the defendant's state of mind is not necessary for a conviction of manslaughter by gross negligence. This does not, however, mean that the offence of manslaughter by gross negligence is a strict liability offence. The fault element required for this offence is negligence that is gross.

### Example 1

Consider the following example. Sarah, a nurse, fails to give Zack, a diabetic under her care, his insulin. Zack dies as a result.

In this example you would need to consider:

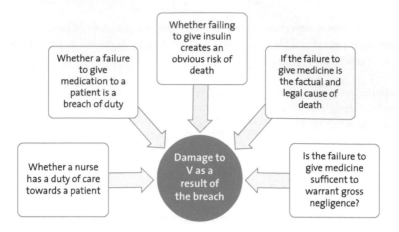

## Example 2

Now consider the following example. Use the flow chart below to work through your answer.

A road worker has dug a hole in the pavement to lay a cable, but she forgets to cover it over at night. Paul is walking on the pavement at night, does not see the hole and falls in. Paul fractures his skull and dies.

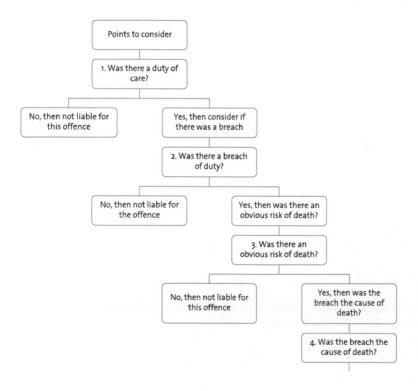

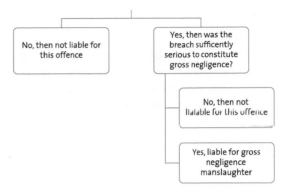

A summary of the points we have covered in this section:

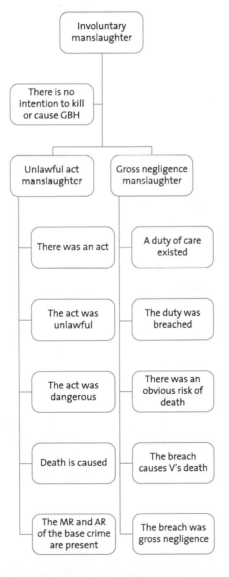

# Putting it into practice

## Question

Raj suffers from depression and is on medication. He recently lost money to Simon after playing poker. Raj cannot now pay his rent, and his depression has worsened. He sees Simon in the street and, taking a knife, goes outside. Raj says, 'Give me my money back or I will kill you.' Simon refuses, and Raj stabs him with the knife, killing Simon.

Discuss whether Raj would be liable for the offence or murder or voluntary manslaughter.

## Suggested solution

To identify whether Raj would be liable for murder or manslaughter, you need to work through the liability for each offence. For the offence of murder you would need to consider:

❖ The definition of murder.
❖ The *actus reus* of the offence.
❖ *Causation*.
❖ The *mens rea* of the offence – malice aforethought – in particular the question makes it clear that the MR for murder is present.

In order to ascertain whether Raj would be liable for voluntary manslaughter you would need to determine whether one of the special partial defences would apply in this case.

You should note that the AR and MR for the offence of voluntary manslaughter are the same as for the offence of murder. You should explain the impact of the successful use of one of these defences. In particular you should note that successfully running one of these defences does not result in an acquittal!

The special partial defences are:

❖ diminished responsibility;
❖ loss of self-control (previously referred to as provocation);
❖ suicide pact.

From these, you could consider both loss of self-control and diminished responsibility. You must define both of these special defences and work your way through each of the ingredients for each defence.

In particular you should focus on diminished responsibility. Consider whether depression is a recognised medical condition and whether Raj could effectively use this as a defence. Remember that this defence is the difference between the offence of murder and voluntary manslaughter, and this would need to emerge from your discussion.

# Key Points Checklist

| | |
|---|:---:|
| The term homicide is used as an overarching term under which a number of specific offences are grouped. Suspects are not charged with homicide or convicted of homicide. | ✓ |
| Murder is a common law offence. As such the definition of murder is not located in the statute books. Rather it is located in the decisions of the courts. Murder is the unlawful killing of a human being with malice aforethought (intention to kill or cause GBH). The sentence upon conviction for murder is a mandatory life sentence. | ✓ |
| The *actus reus* for murder is the unlawful killing of a human being. Murder is a result crime and this means that a chain of causation must be established from the defendant's conduct to the resulting death of the victim. The *mens rea* for murder is 'malice aforethought': this simply means intention to kill or cause GBH. Direct or oblique intent will suffice as per *Woollin*. | ✓ |
| There are three special partial defences to a charge of murder. If these defences are successfully run they reduce the charge of murder to voluntary manslaughter. This reduction in charge enables the judge to exercise discretion in sentencing. These special partial defences are: loss of self-control; diminished responsibility; and suicide pact. These defences are only applicable to a charge of murder. | ✓ |
| Manslaughter is another form of unlawful killing. Like homicide it is a general term. There are two species of manslaughter: voluntary manslaughter as described above; and involuntary manslaughter. What distinguishes these offences is the presence of malice aforethought for voluntary manslaughter and its absence for involuntary manslaughter. | ✓ |
| In circumstances where an unlawful killing has taken place and the defendant does not have the requisite *mens rea* for murder an alternative charge would be involuntary manslaughter. | ✓ |
| There are three forms of involuntary manslaughter: constructive manslaughter, also known as unlawful act manslaughter; manslaughter by gross negligence; and reckless manslaughter. | ✓ |
| Unlawful act manslaughter requires: an unlawful act (not an omission); the act must be a crime; the act must be the cause of the victim's death; the elements of the base level offence must be made out; the *mens rea* for this offence is the *mens rea* for the base offence. | ✓ |
| Gross negligence manslaughter: the defendant must owe the victim a duty of care; there must be a breach of the duty of care; the breach must cause the victim's death; the negligence must be gross. | ✓ |

# Table of key cases referred to in this chapter

| Key case | Brief facts | Principle |
|---|---|---|
| *R v Jordan* [1956] 40 Cr App R 152 | V was stabbed, but died from the treatment and not from the stab wound | Causation and intervening acts |
| *A (Children) (Conjoined Twins)* [2001] 2 WLR 480 | Conjoined twins, one of whom would not survive separation, but was having a detrimental effect on the other twin | Human being and necessity |
| *Martin* [2001] EWCA Crim 2245 | D shot and killed an intruder entering his home | Murder is an unlawful act and self-defence |
| *Byrne* [1960] 2 QB 396 | D murdered and mutilated V while experiencing impulses to do so | Diminished responsibility |
| *Hobson* [1997] Crim LR 759 | Stabbed and killed her abusive husband. Psychiatric reports found she was suffering from battered woman's syndrome. | Diminished responsibility – battered woman's syndrome |
| *Sanderson* (1993) CR App R 325 | D beat and killed his girlfriend. Psychiatric reports found that he suffered from paranoid psychosis. | Diminished responsibility – paranoid psychosis |
| *Gittens* (1984) 79 Cr App R 272 | D was suffering from depression, and killed his wife when on a home visit. | Diminished responsibility – depression |
| *Campbell* (1986) 84 Cr App R 255 | D killed V and was found guilty. On appeal medical evidence of his epilepsy was discovered, and a retrial ordered. | Diminished responsibility |
| *Dowds* [2012] EWCA Crim 281 | D killed V after a binge drinking session. | Diminished responsibility and intoxication |
| *R v Ahluwalia* [1992] 4 All ER 889 | D killed V, her husband, after a long period of physical and mental abuse. | Provocation (old law) |
| *R v Doughty* [1986] 83 Cr App 319 | D killed his baby son when he would not stop crying | Provocation (old law) |
| *DPP v Camplin* [1978] 2 All ER 168 | D was raped by V, who then laughed at him. D hit V over the head with a pan and killed him. | Characteristics of the reasonable man |

| Luc Thuet Thuan [1997] AC 131 | D said that V, his girlfriend owed him money. Her made her withdraw the money and then stabbed her. | Characteristics of the reasonable man |
|---|---|---|
| Smith R v Smith (Morgan) [2000] 3 WLR 654 | D suffered from depression, and killed V after an argument | Characteristics of the reasonable man |
| Attorney General for Jersey v Holley [2005] 3 WLR 29 | D and V were separated and both alcoholic. After a day drinking alcohol D killed V after she had slept with another man. | Characteristics of the reasonable man |
| R v James & Karimi [2006] 2 WLR 887 | D killed V, his wife, after she had formed a relationship with another man | Characteristics of the reasonable man and use of provocation |
| R v Franklin [1883] 15 Cox CC 163 | D killed V by throwing an item into the sea | An unlawful act is required |
| R v Dias [2002] Crim LR 390 | D prepared a syringe for V who injected himself and died of an overdose | What constitutes an unlawful act |
| R v Church [1966] 1 QB 59 | V mocked D's sexual ability, and he killed her | A dangerous act |
| Reid [1992] 1 WLR 793 | D dived into a pool and killed a swimmer underneath | Gross negligence |
| R v Adomako [1995] 1 AC 171 (HL) | D did not attach a tube during an operation, resulting in the death of V | Gross negligence |

---

@ Visit the book's companion website to test your knowledge

❖ Resources include a subject map, revision tip podcasts, downloadable diagrams, MCQ quizzes for each chapter, and a flashcard glossary

❖ www.routledge.com/cw/optimizelawrevision

# 6

# Theft and Related Offences

**Understand the law**
- Can you identify the different sections of the Theft Act 1968, and apply these to the offences of theft, robbery and burglary?

**Remember the details**
- Can you remember the definitions for each offence?
- Can you remember the *actus reus* and *mens rea* for each offence?
- Can you define these elements using case law?

**Reflect critically on areas of debate**
- Do you understand the definition of appropriation, and can you critically discuss the meaning of appropriation in relation to consent and the assumption of the rights of an owner?
- Do you understand the test for dishonesty and are you able to critically reflect on the limitations of the definition?

**Contextualise**
- Can you relate the offences in this chapter to other offences such as non-fatal offences against the person or sexual offences?

**Apply your skills and knowledge**
- Can you complete the activities in this chapter, using statutes and cases to support your answer?

# Chapter Map

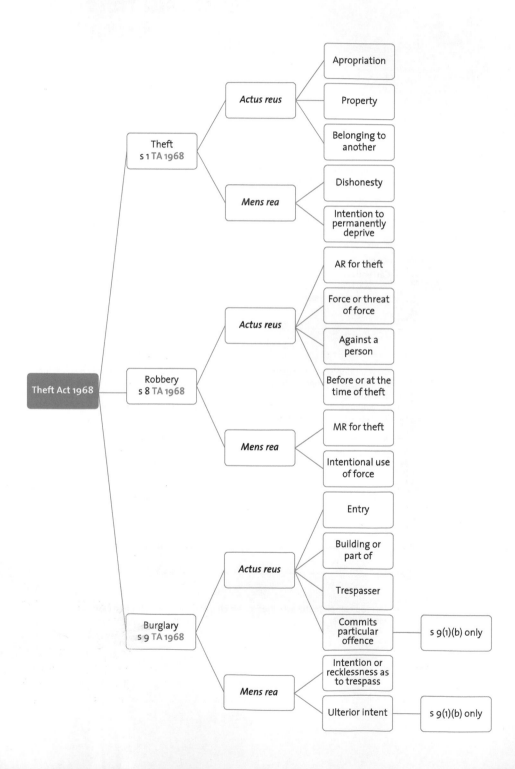

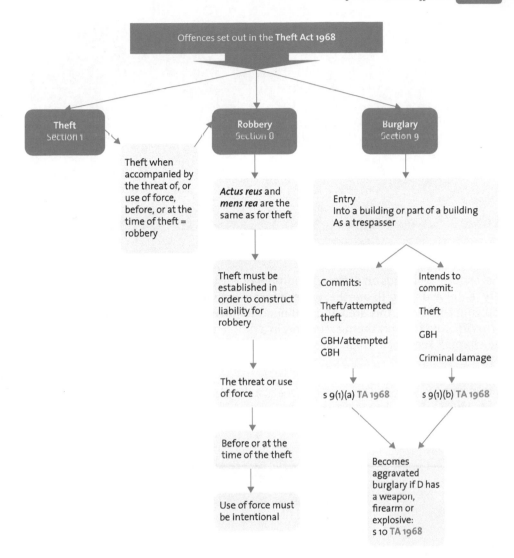

Offences set out in the **Theft Act 1968**

**Theft**
Section 1

**Robbery**
Section 8

**Burglary**
Section 9

Theft when accompanied by the threat of, or use of force, before, or at the time of theft = robbery

*Actus reus* and *mens rea* are the same as for theft

Entry
Into a building or part of a building
As a trespasser

Theft must be established in order to construct liability for robbery

Commits:

Theft/attempted theft

GBH/attempted GBH

Intends to commit:

Theft

GBH

Criminal damage

The threat or use of force

s 9(1)(a) TA 1968

s 9(1)(b) TA 1968

Before or at the time of the theft

Becomes aggravated burglary if D has a weapon, firearm or explosive:
s 10 TA 1968

Use of force must be intentional

*Relationship between the different offences*

# Introduction

In this chapter we will consider theft and related offences. You can see in the diagram above that we have illustrated the connection between the different offences. It is important that you do not revise theft in isolation as examiners frequently seek to test students' knowledge of the connectivity between these offences. The offences in this chapter are statutory in nature, and this means that all you need do when faced with a problem question, or an essay question is work your way methodically through the different statutory provisions using relevant case law to illustrate your answer.

## Aim Higher

Examiners may sometimes set a theft scenario which draws on other areas of law, such as property law, contract law or tort law.

It is important to remember to stay focused on the subject you are being examined on (theft and criminal law), try not to stray into other areas of law, as these can distract from the central issues. That is not to say that you should not note the overlap – and this will demonstrate a rounded understanding of all the issues for the examiner – but do ensure that the vast majority of your answer is in relation to the criminal law! If you wander too far off on a tangent you will limit the award of marks that the examiner can make.

This chapter will focus on defining a number of key terms such as 'property', 'dishonesty' and 'belonging to another'. These terms are vital to fully understanding and applying the law in this area and you need to have a solid understanding of these terms in order to apply them accurately in a problem question. As you work through the chapter, keep focused on these terms, and then test your understanding in the activities at the end.

In this chapter we will focus on the Theft Act 1968, and the subsequent Theft Act 1978, which refined the 1968 Theft Act.

The Theft Act 1968 brought together the main theft offences for the first time, clarifying the *actus reus* and *mens rea* for each.

The offences in the Theft Act 1968 that we will consider in this chapter are:

* theft
* robbery
* burglary – including aggravated burglary
* trespass with intent to commit a sexual offence – an overview.

## Theft

The definition of theft is set out in s 1 of the Theft Act 1968:

(1) A person is guilty of theft if he dishonestly appropriates property belonging to another with the intention of permanently depriving the other of it . . .

(2) It is immaterial whether the appropriation is made with a view to gain, or for the thief's own benefit.

The *actus reus* and *mens rea* for theft are:

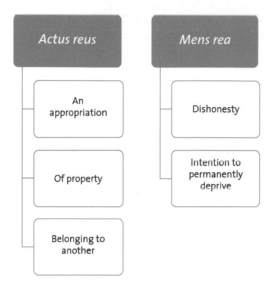

We will now consider each of these five elements in detail.

## Appropriation

It is this element of theft that causes the most difficulty for students. At first glance, it might be assumed that the term means the physical removal of property, such as physically removing a purse from a handbag. However, appropriation actually has a much broader meaning.

Section 3(1) of the 1968 Act defines appropriation as:

> Any assumption by a person of the rights of an owner amounts to an appropriation, and this includes, where he has come by the property (innocently or not) without stealing it, any later assumption of a right to it by keeping or dealing with it as owner.

The discussion focuses in relation to appropriation around the phrase 'any assumption by a person of the rights of an owner', that is, dealing with the property in a way which only the owner has a right to.

Appropriation is seen as a continuing act, as confirmed in the case of *R v Hale* (1978) (when revising, you might find it helpful to remind yourself of this concept in relation to the case of *Fagan* and the concept of a 'continuous act' in this case in relation to appropriation).

It is not easy to articulate precisely what behaviour, or acts will constitute an appropriation. The courts have discussed this concept in great detail in a number of different cases. We will consider a number of cases where the issue of appropriation has been considered in cases where there is consent.

## Consent

A common issue that has arisen in relation to the concept of appropriation is what happens when the owner of the property has consented to the appropriation? Does the existence of consent invalidate the appropriation in some way?

---

**Case precedent – *Lawrence v Metropolitan Police Commissioner* [1972] AC 626**

**Facts:** V opened his wallet to allow D, a taxi driver, to take the fare from the wallet. D took more money than he was entitled to. In his defence, D highlighted that V gave him the money voluntarily.

**Principle:** The impact of consent on appropriation

**Application:** It was held by the House of Lords that appropriation can occur even where V consented.

---

As a consequence of the decisions in *Lawrence v Metropolitan Police Commissioner* (1972), *Morris* (1984), *Gomez* (1993) and *Hinks* (2001), the meaning of consent has been expanded significantly. Therefore in the following circumstances appropriation may have occurred:

- Where there is no misappropriation
- With or without the consent of the owner
- With or without the property being physically taken or removed
- Where a valid gift has been made by the property owner
- Where there has been an assumption of any one right of the owner

Therefore, the significant factor that turns a lawful appropriation into an unlawful appropriation is the *mens rea* of the defendant. You should highlight this in any assessment question on theft when discussing appropriation.

The three key points to remember on consent are:

1. Appropriation can take place even if there is consent ⇨ 2. Consent is therefore irrelevant to appropriation ⇨ 3. It is the *mens rea* of D at the time of the appropriation, not the existence of consent, that is significant

## Appropriation and suffered a loss

It is also important to note that V does not have to suffer a loss in order for an appropriation to take place. This was confirmed in *Corcoran v Anderton* (1980), where D grabbed V's handbag and dropped it then ran off. The Court held that by grabbing the handbag, D did assume the rights of the owner (and a conviction for robbery was upheld). In this case V had not suffered a loss as the defendant quickly abandoned the bag.

This principle was later applied in *Ex parte Osman* (1990), which established that even if the victim does not suffer any loss there may still be an appropriation.

## Appropriation and assuming the rights of the owner

The essence of an appropriation is the assumption of any one (or more) of the owner's rights. In *R v Morris* (1983) the two defendants were convicted when they switched the price tags on items in a shop. One was arrested before paying for the goods, the other after paying for the goods.

Switching the labels was something that only the owner had the authority to do, therefore the defendants assumed the rights of the owner (and an appropriation had taken place) the moment the labels were switched.

It was highlighted that there only needs to be any one right of the owner that is assumed.

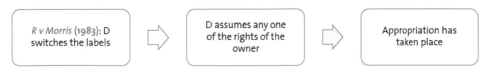

*R v Morris* (1983): D switches the labels ⇨ D assumes any one of the rights of the owner ⇨ Appropriation has taken place

## Appropriation and gifts

An appropriation can also occur in circumstances where the owner has made a gift of the property to the defendant. This will occur in circumstances where the defendant has acted dishonestly in relation to the transaction.

For example, in the case of *R v Hinks* (2000), D persuaded V, a person of limited intelligence, to give them monetary gifts. The court held that an appropriation could still occur where property has been gifted, even when indefeasible gifts are given.

In the next section we will consider the *actus reus* element of theft, which is that the appropriation must be of property.

## Property

According to s 4 of the Theft Act 1968, property is:

> Section 4(1) 'Property' includes money and all other property, real or personal, including things in action and other intangible property.
>
> (2) A person cannot steal land, or things forming part of land and severed from it by him or by his directions, except in the following cases, that it to say—
>
> > (a) When he is a trustee or personal representative, or is authorised by power of attorney, or as liquidator of a company, or otherwise, to sell or dispose of land belonging to another, and he appropriates the land or anything forming part of it by dealing with it in breach of the confidence reposed in him; or
> >
> > (b) When he is not in possession of the land and appropriates anything forming part of the land by severing it or causing it to be severed, or after it has been severed; or
> >
> > (c) When, being in possession of the land under a tenancy, he appropriates the whole or part of any fixture or structure let to be used with the land.
>
> (3) A person who picks mushrooms growing wild on any land, or who picks flowers, fruit or foliage from a plant growing wild on any land, does not (although not in possession of the land) steal what he picks, unless he does it for reward or for sale or other commercial purpose.
>
> For purposes of this subsection 'mushroom' includes any fungus, and 'plant' includes any shrub or tree.
>
> (4) Wild creatures, tamed or untamed, shall be regarded as property; but a person cannot steal a wild creature not tamed nor ordinarily kept in captivity, or the carcase of any such creature, unless either it has been reduced into possession by or on behalf of another person and possession of it has not since been lost or abandoned, or another person is in course of reducing it into possession.

This can be summarised as:

| Property is: | Property is not: |
| --- | --- |
| Tangible and intangible items | Land, in relation to stealing, with exceptions |
| Wild and tamed animals reduced into the possession of others | Picking wild flowers or fruit, except for a financial reward |

It is clear from s 4 that there are a number of detailed stipulations regarding what does and does not constitute property for the purposes of this offence. It is important to note that the meaning of property can differ between different offences. A number of cases have refined our understanding of what constitutes property for the purposes of theft. These are set out in the table below:

| Item | Position in relation to the Theft Act 1968 with refinements |
|---|---|
| Personal property | Personal property can be classified as movable property, and can therefore be tangible and intangible |
| Tangible property | Includes movable and non-movable property |
| Intangible property | Exists as a right, and can be enforced by law |
| Money | Includes notes and coins. There is an intention to permanently deprive unless the exact same money (the exact notes and coins that had been taken) as the same ones were going to be returned, as set out in *R v Velumyl* [1989] Crim LR 299. |
| Unlawful possession of property | Property can amount to something that is in unlawful possession, such as stealing illegal drugs. Demonstrated in *R v Smith & Ors* [2011] 1 Cr App R 30. |
| Body parts | Body parts are also regarded as property of the person whose parts they are, confirmed in *R v Kelly* [1998] 3 All ER 741. There was previous debate regarding classification of a corpse, and this is also now regarded as property. |

If you need help understanding the difference between tangible and intangible property, consider the example below.

**Example:** think about a banker's cheque: as a piece of paper it is tangible property because you can touch it and see it; however, it also represents something else. It represents more than a tangible piece of paper, because it also represents the transfer of money between two people. That representation is an example of a 'thing in action', which is intangible.

It is important to highlight the following case that also concerned intangible property.

For example, in the case of *Oxford v Moss* (1979), it was held that confidential information cannot be stolen. In this case a student accessed a forthcoming exam paper. There was no intention of permanently depriving the university of the paper (the tangible property); it was the information on the paper that was of interest, and this was intangible property. Therefore, the offence of theft could be made out in this case.

## Common Pitfall

Aside from checking your understanding of the law relating to property, a common question asked can relate to s 4(3) of the **Theft Act 1968**. An examiner may pose a question asking you to consider whether is it theft to pick mushrooms growing wild on land, or whether a person who picks flowers, fruit or foliage from a plant growing wild on any land, commits theft. The key to remember here is that the above are not considered property for the purposes of the **TA 1968** UNLESS D does it for reward, sale or other commercial purpose.

We are now moving on to consider the third element of the *actus reus* for the offence of theft, and that is the requirement that the appropriated property belongs to another.

## Belonging to another

This element of the *actus reus* relates to the property that has been appropriated belonging to another person. The emphasis here is on the word 'belonging'. We will see in this section that the meaning of 'belonging' has a different meaning to the meaning that we would normally attribute to this word. That is because in the context of theft the meaning of 'belonging' is much broader, as it encompasses a person who is in **possession** or in **control** of the appropriated property.

Section 5 of the 1968 Act states:

(1)    Property shall be regarded as belonging to any person having possession or control of it, or having in it any proprietary right or interest (not being an equitable interest arising only from an agreement to transfer or grant an interest).

(2)    Where property is subject to a trust, the persons to whom it belongs shall be regarded as including any person having a right to enforce the trust, and an intention to defeat the trust shall be regarded accordingly as an intention to deprive of the property any person having that right.

(3)    Where a person receives property from or on account of another, and is under an obligation to the other to retain and deal with that property or its proceeds in a particular way, the property or proceeds shall be regarded (as against him) as belonging to the other.

(4)    Where a person gets property by another's mistake, and is under an obligation to make restoration (in whole or in part) of the property or its proceeds or of the value thereof, then to the extent of that obligation the property or proceeds shall be regarded (as against him) as belonging to the person entitled to restoration, and an intention not to make restoration shall be regarded accordingly as an intention to deprive that person of the property or proceeds.

(5)    Property of a corporation sole shall be regarded as belonging to the corporation notwithstanding a vacancy in the corporation.

## *Belonging can mean in possession or control*

This effectively means that a person does not have to own the property for it to belong to him (s 5(1)), for the purpose of theft. It can be enough that V has possession or control of the property. Thus it is possible for a defendant to be convicted of stealing his own property!

**Example:** Nihal asks Peter to look after his mobile phone while he is at the gym. Surya steals the phone from Peter's bag when he is not looking. In this example, Peter is in possession of the mobile phone for Nihal, and Surya steals the phone while it is in the possession of Peter, even though it is not his phone.

| Theft can occur if: | the property is in the possession of V | V has control of the property |
|---|---|---|

Many criminal law students are surprised by the revelation that a defendant can be convicted of stealing their own property from a person that is looking after it. An example of this situation can be seen in the case of *Turner (No 2)* (1971).

---

**Case precedent – *R v Turner (No 2)* [1971] 1 WLR**

**Facts:** D left his car at a garage for repairs. The defendant did not want to pay for the repairs so simply collected his car without paying or notifying the owners of the garage.

**Principle:** D can steal his own property if it is in the possession or under the legal control of another.

**Application:** D was guilty of theft as he was interfering with the garage owners' right of possession over the car, until payment for the repairs is made by the owner.

---

## *Instructions*

Section 5(3) of the Theft Act 1968 highlights that where a person has specific instructions to deal with the appropriated property in a certain way, any deviation from these instructions can amount to theft. The central issue is whether the instructions are clear. This was decided in *R v Hall* (1973).

If you are answering a question which includes a set of instructions, you will need to identify that:

❖ the instructions were clear;
❖ they were understood;
❖ D did not follow these instructions.

## Property received by mistake

Section 5(4) of the Theft Act 1968 states that where a person receives property by mistake and they are under an obligation to return the property, a failure to do so can amount to theft. This principle is outlined in *A-G's Ref (No 1 of 1983) (1985)*.

For example, Rita's bank pays money into her account in error. They actually intend to pay the money into Paul's account. Rita goes to a cash machine and discovers that she has £15,000 more than she expected in her account. Rita knows that this must be an error, but she decides to buy a new car with the money.

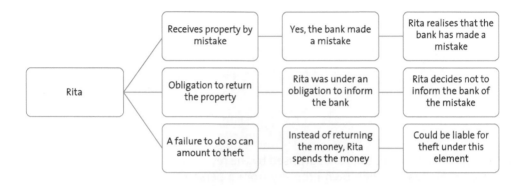

Section 5(4) operates only in circumstances where the giver of the property has made a mistake. It is also important to note that s 5(4) does not apply unless the obligation to return the property is a legal obligation: *Gilks (1972)*.

## Abandoned property

The *actus reus* of theft stipulates that the appropriated property must belong to another. Abandoned property does not 'belong to another' and therefore property that is abandoned cannot be stolen for the purposes of s 1 of the Theft Act 1968. In the case of *Ricketts v Basildon Magistrates (2011)* the court dealt with the issue of abandoned property. In this instance the defendant took donation bags left outside a charity shop. The court held that the donor of the bags intended the charity shop to take ownership of the items. As such the bags had not been abandoned.

It is important to note that lost property is not abandoned property: *Hibbert v McKiernan (1948)*.

For example, Sam accidentally leaves her iPhone on the train. Kyle, who has been sitting opposite her, sees the phone and takes it. In this situation Sam has not abandoned her phone, therefore the phone still belongs to her, even though it is not in her possession.

Abandonment of property suggests that the owner no longer has an interest in the property: it does not matter to the owner what happens next to the property or who appropriates it.

For example, DJ purchases a magazine at the train station. He reads the magazine on the train and once he has finished reading it he deliberately leaves the magazine on the train seat in order that someone else can read it. Sarah sits in DJ's seat and picks up the magazine; she takes the magazine home with her. In this situation DJ has abandoned the magazine – he does not care what happens to it next, whether it is disposed of or whether someone else appropriates it. In this case Sarah could not be liable for theft because the property does not 'belong to another': it has been abandoned.

So, when you are determining whether the property belongs to another, remember to consider:

Having considered the three elements of the *actus reus* of theft, we must now consider the two *mens rea* requirements for the offence.

## Dishonesty

The first *mens rea* requirement for the offence of theft is that the appropriation of property must be dishonest. Dishonesty is therefore a key concept not only in relation to theft but also in relation to other 'dishonesty offences'. It is therefore very important that you understand the concept of dishonesty and that you are able to apply it to a range of situations.

The **Theft Act (TA) 1968** does not provide a definition of theft. It does however, set out a number of situations in which a defendant will **NOT** be considered dishonest. Section 2 sets out:

(1) A person's appropriation of property belonging to another is not to be regarded as dishonest–

    (a) if he appropriates the property in the belief that he has in law the right to deprive the other of it, on behalf of himself or a third person; or

    (b) if he appropriates the property in the belief that he would have the other's consent if the other knew of the appropriation and the circumstances of it; or

    (c) (except where the property came to him as trustee or personal representative) if he appropriates the property in the belief that the person to whom the property belongs cannot be discovered by taking reasonable steps.

(2) A person's appropriation of property belonging to another may be dishonest notwithstanding that he is willing to pay for the property.

It is important to note that these situations are not the only situations in which a defendant would not be considered dishonest. When discussing whether an appropriation is dishonest you should start with s 2 TA 1968: if the D held any of these beliefs then he would not have acted dishonestly.

## Aim Higher

Remember that there is only a need for a **genuine belief** to be demonstrated in relation to s 2 of the **Theft Act 1968** – it does not matter whether the belief is reasonable. This was established in *R v Holden* [1991] Crim LR 478.

Section 2(2) also establishes that D may be dishonest, even if he is willing to pay for or replace the property which he has appropriated. For example, Ryan takes Jo's Kindle without asking, he accidentally breaks the Kindle, and Jo discovers that Ryan has taken and broken his Kindle. Ryan then offers to pay for another Kindle. Ryan could still be liable for theft even though he is willing to pay for it.

## What is dishonesty?

What does dishonesty actually mean? The Court of Appeal insists that dishonesty is an ordinary word in everyday use. It is a word that can be understood by the average person without a need for a definition: *R v Feely* (1973).

In the case of *Ghosh* (1982) a two-stage test for dishonesty was established. This test for dishonesty applies to other dishonesty offences.

### Case precedent – *R v Ghosh* [1982] QB 1053

**Facts:** D was a doctor, and claimed fees from patients for surgical operations that he had not carried out.

**Principle:** Two-stage test for dishonesty

**Application:** The Court of Appeal held that the jury should be directed towards answering the following questions:

(1) Was D's conduct dishonest according to the current standards of ordinary decent people? and

(2) Did D realise that his conduct was dishonest by the current standards of ordinary decent people?

If D answers yes to both questions then D has been dishonest; but if D answers NO to EITHER question then D is not dishonest.

You will see that this is a twofold test, which contains subjective and objective elements. It is commonly called the 'Ghosh Test', and you will see this test applied to other areas of law where dishonesty is part of the *mens rea*.

**Example:** Danny regularly borrows money from his manager's shop till to buy his lunch. He repays all of the money at the end of the week. This has been going on for many months. The manager discovers this and accuses Danny of theft. Look at the two-part test above, and think about whether Danny would be dishonest according to the Ghosh Test.

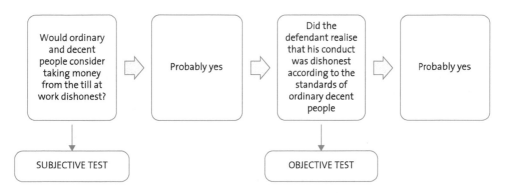

It is for the jury to decide whether the test has been met.

## Common Pitfall

When applying the Ghosh Test make sure that you fully work through the subjective and objective elements of the Test as well as s 2 of the **Theft Act 1968**. Some students conclude that D is dishonest in relation to one stage of the Ghosh Test but not dishonest in relation to the other element. They then go on to conclude that D is to be deemed dishonest.

This is incorrect: D must pass BOTH elements of the Ghosh Test in order to be dishonest.

Having considered the first *mens rea* element for theft we will now consider the second element of the *mens rea*, which is the intention to permanently deprive.

### Intention to permanently deprive
The intention to permanently deprive the owner of the goods is an essential element of theft. It is a unique element of the *mens rea* for theft offences, so it is important that you pay particular attention to this element in any answer, to differentiate the offence of theft from other offences.

### Intention
It is important to note that it is not necessary to show actual deprivation of the property – just an intention to bring about such deprivation.

## Common Pitfall

The key element is 'if his intention is to treat the thing as his own to dispose of'.

But be aware, this is not the same as D intending to keep the property for themselves – it effectively means an intention to deprive V of their property.

Intention is outlined in s 6 of the 1968 Act, which states:

6(1) A person appropriating property belonging to another without meaning the other permanently to lose the thing itself is nevertheless to be regarded as having the intention of permanently depriving the other of it if his intention is to treat the thing as his own to dispose of regardless of the other's rights; and a borrowing or lending of it may amount to so treating it if, but only if, the borrowing or lending is for a period and in circumstances making it equivalent to an outright taking or disposal.

(3) Without prejudice to the generality of subsection (1) above, where a person, having possession or control (lawfully or not) of property belonging to another, parts with the property under a condition as to its return which he may not be able to perform, this (if done for purposes of his own and without the other's authority) amounts to treating the property as his own to dispose of regardless of the other's rights.

### Case precedent – *DPP v Lavender* [1994] Crim LR 297

**Facts:** D removed some doors from a council property and put them in his girlfriend's house (which was also owned by the council).

**Principle:** Intention to permanently deprive

**Application:** D treated the doors as his own to dispose of (as set out in s 6(1)), regardless of the council's (owner's) rights, therefore he was guilty of theft.

In this case, D intentionally treats the property as his own, regardless of the rights of the owner.

### Borrowing

It is important that you are able to draw a distinction between *borrowing* and *depriving*, as this is a popular examination issue. The defendant must have an intention to permanently deprive the owner of their property; it is no defence that the defendant had a change of heart and returned the property: *McHugh* (1993).

It can sometimes be difficult to determine the difference between the intention to permanently deprive and borrowing.

**Example:** Dean steals a car as a getaway vehicle for a robbery. Dean uses the car and then abandons it.

In this case we can see that the defendant has no intention to permanently deprive the owner of the car. Dean simply intends to use the car in order to escape. In this case liability for theft cannot be made out (that is not to say that liability for other offences does not exist). Can you differentiate between borrowing and intention to permanently deprive here?

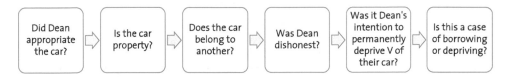

To help you clarify your understanding, look at the case of *R v Mitchell* (2008). You will see that the facts of the case are very similar. In *Mitchell* D was found not guilty. This is because D intended to use the car as a getaway vehicle, so there was no intention to permanently deprive.

In order to constitute borrowing there must be an intention to return the exact property in the same state/condition and the property must retain the same value.

* Borrowing money with the intention of replacing it at a later date meets the criteria for intention to permanently deprive unless the defendant intends to replace the exact same notes/coins: *Velumyl* (1989).
* Borrowing a ticket and returning it after the event to which it applies has taken place, will constitute an intention to permanently deprive: *Coffey* (1987).
* Borrowing a device and draining its goodness/value can amount to an intention to permanently deprive.

### *Permanently*

The concept of intention to permanently deprive will also require you to consider what 'permanently' means for the purposes of the Theft Act 1968.

Broadly speaking, it does not need to be established that the deprivation is permanent, as it can also be temporary: for example, stealing a chainsaw from a building site and returning it three years later. Would this be considered permanent or temporary deprivation?

Consider the case below.

| Case precedent – *R v Lloyd* [1985] QB 829 (CA) |
| --- |

**Facts:** V was taking films from his employer, a cinema, giving them to a friend to copy and then returning them in the same condition to the cinema.

**Principle:** Intention to permanently deprive

**Application:** D was found guilty, but this was overturned on appeal, as the films were returned in the same condition, so there was no intention to permanently deprive the owner of the property in question.

In reality the concept of intention to permanently deprive is quite broad. Section 6 creates the possibility that something less than permanent deprivation can suffice.

## Conditional intention to permanently deprive

Before concluding this section it is important to briefly address the situation where a defendant has a conditional intention to permanently deprive. For example, imagine that Leigh looks through Monique's bag with the intention of ascertaining whether there is anything in the bag worth stealing. In this case Leigh has a conditional intention to permanently deprive Monique of property in the event that he finds anything of value. In *Eason* (1971) and *Husseyn* (1977) it was held that a conditional intent was insufficient. The correct charge here would be attempted theft.

## Common Pitfall

It is not uncommon for criminal law students to reach the wrong conclusion not because their understanding of the law is flawed, but because they feel that the defendant should be held responsible. In this situation the application of law is often good, but at the last moment, despite having already established that a key element of liability is missing, a student will conclude that the defendant is liable.

Remember that your conclusion should always flow from your working out. If all the indicators suggest no liability then there is in all likelihood no liability – BUT that is in relation to the specific offence that you have been considering. It DOES NOT mean that the defendant would escape all criminal liability. It is often the case that liability exists for a lesser or alternative offence.

In many ways constructing criminal liability is a little like solving a mathematical problem.

❖ You should always show your working out – this is where the examiner awards the majority of the marks.
❖ Your answer/conclusion should always flow from your working out.
❖ Worst case scenario – if you come to the wrong conclusion you will still have been awarded marks for your working out!

A summary of the points we have covered in this section is:

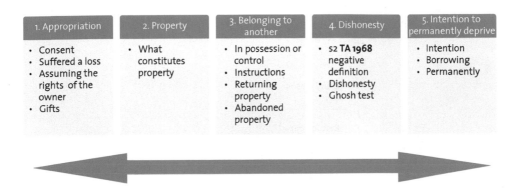

**Section 1 Theft Act 1968**

Theft is the dishonest appropriation of property belonging to another with the intention of depriving the owner of it.

| 1. Appropriation | 2. Property | 3. Belonging to another | 4. Dishonesty | 5. Intention to permanently deprive |
|---|---|---|---|---|
| • Consent<br>• Suffered a loss<br>• Assuming the rights of the owner<br>• Gifts | • What constitutes property | • In possession or control<br>• Instructions<br>• Returning property<br>• Abandoned property | • s2 **TA 1968** negative definition<br>• Dishonesty<br>• Ghosh test | • Intention<br>• Borrowing<br>• Permanently |

We are now moving on to consider a theft-related offence, the offence of robbery.

# Robbery

The offence of robbery is also contained in the Theft Act 1968. Section 8 states:

(1) A person is guilty of robbery if he steals, and immediately before or at the time of doing so, and in order to do so, he uses force on any person or puts or seeks to put any person in fear of being then and there subjected to force.

In order to understand the components of robbery you must understand the *actus reus* and *mens rea* of theft. Once you understand the elements of theft, the offence of robbery is easily understood. Essentially, robbery comprises the following elements:

What distinguishes the offence of robbery from theft is the threat of, or the use of, force in order to steal. You will sometimes see robbery referred to as an aggravated form of theft. It is a more serious offence than theft, and one which attracts a more significant sentence upon conviction.

The elements of the offence are:

## *Actus reus* of theft

In order to construct liability for robbery the prosecution must be able to establish the *actus reus* (AR) for theft. In a problem question you will need to outline the AR elements of theft, which are:

* appropriation
* of property
* belonging to another.

---

**Case precedent – *R v Robinson* [1977] Crim LR 173**

**Facts:** D had a genuine belief that he had a right to the property, and he used force to obtain the property from the victim.

**Principle:** Liability for robbery can only arise where liability for theft is established.

**Application:** The defendant's genuine belief in his right to the property meant that D was not dishonest (as under s 2(1)(a)). As theft was not committed, the offence of robbery could not be made out.

---

If the offence of theft cannot be made out, liability for robbery will not exist. If you face this situation in a problem question you can consider a non-fatal offence against the person as an alternative charge (for the threat/use of force).

Try to remember this as:

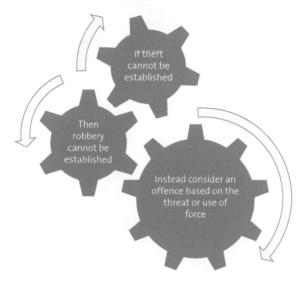

If theft cannot be established

Then robbery cannot be established

Instead consider an offence based on the threat or use of force

The authority for the principle that liability for robbery flows from liability for theft is *Corcoran v Anderton* (1980).

## *Force or threat of force to any person*

The second element of the *actus reus* of theft is that D must threaten or use force. The term *force* is an ordinary word that does not require definition. It is a question of fact for the jury: *Dawson* (1976). It is irrelevant whether the victim actually feels threatened; it is the intention of D that is important here: *B v DPP* (2007).

In the case of *R v Dawson & James* (1976), V was nudged off balance by D in order for the second defendant to steal his wallet. This amounted to an offence of robbery. From this case it can be seen that a relatively low level of force was all that was needed.

## Up for Debate

if we consider that it is the role of the jury to determine whether force has been used or the threat of it, is it possible that different juries could come to different conclusions in cases involving the same facts?

Do you think that there should be some guidance given to the jury in order to obtain some form of consistency?

The force may also be directed somewhere else, in order to steal. For example, in *R v Clouden* (1987), D wrenched a handbag from V's hands. Although the force used was on the handbag, in order to pull it away from the victim, the court held that this could amount to robbery.

We can see these cases in the following timeline:

*R v Dawson & James* (1976)    *R v Clouden* (1987)    *R v DPP* (2007)

### The threat of force

There is no need for D actually to use force against the victim; the threat of force is sufficient. The threat of force may be express (a verbal threat, actual force) or implied (threatening, or menacing behaviour).

It is useful to refer back to the chapter on non-fatal offences (Chapter 3), in particular the offence of technical assault. In a technical assault V apprehends immediate unlawful violence. If the other elements of the offence of robbery are not made out it is possible that liability for an offence against the person (technical assault, battery or an aggravated offence) may be made out.

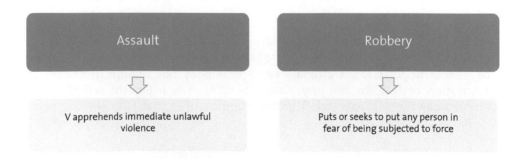

Assault    Robbery

V apprehends immediate unlawful violence    Puts or seeks to put any person in fear of being subjected to force

### The force can be against 'any person'

It is not necessary for the force to be directed against the owner of the property itself. It can be directed against 'any person'.

## Immediately before or at the time of the theft

The use of force or threat of force must be immediately before, or at the time of the theft. If a defendant uses force after the theft this will not amount to robbery.

> ### Case precedent – *R v Hale* [1978] Cr App R 415 D1
>
> **Facts:** D1 went upstairs and appropriated jewellery, whilst D2 was downstairs with V. D1 rejoined D2 downstairs, where they tied up V.
>
> **Principle:** Appropriation is a continuing act. Force or threat of force immediately before or at the time of the theft.
>
> **Application:** The issue related to whether this was a use of force immediately before or at the time of the theft.

Thus, in the above case, the theft of the jewellery was a continuing act: D1 had appropriated the jewellery, and still had the jewellery when the victim was tied up. As a result D1 and D2 were convicted of robbery.

Another useful case is *R v Lockley* (1995), where it was held that, as in *Hale*, there was a continuing act where the defendant used force to escape. Therefore force can be used in order to steal AND in order to escape once the theft has been committed.

We can summarise this as:

## The mens rea *for theft*

The *mens rea* for theft must be made out. The elements that need to be established are:

❖ dishonesty;
❖ intention to permanently deprive.

## The force or threat of force is intentional

In addition to the *mens rea* requirements for theft it must be established that the use of force or the threat of force by D is intentional. Thus accidental force will not suffice. The use of force must be in order to steal.

A summary of the points we have covered in this section is:

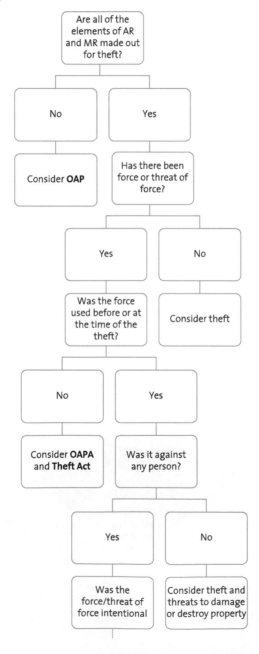

# Burglary

In this next section we are going to consider another offence in the Theft Act 1968: the offence of burglary. This is an offence under s 9 of the Theft Act 1968. It is not uncommon for students to think that burglary is simply breaking into a property in order to steal. This is an oversimplification of the offence of burglary. In reality the offence is more sophisticated than this.

Section 9 of the Theft Act 1968 provides:

(1)  A person is guilty of burglary if –

   (a)  he enters any building or part of a building as a trespasser and with intent to commit any such offence as is mentioned in subsection (2) below; or
   (b)  having entered into any building or part of a building as a trespasser he steals or attempts to steal anything in the building or that part of it or inflicts or attempts to inflict on any person therein any grievous bodily harm.

(2)  The offences referred to in subsection (1)(a) above are offences of stealing anything in the building or part of a building in question, of inflicting on any person therein any grievous bodily harm, and of doing unlawful damage to the building or anything therein.

## Common Pitfall

Note: this section used to include the offence of rape, but this has now been repealed by the Sexual Offences Act 2003.

(3)  A person guilty of burglary shall on conviction on indictment be liable to imprisonment for a term not exceeding –

   (a)  where the offence was committed in respect of a building or part of a building which was a dwelling, fourteen years;
   (b)  in any other case, ten years.

## The types of burglary

There are two different ways in which burglary can be committed. These are:

**The Common Elements**

- enters a building or part of
- as a trespasser

| Section 9(1)(a) Burglary | Section 9(1)(b) Burglary |
|---|---|
| • Intent to commit any one or more of the three offences; theft, criminal damage, GBH | • Commits theft or attempted theft, or inflicting or attempting to inflict GBH |

In the case of s 9(1)(a) the offence is committed upon 'entry' to the building, as a trespasser, where D has the ulterior intent to commit one of the following offences: theft, GBH or criminal damage. In the case of s 9(1)(b) the offence is committed when one of the specific offences is actually committed (i.e. theft/attempted theft, GBH/ attempted GBH). Either way D must have entered the building or part of a building as a trespasser and must have intended or have been reckless as to the trespass.

**Example:** Carlo and David enter a building site as trespassers to skateboard on the site. While they are there, they decide to take some building materials home in order to construct jumps and ramps to practise on. They have therefore committed a s 9(1)(b) offence, as they trespassed first, and then decided to steal the pipe.

However, if Carlo and David entered the building site with the intention of stealing the pipe, this would be a s 9(1)(a) offence.

We will now look at the individual elements of the offence of burglary.

## Entry

The defendant must make a 'substantial and effective entry' into a building or part of a building: *Collins* (1973). There are two critical issues in this context:

❖ How much of the defendant must have entered the building or part of the building in order for entry to occur? It is sufficient for only part of D's body to have entered the building or part of it.

❖ What if the defendant uses an object or innocent agent to enter the building: is this sufficient? Entry can be substantial and effective where it is achieved through an innocent agent or a device.

---

**Case precedent – *R v Ryan* [1996] Crim LR 320**

**Facts:** D tried to burgle a house, and was found wedged in the open window where he was stuck. Part of his body was in the house.

**Principle:** Effective entry

**Application:** D was convicted of burglary and appealed on the basis that he was stuck, therefore entry was not effective. The conviction was upheld, as part of his body was inside the house.

---

## Building or part of a building

The entry must be into a building or part of a building. Therefore it is important to understand what constitutes a building or part of a building.

The definition of a building is broad: it includes a house, a flat, a caravan, an office block, etc. An immobile container can also be considered a building, as illustrated in the following case.

---

**Case precedent – *B and S v Leathley* [1979] Crim LR 314**

**Facts:** D stole from a container, which had been in the same position for a number of years.

**Principle:** Definition of a building

**Application:** That an immobile container can be classed as a building.

---

There are a number of other cases which have refined the term *building*, and it is important to remember the key rule is:

### A building is a permanent structure

In order to constitute a building, part of the structure must be a permanent structure. This explains why the container in the above case was considered a permanent structure: because it had been there for many years. The diagram below identifies permanent and temporary structures:

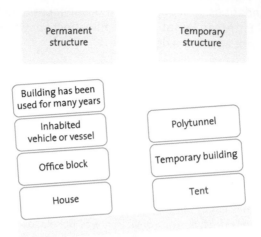

## Part of a building

It is also possible to commit this offence by entering part of a building. For example, a trespasser may have permission to enter a particular building because it is open to the public. However, that permission does not extend to all parts of the building. It may not apply to:

❖   the staff room
❖   the stock room
❖   behind the till/cashiers.

The notion of a private area was clarified in *R v Walkington* (1979), which found that there does not need to be a physical separation of part of a building: a counter or a line will suffice: for example, walking behind the counter of a shop to steal from the till, or entering a room marked private, which they have not been given permission to go into.

**Example:** JJ is shopping for a new TV, when he walks past a window through which he can see a table set up with lots of cupcakes. JJ is hungry and decides that he wants to take some of the cakes with him. He enters a door marked 'Private Staff Only'. JJ fills his backpack with the cupcakes and walks back into the shop and continues shopping for a TV. Eventually JJ leaves the shop.

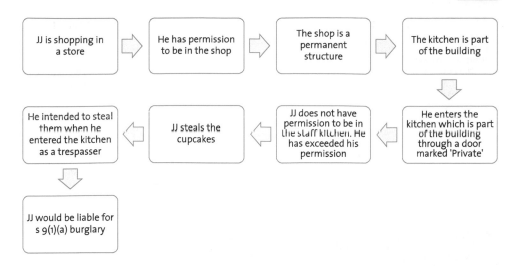

## Trespasser

In civil law, a person is a trespasser when they are on land/property without permission. Clearly someone breaking into a property is a trespasser, but what if someone enters the building legally? We have touched on this point briefly under the previous heading.

For example, it may be that a defendant enters one part of the building with the permission of the owner, but then proceeds to an area where they do not have permission. Or it may be that they have permission to enter the building generally, but they then go on to do something that they do not have permission to do. In these situations the response of the courts has been to treat the defendants as having **exceeded their licence or permission**.

> #### Case precedent – *R v Jones and Smith* [1976] 2 All ER 412
>
> **Facts:** D1 and D2 were at their parents' house with their permission, and stole a television.
>
> **Principle:** Trespass and exceeding permission
>
> **Application:** The permission to be in the dwelling was exceeded when D1 and D2 stole the television. Therefore they were classed as trespassers.

Based on the case law that we have discussed this for, look at the example below to work through the concept of trespass:

**Example:** Karen works in a hotel as a beauty therapist. Unknown to the management, Karen frequently goes into the kitchen and takes food, which she eats when she gets home. Would this be classed as trespass? Work your way through the following steps to determine whether Karen is a trespasser:

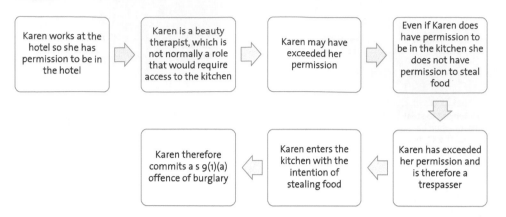

## Intentional or reckless as to trespass

The *mens rea* requirement for burglary is that the defendant is intentional or reckless as to the trespass; as mentioned above, this rules out accidental trespass. It is therefore essential that D knows that he or she does not have permission, or that they are at least reckless as to whether permission exists: *Walkington* (1979).

We are now going to consider the offence of aggravated burglary.

## Aggravated burglary

Section 10 of the **Theft Act 1968** creates an offence of 'aggravated burglary'. It provides that an offence of aggravated burglary is committed where a person commits burglary and **has with him at the time**:

❖ a firearm;
❖ an imitation firearm;
❖ any other 'weapon of offence'; or
❖ an explosive.

A weapon of offence means an object that can be construed as a weapon, if the accused intended it to be used for that purpose. This could be a knife, screwdriver etc.

This is a common mistake, so in a problem question check where the weapon is, and who is in possession of it.

In order to construct liability for this offence it must first be established that a burglary has taken place, under either s 9(1)(a) or s 9(1)(b). If liability for burglary cannot be demonstrated, then D would not be liable for aggravated burglary. The key additional factor differentiating burglary from aggravated burglary is the possession of the firearm/weapon/explosive.

| D must be liable for the offence of burglary | for the offence of aggravated burglary to be considered |
|---|---|

Remember that D only needs to be in possession of the weapon. It does not need to be proven that D intended to use it, only that D had it at the time of the burglary.

**For example**, Harold sees a house window open so climbs inside. Pearl is inside, and Harold grabs a knife from the kitchen table and tells Pearl to give him her money, which she does. Do you think this would constitute 'at the time has with him'?

According to case law this would be sufficient. There is in fact a very similar case, the case of *R v O'Leary* (1986), which held that as stealing is a continuous offence, when D picked up the knife, the offence changed from burglary to aggravated burglary.

A summary of the points we have covered in this section is:

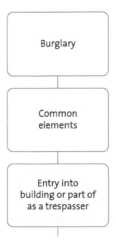

Burglary

Common elements

Entry into building or part of as a trespasser

## Trespass with intent to commit a sexual offence

This offence spans the areas of theft and also sexual offences. More information on sexual offences and the different types of offence can be found in the chapter on sexual offences (Chapter 4). Below we will consider a very specific offence linked to trespass.

Section 63 of the Sexual Offences Act 2003 provides:

(1)  A person commits an offence if –

   (a)  he is a trespasser on any premises,
   (b)  he intends to commit a relevant sexual offence on the premises, and
   (c)  he knows that, or is reckless as to whether, he is a trespasser.

(2)  In this section –

   'premises' includes a structure or part of a structure;
   'relevant sexual offence' has the same meaning as in section 62;
   'structure' includes a tent, vehicle or vessel or other temporary or movable structure.

This offence replaces the offence of burglary under s9(1)(a) of the Theft Act 1968, where D entered as a trespasser with intent to rape. The Sexual Offences Act 2003 widened the definition to 'relevant sexual offence' to mean that all the sexual offences would be included within this one offence.

# Putting it into practice

## Question

Consider the case of *R v Gomez* [1993] AC 442 – research the facts of the case and the case summary:

❖ **Which aspect of theft does this case focus upon?**
❖ **Explain why this case is important in the offence of theft.**

## Suggested solution

D was an assistant manager at a retail store. He accepted cheques from X, knowing that they were worthless. He told the manager that the cheques were as good as cash. As the manager handed over the property with consent D argued that no appropriation could have been found. On appeal to the House of Lords, they stated that consent is not relevant to appropriation (following *Lawrence*).

This case focuses on when appropriation takes place, i.e. when goods are transferred from the owner with the owner's consent. In this case, this was when the owner was led to believe that the cheques were sound. The fact that the cheques were dishonest then calls into question the appropriation of the goods from the owner, and the time that this occurred.

Prior to the *Gomez* case, the law was that if D used deceit in obtaining the goods from the owner, then they were not liable for theft because they were the owner of the goods. However, the judge in the case of *Gomez* turned this on its head, and argued that the act led to appropriation of the goods by D. This is because the judge ruled that appropriation can take place if the owner consents.

As a result of this case, the law on appropriation was clearer to interpret and apply in case of appropriation occurring at different times.

## Problem question

George sees that his local museum is hosting an art exhibition by his favourite painter. George decides that he wants to take his favourite painting to hang on his wall. So, in the evening when the museum is closed he sneaks into the museum through a back door marked 'Staff Only', and takes the painting off the wall. As he is walking back, a guard confronts George, telling him to put the painting back. George looks around and picks up an ancient dagger from a cabinet, points it at the guard and runs out of the museum with the picture and dagger.

Identify what offence George would be liable for and why.

Remember to follow the structure that we have practised in earlier chapters:

1. **Identify the crime.**
2. **Define the crime.**
3. **Address all elements of the *actus reus*.**
4. **Address all elements of the *mens rea*.**
5. **Deal with potential defences.**
6. **Deal with alternative/lesser charges.**

As a general rule you should always start with the most serious potential offence. In this case the most serious offence would seem to be aggravated burglary. However, in order to establish aggravated burglary we must first establish that George is liable for the offence of burglary, so we need to work through the elements to ensure that they are satisfied.

Following the above structure, work your way through each element of the AR and MR of the offence. In this case, it would be the s 9(1)(a) burglary offence, as George had the intention to steal the painting before he went to the museum – it was his intent before he entered the museum. The elements we then need to focus on are:

❖ **entry;**
❖ **into a building or part of a building;**
❖ **as a trespasser;**
❖ **intention or recklessness as to the trespass**.

Trespass – George trespassed into the museum because he entered the museum when it was closed in the evening, and he should not have been there.

The building – the museum is a building and is a permanent structure. George enters through a door marked 'Staff Only', and he crosses the line, so not only should he not be in the building, but he should definitely not be in the 'staff only' part of the building.

Entry – George's entrance is effective as he enters the building and removes the picture.

Therefore George fulfils the elements of burglary, which are required before the offence of aggravated burglary can be considered. The offence changes from burglary to aggravated burglary (s 10 **TA 1968**) when George picks up the dagger in response to the guard. A dagger is classed as a weapon of offence, so meets the criteria. Remember that George does not need to show intent to use the dagger, but it must be in his possession, as seen in *R v O'Leary* (1986).

## Key Points Checklist

| | |
|---|---|
| ❖ Theft is defined in s 1 of the Theft Act (TA) 1968. Theft is the dishonest appropriation of property belonging to another with the intention to permanently deprive the owner of it. | ✓ |
| ❖ Section 2 of the TA 1968 provides a negative definition of dishonesty. In essence it outlines a number of situations in which a defendant will not be deemed to have been dishonest. | ✓ |
| ❖ In the event that the defendant's situation is not captured by s 2 of the TA 1968 the Ghosh test will apply. The Ghosh test is a two-stage test with a subjective and objective element. The defendant must pass through both stages of the test. | ✓ |

❖ Robbery is closely related to the offence of theft. It is defined in s 8 of the TA 1968. In order to establish liability for robbery you must first establish liability for theft. What differentiates robbery from theft is the threat or use of force in order to steal. Thus once the *actus reus* and *mens rea* of theft have been established it must additionally be shown that D: threatened or used force; before or at the time of the theft; against any person; and that the threat of force or force was intentional. ✓

❖ Burglary is defined in s 9(1)(a) and s 9(1)(b) of the TA 1968. The common elements of the offence are: that D enters; property or part of; as a trespasser, intending or being reckless as to the trespass. In order to make out s 9(1)(a) the defendant must have an ulterior intent to commit: theft, GBH or criminal damage. In relation to s 9(1)(b), having entered the property or part of as a trespasser D must go on to commit: theft/attempted theft or GBH/attempted GBH. ✓

❖ An aggravated species of burglary is contained in s 10 of the TA 1968. It provides that D commits an offence when they commit burglary whilst in possession of one or more of the following: firearm; imitation firearm; explosive; or weapon. ✓

# Table of key cases referred to in this chapter

| Key case | Brief facts | Principle |
|---|---|---|
| *R v Lawrence* [1972] AC 626 | V gave D his purse to take a taxi fare, and D took more money than he was entitled to | Consent in theft |
| *R v Gomez* [1993] AC 442 | D informed V that the cheques were good, when he knew that they were worthless | Consent in theft |
| *R v Hale* [1978] 68 Cr App R 415 | D burgled V's house, stealing jewellery and tying up V | Appropriation is a continuing act |
| *R v Hinks* [2000] 3 WLR 1590 | D persuaded V to give out gifts of money | Gifts can be classed as appropriation |
| *Oxford v Moss* [1979] 68 Cr App Rep 183 | D accessed an exam paper due to be set by the university | Classification of tangible and intangible property |
| *R v Turner (No 2)* [1971] 1 WLR | D removed his car from a garage, without paying for the repairs | Possession of property |

| Key case | Brief facts | Principle |
|---|---|---|
| *Ricketts v Basildon Magistrates* [2011] 1 Cr App Rep 15 | D took bags left outside a charity shop | Abandoned property – belonging to another |
| *DPP v Lavender* [1994] Crim LR 297 | D took doors from his council property and put them in his girlfriend's house | Intention to permanently deprive |
| *R v Lloyd* [1985] QB 829 (CA) | D took films from the cinema where he worked to copy, and then returned them | Intention to permanently deprive |
| *R v Robinson* [1977] Crim LR 173 | D believed he had a right to the property, and used force | Theft must be proved for the offence of robbery |
| *R v Dawson & James* [1976] 64 App R 150 | D nudged V, while another stole V's purse | The level of force required for robbery |
| *R v Clouden* [1987] Crim LR 56 | D pulled on V's handbag to pull it away | Use of force can be applied to the handbag |
| *R v Hale* [1978] Cr App R 415 D1 | D1 stole jewellery while D2 was with V. D1 & D2 tied up V afterwards | Immediately before or at the time |
| *R v Lockley* [1995] Crim LR 656 | D used force to escape after stealing V's property | Force used to escape after the property is stolen |
| *R v Jones and Smith* [1976] 2 All ER 412 | D1 and D2 stole a television from a dwelling they had permission to be in | Definition of trespass |
| *B and S v Leathley* [1979] Crim LR | D stole from a container, which had been in the same position for many years | Definition of a building |
| *R v Walkington* [1979] 1WLR 1169 | D stole from within a private area | Definition of a private area |
| *R v Ryan* [1996] Crim LR 320 | D tried to burgle a house, and was found stuck in the window, halfway into the house | Effective entry |

---

@ **Visit the book's companion website to test your knowledge**

❖ Resources include a subject map, revision tip podcasts, downloadable diagrams, MCQ quizzes for each chapter, and a flashcard glossary

❖ www.routledge.com/cw/optimizelawrevision

# 7 Criminal Damage

**Understand the law**

- Do you understand the definition for criminal damage and aggravated criminal damage in the Criminal Damage Act 1971?

**Remember the details**

- Can you remember the *actus reus* and *mens rea* for criminal damage?
- Can you remember the *actus reus* and *mens rea* for aggravated criminal damage?

**Reflect critically on areas of debate**

- Do you understand the definition of arson, and can you critically discuss the difference between arson and the basic offence of criminal damage?

**Contextualise**

- Can you relate criminal damage to other property offences?

**Apply your skills and knowledge**

- Can you complete the activities in this chapter, using statutes and case law to support your answer?

# Chapter Map

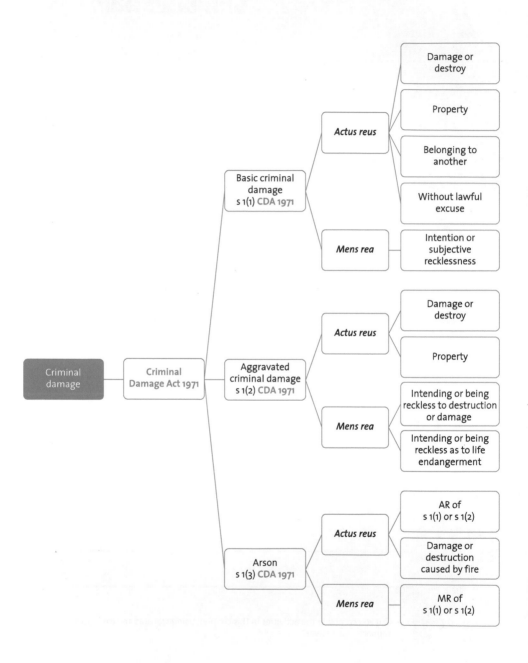

# Introduction

In this chapter we are going to consider criminal damage. This offence can take several forms, and these different offences are all set out in s 1 of the Criminal Damage Act 1971. The Act sets out three types of offence, which are:

- ❖ basic (s 1(1))
- ❖ aggravated (s 1(2))
- ❖ arson (s 1(3))

We will consider each of these offences in turn. As is our normal practice we will break the definitions of each offence down into the *actus reus* and *mens rea* and consider how each offence can be applied, particularly in the context of a problem question.

As you consider the different offences, you will find it helpful to reflect on other property offences such as theft, as these offences can sometimes be linked together in a problem question. It is also worth noting that there are similarities between the definitions of the different property offences. Think about the circumstances in which different property offences may be linked, and how you would approach this in an exam or assessment.

## Aim Higher

As you progress through this chapter, consider the **Theft Act 1968**, and the similarities between the different property offences. Make sure that you are clear as to the similarities and differences.

The key legislation that you must be familiar with is the Criminal Damage Act (CDA) 1971.

# Simple criminal damage

Section 1(1) of the Criminal Damage Act 1971 creates an offence of 'simple' criminal damage. It provides:

> *A person who without lawful excuse destroys or damages any property belonging to another intending to destroy or damage any such property or being reckless as to whether any such property would be destroyed or damaged shall be guilty of an offence.*

The basic offence is a triable-either-way offence with a maximum sentence of ten years' imprisonment: s 4(2) CDA 1971.

## Aim Higher

A good way of picking up additional marks in an assessment question is to demonstrate knowledge of the following:

1. Whether the offence is a common law or statutory offence.
2. Whether the offence is a summary offence, a triable-either-way offence or an indictable offence.
3. The maximum sentence upon conviction for the offence.

It is worth noting that s 30(1) of the Crime and Disorder Act 1998 creates a racially aggravated form of criminal damage, which is also a triable-either-way offence and has a maximum sentence of 14 years' imprisonment. Although we will not consider the racially aggravated form of criminal damage, it is worth noting this offence, particularly in an essay question, or where the facts of the question give rise to the possibility that the criminal damage has been racially aggravated.

Section 1(1) can be split into the following *actus reus* and *mens rea* elements:

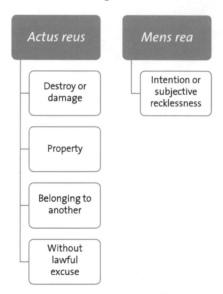

In order for a defendant to have committed the *actus reus* for the offence of simple criminal damage the defendant must have:

1. Damaged or destroyed
2. Property
3. Belonging to another
4. Without lawful excuse.

We will now look at each of these elements in turn.

## Destroy or damage

The question as to whether property has been destroyed or damaged is a question of fact for the jury/magistrates. This element of the *actus reus* allows for:

❖ the destruction, or
❖ damage of property.

The term destruction is self-explanatory in so far as it indicates a sense of finality and irreparable repair. The term damage requires further explanation.

❖ Damage does not need to be permanent: *Roe v Kingerlee* (1986).
❖ Damage can be temporary: *Roper v Knott* (1898).
❖ The damage does not have to be tangible or visible provided that the value of the property is affected: *Cox v Riley* (1986).

You can remember these points as:

The key points to remember in relation to the term *damage* is that as a result of the defendant's actions, the property must suffer from:

❖ a reduction in value, or
❖ a reduction in its usefulness.

**Example:** Lucy and Lee have just got married and go on honeymoon. When they come back, they find that the best man has painted their house windows pink as a welcome home joke. Lucy and Lee are very unhappy – would this constitute criminal damage? Look at the list above, and see whether damage or destruction has occurred.

If you are working through a problem question and you are considering whether damage or destruction has taken place, working through the above list will help you to determine if it has taken place, and whether it would be considered damage or destruction.

## Up for Debate

Contrast the following cases relating to damage. In *A (A Juvenile) v R* (1978) spit was not regarded as damage, whereas in *Samuels v Stubbs* (1972) jumping up and down on a policeman's cap was held to be damage.

Does this provide enough guidance on what constitutes damage, or should there be greater guidance on the definition of damage? This is a useful critical point to refer to in an essay question.

We are now moving on to consider the second element of the *actus reus* of simple criminal damage which is property.

### Property

The defendant must destroy or damage *property*. The meaning of property for criminal damage is set out in s 10(1) of the Criminal Damage Act (CDA) 1971, and it is similar, *but not identical*, to the definition of property for theft contained in s 4 of the Theft Act 1968. The definition of property in the CDA 1971 is broader than the definition of property in the Theft Act 1968.

For the purposes of criminal damage property, does not include the following:

❖ mushrooms and fungi growing wild on any land;
❖ flowers, fruit, foliage, plants, shrubs or trees growing wild on any land;
❖ intangible property such as copyright.

We will now consider the next *actus reus* element of the offence of simple criminal damage which is that the property must belong to another (this AR element is exclusive to the offence of simple criminal damage).

### Belonging to another

The meaning of 'belonging to another' is set out in s 10(2) of the Criminal Damage Act 1971, which states that property belongs to another person if that person:

❖ has custody or control of it;
❖ has in it any proprietary right or interest (such as a lessee but not an equitable right);
❖ has a charge on it.

It is important to note that it is possible for a person to be convicted of criminal damage if it is owned, at the same time, by someone else, e.g. joint ownership or shared ownership. It is also worth noting that, under s 10(3), trust property belongs to anyone who has a right to enforce the trust.

**Example:** Sam asks Layla to look after his iPad while he is swimming. Mollie swipes the iPad from Layla and stamps on it with her foot, damaging the device. Would Mollie be liable for criminal damage in this example? Work through the steps below in relation to property:

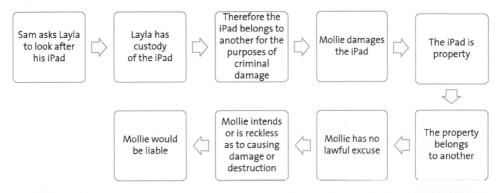

Sam asks Layla to look after his iPad ⇨ Layla has custody of the iPad ⇨ Therefore the iPad belongs to another for the purposes of criminal damage ⇨ Mollie damages the iPad ⇨ The iPad is property ⇩

Mollie would be liable ⇦ Mollie intends or is reckless as to causing damage or destruction ⇦ Mollie has no lawful excuse ⇦ The property belongs to another

We are now going to consider the final element of the *actus reus* for criminal damage and that is that the damage or destruction of property belonging to another must have taken place without lawful excuse.

We have included this as an element of the *actus reus* of the offence for the sake of simplicity. However, it is perhaps more accurate to describe this requirement as a defence as opposed to an element of the AR of the offence.

### Lawful excuse

The phrase *lawful excuse* is set out in s 5(2) of the **Criminal Damage Act 1971**, and provides for two specific defences to criminal damage. These are now considered below:

Section 5(2) of the **Criminal Damage Act 1971** provides that a person charged with an offence to which the section applies will be treated as having a lawful excuse if:

> **Section 5(2)(a):** D believed that the person or persons entitled to consent to the damage or destruction either had consented, or would have consented to the damage or destruction of the property.

Section 5(2)(a) stipulates that D must honestly believe that a certain person (or persons) would have consented to the damage or destruction (set out in s 5(3)). You will see here that the words centre on D's belief.

The case of *Jaggard v Dickinson* (1980) focuses on D's belief that the owner had or would have consented to cause the damage. In this case, D was out late at night and lost her keys. She broke into her friend's house, believing that her friend would agree to this action and the damage caused. She had in fact broken into the wrong house. Thus the belief in consent is a subjective one. The key question here is: did D have an honest belief in the owner's consent, or an honest belief that the owner would have consented?

Therefore D need only show a valid belief of consent.

Another useful case to use here is *Denton* (1982), where D1 asked D2 to burn down his factory, so he could make a claim against the insurance. In this case, D2 was found not guilty, as it was proven that D1 (the owner of the factory) had indeed asked D2 to set fire to the factory, thereby giving his consent.

## Up for Debate

The interesting aspect of this case is that D2 was found not guilty of criminal damage, as it was found that he believed he had the consent of D1, who was the owner of the factory.

Therefore D1, as the owner of the factory, was also acquitted of criminal damage because he was the owner of the building, and could therefore damage the building if he wished – it is his property to do as he wished with (i.e. not belonging to another).

What do you feel about this decision? It is worth noting that although the defendants were not liable for criminal damage that is not to say that they were not liable for any criminal offences! We will consider the issues raised here later in the chapter.

We will now consider s 5(2)(b) of the CDA 1971. This provides that the defendant should be treated as having a lawful excuse where:

> **Section 5(2)(b)** – D believed that property belonging to himself or another was in immediate need of protection, and so D damaged or destroyed other property in order to protect it, where D believed that the means of protection used were reasonable.

What is significant in relation to s 5(2)(b) is that the test in relation to the above section is a subjective test. The question is not whether the actions of D were reasonable but whether believed those actions to be reasonable: *Hunt* (1977).

This defence is broad, due to the range of circumstances which could apply – it is key that D must have had a genuine belief that the property was at risk, the requirement for protection was immediate, and D believed that his actions were reasonable. You can remember these four key parts as:

It may not always be clear whether all four elements are contained within D's lawful excuse. Look at the example below and see if you can identify them:

**Example:** Tom and Abbey are neighbours, but the vehicular access across Tom's land to Abbey's house is disputed. Tom builds a wall across the land, blocking in Abbey's car. Abbey knocks down the wall, arguing that this was to protect her vehicular rights without delay.

❖  Can you identify the four elements here?
❖  What would you argue would be the outcome from this example?

This is in fact a real case, and is *Chamberlain v Lindon* (1998).

But – be careful how broadly you apply these four elements, as seen in the case below:

---

**Case precedent – *Hill and Hall* (1989) 89 Cr App R 74**

**Facts:** D1 and D2 intended to cut wires around the perimeter of a nuclear base. They argued that if the base was bombed, their homes could be damaged. By cutting the fence, they could persuade the base to move elsewhere. D1 and D2 used lawful excuse because they were concerned about the potential damage to their homes.

**Principle:** Lawful excuse

**Application:** D1 and D2 were found guilty of criminal damage, as the claim was spurious and the potential for damage too remote (i.e. not immediate).

We will now consider the two tests used in lawful excuse in a little more detail.

### D damaged or destroyed (other) property in order to protect property

For example, consider the case of *Hunt* (1977). In this case set fire to bedding in order to draw attention to a defective fire alarm at an old people's home. The defendant in this case was held not to have reasonably believed that setting fire to bedding would have protected property. He was therefore not protecting the property, he was demonstrating that the fire alarm was not working, and hence was found guilty.

### D believed that the means used were reasonable

As we have already discussed this test is subjective: D must honestly believe that the means of protection adopted was reasonable.

Look at the example below, and work through whether the subjective test (for reasonableness) would apply here.

**Example:** Julie is sitting having a glass of lemonade when she notices that her next door neighbour's car is rolling backwards out of the drive. The car is travelling towards two cars parked on the opposite side of the road. Julie rushes out of her house, catches up with the car and pulls on the handbrake sharply, stopping the car but damaging its electronic braking system.

Work through the steps below to see if Julie could use lawful excuse in this case:

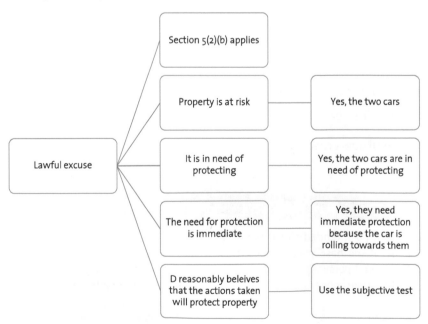

Having discussed the four elements of the *actus reus* we will now move on to consider the *mens rea* for the basic offence of criminal damage. Remember that both AR and MR must be present to successfully construct liability for the offence.

## *Mens rea*: intention or being reckless as to the damage

Simple criminal damage is a crime of basic intent. That means that either intention on behalf of the defendant or recklessness will suffice. The *mens rea* required for the simple offence of criminal damage is set out within s 1(1) of the Criminal Damage Act 1971. It is:

Intention or recklessness
- **intention** to destroy or damage property belonging to another, or
- being **reckless** as to whether any such property would be destroyed or damaged

We will now consider the meaning of these two key terms in more detail.

### *Intention*

Intention is an important concept here, and it is covered more fully within the section on *mens rea* in Chapter 2. For criminal damage, it must be proved beyond a reasonable doubt that the D intended to cause the criminal damage. You will remember from our earlier discussion on intention that the meaning of intention encapsulates both direct and oblique intention. Remember the definition of direct and oblique intention as:

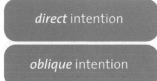

*direct* intention
- intention as an aim, purpose or desire

*oblique* intention
- foresight of a virtual certainty

### *Recklessness*

A defendant can cause criminal damage intentionally *or* by being reckless. Again, the principles of recklessness are discussed in more detail in the section on *mens rea* in Chapter 2, and these principles would also apply to criminal damage.

You will recall that there are two types of recklessness – subjective and objective. These mean:

| Subjective test | Objective test |
|---|---|
| • Proof that D is aware of, or foresees the risk of harm and nevertheless goes on to take that risk. The risk is an unjustifiable risk. | • The reasonable man would have foreseen the risk of harm. |

For a significant period of time the courts determined that test for recklessness in the case of criminal damage was an objective one: *Caldwell* (1982). This meant that the risk of harm needed only to be obvious to the reasonable man. Thus if the accused through lack of age/experience or infirmity lacked the ability to foresee the obvious risk he or she would still be held liable: *Elliot v C* (1983).

However, in the case of *G* (2004) the objective test for recklessness was overruled and the subjective test for recklessness was reinstated. It is worth noting that D does not need to:

- ❖ foresee the extent of the damage: *G* (2004); or
- ❖ realise that what they are doing to the property constitutes damage: *Seray-Wurie v DPP* (2012).

The House of Lords in *G* (2004) set out the meaning of subjective recklessness in relation to criminal damage as:

- ❖ a circumstance when he is aware of a risk that exists or will exist;
- ❖ a result where he is aware of a risk that it will occur; and
- ❖ it is, in the circumstances known to him, unreasonable to take the risk.

The following illustration outlines the timeline for recklessness in relation to criminal damage:

Cunningham (1957) → Caldwell (1981) → Elliot v C (1983) → G and Another (2004)

The more recent case of *Seray-Wurie v DPP* (2012) mentioned above is a useful and recent case to consider when considering the *mens rea* requirement for criminal damage.

> ### Case precedent – *Seray-Wurie v DPP* [2012] EWHC 208 (Admin)
>
> **Facts:** D wrote on parking tickets with a black pen, which could not be erased.
>
> **Principle:** D need not appreciate that his actions constitute damage for the purpose of criminal damage.
>
> **Application:** The judge ruled that the prosecution must prove D intended or was reckless (subjectively) in causing the damage to the property in question. However, the prosecution does not need to prove that D *knew* that his actions constituted damage for the purpose of criminal damage.

**Example:** Ashley, aged 11, used a can of spray paint to write the name of Liverpool FC onto a bridge over a railway track, showing off to his friends. Ashley claims that he honestly believed that when his friends had gone home, he would be able to remove the paint with water from his drink bottle. He had seen his dad remove paint from a wall at their house with water. Being only 11, Ashley did not understand that when his dad cleaned the paint off the wall at home the paint had been water-based paint and not oil-based, as was the case with the spray paint. The paint on the bridge had to be removed by the rail authorities with a special solvent. Decide whether or not Ashley has committed criminal damage contrary to s 1 CDA 1971.

Work through the following steps to help you come to your conclusion. These are based on the elements of the *actus reus* and *mens rea*, to determine liability, as you would be expected to discuss when considering liability for criminal damage in a problem question:

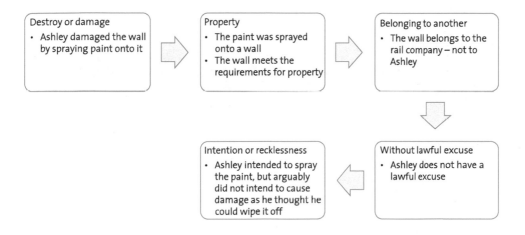

We are now moving on to consider aggravated criminal damage.

## Aggravated criminal damage

Section 1(2) of the Criminal Damage Act 1971 provides for an aggravated form of criminal damage. It stipulates that:

A person who without lawful excuse destroys or damages any property, whether belonging to himself or another –

(a) intending to destroy or damage any property or being reckless as to whether any property would be destroyed or damaged; and

(b) intending by the destruction or damage to endanger the life of another or being reckless as to whether the life of another would be endangered,

commits an aggravated form of criminal damage.

The difference from the simple offence of criminal damage is an aggravating factor. That factor is the ulterior *mens rea* (an intention or recklessness as to whether life is endangered).

## Common Pitfall

Note that this offence does not require proof that the property damaged or destroyed belonged to another, i.e. D can damage his own property, and still be liable for the offence.

The offence of aggravated criminal damage is an indictable offence subject to a maximum term of life imprisonment.

## Aim Higher

The case history relating to this offence has evolved, particularly over the last thirty years in an effort to refine the issue of the damage endangering life. To aid your understanding, research the case of *Steer* **(1987)**, and then compare this to the case of *Warwick* **(1995)**.

The case of *Steer* was recently re-applied in *Luke Wenton* **(2010)**.

Another useful example is the case of *Webster* **(1995)**, where D pushed heavy coping stones onto a moving train, which showered passengers with debris. In this case D was reckless to endangering the lives of the passengers from the roof material hitting them.

## Aim Higher

This offence is often linked in assessments with homicide, and in particular the offence of murder. Look at the chapter on homicide, and re-read the section on murder. This will help you to put both offences in context, and also to link them should this arise in a problem question.

## Liability for aggravated criminal damage

The *actus reus* and *mens rea* for the aggravated offence are similar to the basic offence, but there are number of important differences. It is important that you are aware of these distinctions.

The main difference is that, in contrast to the basic offence, the aggravated offence can be committed where D destroys or damages his own property (in other words the requirement that the property belongs to another is not present in the aggravated form of criminal damage).

**Example:** Dan owns a manufacturing business, and is in financial difficulty. He decides to damage some of the very expensive machinery in order to make a fraudulent insurance claim. Under the basic offence, Dan would not be liable as he is the owner of the property. However if Dan damages machinery in such a way that the damage presents a danger to human life. And he intentionally endangers life or is reckless as to whether it is endangered he will be liable for the aggravated offence.

Now we will consider the individual elements of the aggravated form of criminal damage.

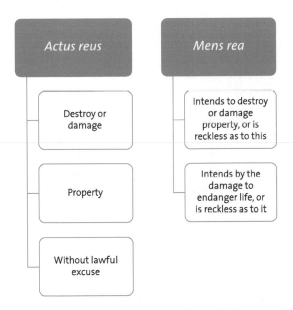

We will now consider each of the individual AR and MR elements.

## Actus reus

### Destroy or damage
The elements of *destroy* and *damage* are the same as for the simple offence of criminal damage, and their meanings are the same.

### Property
The meaning of property is the same as for the simple offence of criminal damage.

## Without lawful excuse

You need to exercise particular caution here because in the context of the aggravated offence the defence of lawful excuse does not apply. This is because a lawful excuse (as defined in s 5(2) of the CDA 1971 cannot be justification for endangering life.

In the context of the aggravated offence, 'without lawful excuse' refers to the operation of other general defences such as self-defence, for example – this requirement applies to all criminal offences even where it is not explicitly mentioned in the definition of an offence.

Now we will consider the *mens rea* elements of the aggravated form of criminal damage.

## Mens rea

We can see here that the *mens rea* requirement for the aggravated offence differs from that of the simple offence of criminal damage. In essence there are two elements to the MR for aggravated criminal damage.

### Intention or recklessness as to the damage or destruction of property

The aggravated form of criminal damage requires intention or subjective recklessness as discussed in relation to the simple offence of criminal damage.

### D intends by the destruction or damage of property to endanger the life of another or is reckless as to whether the life of another is endangered

This component of the *mens rea* is key. It is what transforms basic criminal damage into the aggravated form of criminal damage. It is what justifies the imposition of a much more severe sentence. The defendant must at least have been reckless as to whether life would be endangered by the damage or destruction: *Steer* (1988). The endangerment of life must be a result of the damage or destruction and not merely the danger itself: *Webster* (1995) and *Dudley* (1989).

---

### Aim Higher

Life does not actually have to be endangered by the damage or destruction – it is D's intention or recklessness as to endangerment of life which is important here (D's guilty mind).

---

For example, in the case of *Sangha* (1998), D set fire to furniture in an unoccupied house. D was found guilty of the aggravated offence, despite the fact that the building was constructed in a way that prevented the spread of fire to adjoining properties.

We can see that it was D's intention or that D was reckless as to whether life would be endangered by setting fire to the house. It is this factor that is relevant here – not the construction of the house or that no one was actually hurt.

Now let us look at the case of *Dudley* (1989), and trace the steps in the diagram below:

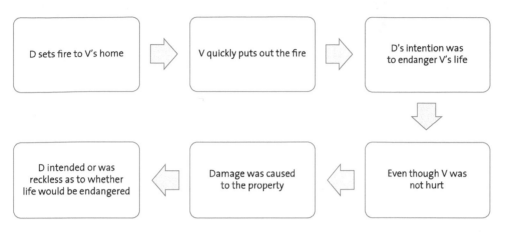

A summary of the points we have covered in this section is:

### Section 1(2) of the Criminal Damage Act 1971

| Destroy or damage | Property | Intending to destroy or damage property or being reckless to this | Intending by criminal damage to endanger life, or being reckless as to this |
|---|---|---|---|

## Arson

We are now going to consider the offence of arson. According to s 1(3) of the **Criminal Damage Act 1971**:

> *An offence committed under this section by destroying or damaging property by fire shall be charged with arson.*

It is important to note that arson under s 1(3) is not a separate offence in its own right, but simply refers to where D commits an offence under s 1(1) or s 1(2) by means of fire (i.e. damaging the property by fire).

Simple arson is a triable-either-way offence punishable with a maximum sentence of life imprisonment. Aggravated arson is an indictable offence also punishable with a maximum term of life imprisonment.

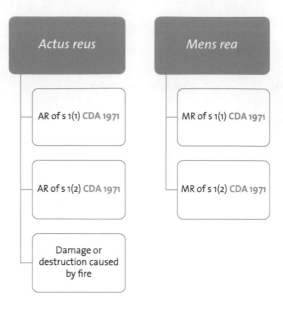

## Actus reus

The *actus reus* for the offence of arson will depend on whether it is a simple or aggravated form of criminal damage.

The added requirement here is that D must destroy or damage the property by fire. It is worth noting that in *Miller* (1954) the House of Lords held that arson was capable of being committed by omission in cases where the fire had initially started accidently and the defendant had taken the decision to do nothing about the fire (such as by failing to call the emergency services).

## Mens rea

If D is charged with simple criminal damage by fire, it must be shown that D intended to damage or destroy or was reckless as to destruction or damage.

If D is charged with an aggravated offence by fire, it must be proved that D intended to endanger the life of another, or was reckless as to whether life would be endangered.

## Establishing offences under the CDA 1971

When answering a problem question, adopt the following structure, which is not necessarily the order of the elements in the statutory wording.

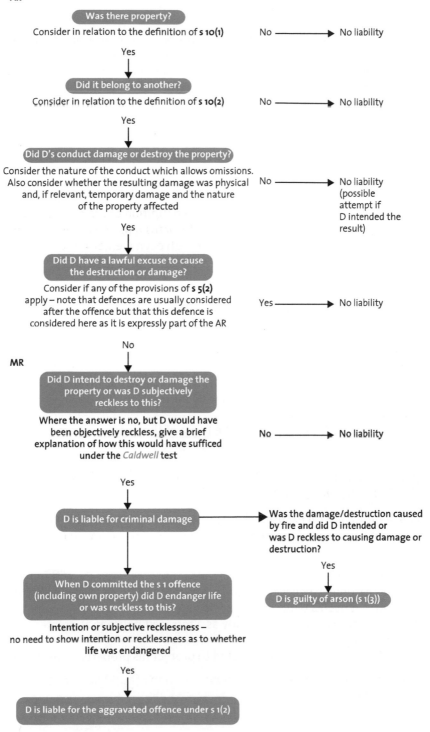

**AR**

**Was there property?**

Consider in relation to the definition of **s 10(1)**          No ————▶ No liability

Yes

**Did it belong to another?**

Consider in relation to the definition of **s 10(2)**          No ————▶ No liability

Yes

**Did D's conduct damage or destroy the property?**

Consider the nature of the conduct which allows omissions.          No ————▶ No liability
Also consider whether the resulting damage was physical                         (possible
and, if relevant, temporary damage and the nature                               attempt if
of the property affected                                                        D intended the
                                                                                result)

Yes

**Did D have a lawful excuse to cause
the destruction or damage?**

Consider if any of the provisions of **s 5(2)**
apply – note that defences are usually considered          Yes ————▶ No liability
after the offence but that this defence is
considered here as it is expressly part of the AR

No

**MR**

**Did D intend to destroy or damage the
property or was D subjectively
reckless to this?**

Where the answer is no, but D would have
been objectively reckless, give a brief          No ————▶ No liability
explanation of how this would have sufficed
under the *Caldwell* test

Yes

**D is liable for criminal damage** ————▶ Was the damage/destruction caused
                                          by fire and did D intended or
                                          was D reckless to causing damage or
                                          destruction?

                                          Yes

**When D committed the s 1 offence
(including own property) did D endanger life          **D is guilty of arson (s 1(3))**
or was reckless to this?**

Intention or subjective recklessness –
no need to show intention or recklessness as to whether
life was endangered

Yes

**D is liable for the aggravated offence under s 1(2)**

# Putting it into practice

## Question

Joe lives in a terraced house, and hears odd noises coming from his neighbour's house. Joe goes into the road, and sees that his neighbour's house is on fire in the kitchen. Worried that the fire will spread to his own house, Joe gets his hosepipe from the garden, opens his neighbour's window and sprays water into the house, and puts out the fire. The water causes significant damage, and more than the fire did.

Would Joe be liable for a criminal damage offence?

## Suggested solution

To determine liability, you must first provide a definition of the offence that you are considering. Then divide the definition into the *actus reus* and *mens rea* elements of the offence. You need to work your way through each element in turn as shown in the above diagram:

Section 1(1) of the Criminal Damage Act 1971

* Destroy or damage – yes, Joe damages his neighbour's house with the water putting out the fire.
* Property – yes, the building itself and the contents inside the kitchen which have not been damaged by the fire.
* Belonging to another – yes, belonging to his neighbour.
* Intention to being reckless – this may be more of a grey area, as Joe could have waited for the fire brigade.
* Without a lawful excuse – this is the focus of the question, because Joe acted out of concern that the fire would spread and damage his own property.
* Did Joe intend to destroy or damage property or was he reckless as to whether it would be destroyed or damaged?

Under s 5(2)(b), a lawful excuse will be present where D believed that the property was in immediate need of protection. The four elements an answer should consider are:

1. Immediate – Yes, the fire could take hold and spread quickly, within minutes.
2. Did Joe reasonably believe that there was a risk to property? – Yes, Joe did not break in, but used a window and a hosepipe.
3. Property is at risk – Yes, particularly as a terraced house is at greater risk of a fire spreading.
4. In need of protection – Yes, Joe acted to protect his property from the fire.

You could consider the case of *Chamberlain v Lindon* (1998) here, as this is a useful case for comparison.

# Key Points Checklist

| | |
|---|---|
| The offence of criminal damage is governed by the Criminal Damage Act 1971. This Act creates two distinct offences: simple criminal damage s 1(1) and aggravated criminal damage s 1(2). Section 1(3) provides that criminal damage caused by fire should be charged as arson. | ✔ |
| The *actus reus* for simple criminal damage is: the damage or destruction of property belonging to another. The *mens rea* for the offence is intention or recklessness. Section 5(2) of the CDA creates a defence of lawful excuse. | ✔ |
| The *actus reus* for aggravated criminal damage is: the damage or destruction of property. The *mens rea* for the offence is intention or recklessness AND intention or recklessness as to whether life would be endangered by the damage or destruction of property. | ✔ |
| Arson s 1(3) can be simple arson (AR + MR for s 1(1)) with the damage or destruction caused by fire; or aggravated arson (AR + MR for s 1(2)) with the damage or destruction caused by fire. | ✔ |

# Table of key cases referred to in this chapter

| Key case | Brief facts | Principle |
|---|---|---|
| *Cresswell v DPP Curry v DPP* [2006] EWHC 3379 | D damaged badger traps to stop the badgers being hurt | Definition of property |
| *R v Smith* [1974] QB 354 | D made home improvements to a rented home, and removed them when he left | Intention and own property |
| *Seray-Wurie v DPP* [2012] EWHC 208 (Admin) | D wrote on parking tickets with a permanent pen | Recklessness |
| *Jaggard v Dickenson* [1980] 3 All ER 716 | D forcibly entered V's house late at night, after losing her keys | Consent to cause criminal damage |
| *Chamberlain v Lindon* [1998] | V built a wall across land blocking in D's car. D knocked down the wall for his vehicular access. | Protecting property – lawful excuse |
| *Hill and Hall* (1989) 89 Cr App R 74 | D1 and D2 intended to cut wires in fencing around an army site, as they were concerned a bomb could damage their homes | Protecting property – lawful excuse |
| *Sangha* [1998] 2 All ER 325 | D set fire to V's house, causing damage and endangering lives | Aggravated offence |
| *Dudley* [1989] Crim LR 57 | D sets light to V's home | Aggravated offence – intent |

@ Visit the book's companion website to test your knowledge

❖ Resources include a subject map, revision tip podcasts, downloadable diagrams, MCQ quizzes for each chapter, and a flashcard glossary

❖ www.routledge.com/cw/optimizelawrevision

# 8 Fraud and Blackmail

**Understand the law**
- Can you identify which sections of the Fraud Act 2006 relate to the principal fraud offences in this chapter?
- Can you identify which section of the Theft Act 1968 refers to the offence of blackmail?

**Remember the details**
- Can you remember the *actus reus* and *mens rea* for each offence?
- Can you define the *actus reus* and *mens rea* using case law?

**Reflect critically on areas of debate**
- Do you understand the definition of dishonesty in relation to fraud, and how dishonesty is tested?

**Contextualise**
- Can you relate the *actus reus* and *mens rea* to other areas of law, particularly theft offences?

**Apply your skills and knowledge**
- Can you complete the activities in this chapter, using liability and case law?

# Chapter Map

# Elements Chart

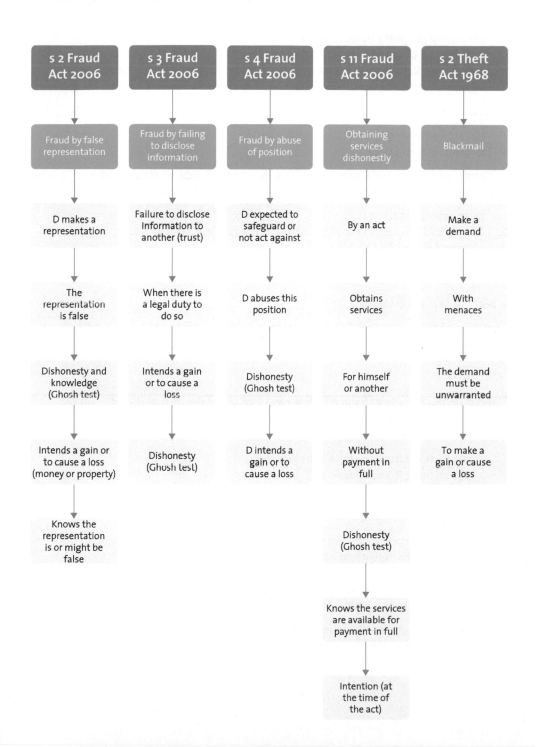

| s 2 Fraud Act 2006 | s 3 Fraud Act 2006 | s 4 Fraud Act 2006 | s 11 Fraud Act 2006 | s 2 Theft Act 1968 |
|---|---|---|---|---|
| Fraud by false representation | Fraud by failing to disclose information | Fraud by abuse of position | Obtaining services dishonestly | Blackmail |
| D makes a representation | Failure to disclose Information to another (trust) | D expected to safeguard or not act against | By an act | Make a demand |
| The representation is false | When there is a legal duty to do so | D abuses this position | Obtains services | With menaces |
| Dishonesty and knowledge (Ghosh test) | Intends a gain or to cause a loss | Dishonesty (Ghosh test) | For himself or another | The demand must be unwarranted |
| Intends a gain or to cause a loss (money or property) | Dishonesty (Ghosh test) | D intends a gain or to cause a loss | Without payment in full | To make a gain or cause a loss |
| Knows the representation is or might be false | | | Dishonesty (Ghosh test) | |
| | | | Knows the services are available for payment in full | |
| | | | Intention (at the time of the act) | |

# Introduction

The offence of fraud is contained in the Fraud Act 2006 [FA 2006]. The FA 2006 came into force on the 15th of January 2007, abolishing the following offences under the Theft Act 1968:

* obtaining property by deception (s 15);
* obtaining a pecuniary advantage by deception (s 16);
* obtaining execution of a valuable security by deception (s 20); and
* obtaining a money transfer by deception (s 15(A)).

The FA 2006 also abolished the following offences under the Theft Act 1978:

* obtaining services by deception (s 1); and
* evasion of liability (s 2).

Section 1 of the FA 2006 created a new general offence of fraud and ss 2, 3 and 4 introduce three offences:

1. false representation (s 2);
2. failure to disclose information where there is a legal duty to do so (s 3); and
3. abuse of position (s 4).

# Fraud introduction

Section 1 of the Fraud Act (FA) 2006 creates a single offence of fraud which can be committed in a number of different ways. Section 1 provides:

(1) A person is guilty of fraud if he is in breach of any of the sections listed in subsection (2) (which provide for different ways of committing the offence).

(2) The sections are –

    (a) section 2 (fraud by false representation),
    (b) section 3 (fraud by failing to disclose information), and
    (c) section 4 (fraud by abuse of position).

(3) A person who is guilty of fraud is liable –

    (a) on summary conviction, to imprisonment for a term not exceeding 12 months or to a fine not exceeding the statutory maximum (or to both);
    (b) on conviction on indictment, to imprisonment for a term not exceeding 10 years or to a fine (or to both).

(4) Subsection (3)(a) applies in relation to Northern Ireland as if the reference to 12 months were a reference to 6 months.

# Fraud by false representation

## Introduction

Fraud by false representation is set out in s 2 of the Fraud Act (FA) 2006, and as you work through the chapter, you will see that the concept of dishonesty, and an intention by the defendant to make a gain (or cause a loss) are key to this offence.

Section 2 FA 2006 stipulates:

(1) A person is in breach of this section if he –

    (a) dishonestly makes a false representation, and
    (b) intends, by making the representation—

        (i) to make a gain for himself or another, or
        (ii) to cause loss to another or to expose another to a risk of loss.

(2) A representation is false if –

    (a) it is untrue or misleading, and
    (b) the person making it knows that it is, or might be, untrue or misleading.

(3) 'Representation' means any representation as to fact or law, including a representation as to the state of mind of –

    (a) the person making the representation, or
    (b) any other person.

(4) A representation may be express or implied.

(5) For the purposes of this section a representation may be regarded as made if it (or anything implying it) is submitted in any form to any system or device designed to receive, convey or respond to communications (with or without human intervention).

The *actus reus* and *mens rea* for false representation are:

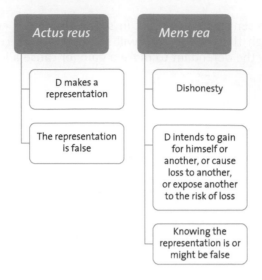

We will now consider the different elements of fraud by representation in detail.

## D makes a representation

The first element of the *actus reus* is that the defendant must have made a representation. The representation can be made in a number of different ways. For example, the defendant can make a representation orally, by conduct, or by silence.

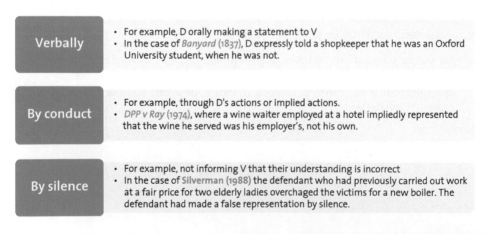

This is a useful checklist for an exam, and you should try to identify the type of representation made by D to strengthen your arguments in a paper – using the case law above to evidence your argument. An examiner will expect you to identify the nature of the representation. You should support your work by reference to relevant cases.

## Aim Higher

You will note in the above diagram the reference to 'implied representation', and it is useful to remember that D's representation can be either implied or express; both are a sufficient form of representation for this offence. Identifying the form of representation will enable the examiner to award more marks.

## Aim Higher

Case law has established that when D uses a credit/debit card, or gives a cheque, D effectively makes an implied representation to the other person that there are sufficient funds available for the payment to go through, and that D has the authority to use the card or cheque.

Providing a credit/debit card or cheque knowing that the payment will not go through, or using a stolen card, can be regarded as a false representation.

Test your understanding of representation with this example:

**Example:** Marco wants to buy a necklace for his girlfriend and sees a gold necklace and pendant. The shop assistant tells Marco that it is 18 carat gold. In fact the necklace is only 9 carat gold, and worth half the price. What type of representation has the shop assistant made?

The shopkeeper made a verbal express representation in this case, by stating the quality (carat) of the necklace.

### Case precedent – *Harris* [1975] 62 Cr App R28

**Facts:** D booked a hotel room, but did not pay the bill.

**Principle:** Representation

**Application:** A person who books a hotel room impliedly represents that they intend to pay for the room. This applies to other such services, such as paying for a meal or using a taxi.

Now look at the case of *Darwin and Darwin* (2008). Can you determine the type of representations which were made and when they are made?

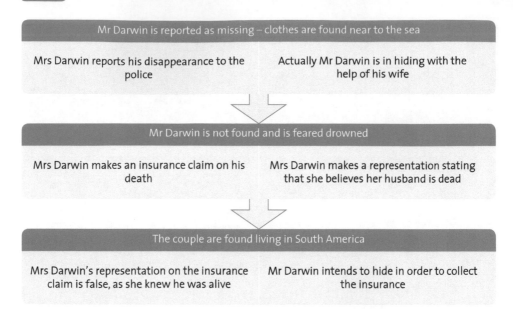

There are two more issues that we must address before moving on to consider the second element of the *actus reus* of this offence.

## Who is the representation made to?

The representation can be made to a person, or to a 'system or device': s 2(5) FA 2006. Sometimes an examiner will pose a problem question involving a machine or system. This might involve a:

❖ vending machine;
❖ cash machine;
❖ computer system.

It is clear from s 2(5) of the FA 2006 that representations to any of the above are included by this section.

## What must the representation contain?

A representation can include a statement of fact, a statement of the law, or a representation as to the state of mind of the person making the representation or any other person (s 2(3)).

The terms *statement of fact* and *statement of law* are fairly straightforward, but it will be helpful to elaborate on the term *state of mind*.

**Example:** Phil is selling DVDs at a car boot sale and he tells prospective buyers that he is saving up for a Christmas present for his daughter, when actually Phil plans to spend the money on alcohol.

In this example, Phil's state of mind (i.e. what D intends to do with the money) is different from the representation he makes to the buyer. Therefore he is making a false representation to the buyer.

## Test your knowledge

We have considered a number of examples of representation above. Now apply your understanding of s 2 **FA 2006** to the following scenarios:

a.  Martina enters a shop and takes a dress she wants to buy up to the counter. Martina gives her debit card to the shop assistant knowing that she has insufficient funds to pay for the dress.
b.  Ivor wants some chocolate from a vending machine. He only has foreign coins in his pocket. He inserts some of the foreign coins into the machine in the hope that they will work.
c.  Gillian applies for a children's bus pass. This discounted bus pass is only available if the applicant is under is under 16 years of age. Gillian sent the form off two days after her 16th birthday.

We are now moving on to consider the second element of the *actus reus* and that is that the representation must be false.

## The representation is false

Under s 2(2) of the **FA 2006**, a representation is false if:

a)  it is untrue or misleading; and
b)  the person making it knows that it is, or might be, untrue or misleading.

Think about the case of *Darwin and Darwin* (2008) that we considered earlier. At what point were the false representations made? In this case, it was when Mrs Darwin informed the police that her husband was missing (because she knew he was not missing), and when she made the claim on life insurance (because she knew that he was still alive). These clearly relate to s 2(b), as Mrs Darwin knew her husband was still alive, and therefore she knew that the representations were false or misleading.

We are now moving on to consider the *mens rea* elements of the offence. It is important to remember that *all three* elements of the MR must be present in order for liability to be constructed. It is the mental state of the defendant that differentiates what would otherwise be lawful conduct from unlawful conduct. The *mens rea* requirements for this offence are:

## Knowing the representation is, or might be false

The first *mens rea* requirement is that D must have known that the representation is, or might be false. In circumstances where the defendant does not know that the representation is false, or may be untrue/ misleading, liability cannot be constructed for this offence. Therefore the following situations would not constitute knowledge for the purposes of this offence:

❖ a defendant who has made a mistake;
❖ a defendant who is confused;
❖ a defendant who makes a statement in good faith believing that his/her representation is accurate.

## D dishonestly makes the false representation

The second element of the *mens rea* is that D must have been dishonest. We considered the test for dishonesty in the previous chapter. The test for dishonesty is the same as that used for the offence of theft – the two-stage Ghosh test. This test includes an objective and a subjective element. The jury will be required to determine the following:

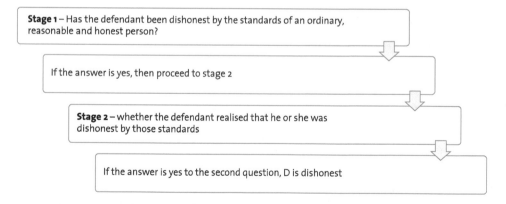

Look at the example below, and then apply the Ghosh test:

**Example:** D is a market trader selling cakes and business has been slow today. V, a diabetic, comes to the stall and asks D if there is sugar in the cakes. Eager to make a sale, D says there is no sugar in the cakes, even though D knows that the cakes contain sugar. V purchases one of the cakes.

Here, in order to establish dishonesty we would need to demonstrate that according to standards of ordinary, reasonable and honest people the defendant was dishonest. If the answer to this stage is yes then we proceed to the second stage and ask: did the defendant realise that he was dishonest according to those standards?

## D intends, by the false representation, to gain for himself or another, or cause loss to another, or expose another to the risk of loss

The definition of gain and loss is set out in s 5 of the **FA 2006**. This is:

(2) 'Gain' and 'loss' –

(a) extend only to gain or loss in money or other property;
(b) include any such gain or loss whether temporary or permanent;
and 'property' means any property whether real or personal (including things in action and other intangible property).

(3) 'Gain' includes a gain by keeping what one has, as well as a gain by getting what one does not have.

(4) 'Loss' includes a loss by not getting what one might get, as well as a loss by parting with what one has.

Note here that the emphasis is on D's intent to make a gain from the false representation – but that you do not need to demonstrate that a gain has actually been made.

This broadens the scope of the offence, so that it includes instances where a false representation was made which did not result in a gain or a loss. It is important to note that the gain or loss can be:

❖ permanent
❖ temporary
❖ retaining property that D already has in their possession.

---

### Case precedent – *R v Wai Yu-tsang* [1991] 4 All ER 664

**Facts:** D was employed by a bank and agreed with other employees that he would not inform the bank that cheques purchased were dishonoured. The defendant in this case agreed with others to not enter information about dishonoured cheques into the bank records.

**Principle:** False representation (intent)

**Application:** In this case D would not make a gain or a loss personally, but his employer would. Under the FA 2006, the intention of the D is considered not whether the D actually caused a gain or loss.

Now look back over the *actus reus* and *mens rea* of this offence and then apply your knowledge to the example below:

**Example:** A charity collector knocked on Diane's door and asked Diane if she had any clothes she could give away. Diane said that she did. Diane ran into her neighbour's back garden and took the clothes off the washing line. Diane did this because she had a grudge against her neighbour, who kept playing loud music.

Applying your knowledge of the FA 2006, determine whether Diane has committed an offence?

Work through the steps below to come to an answer:

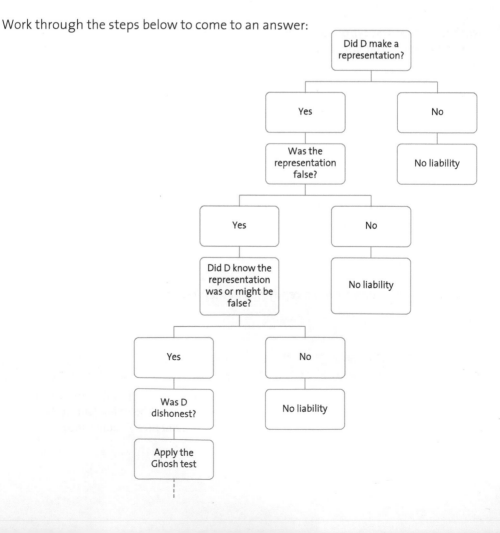

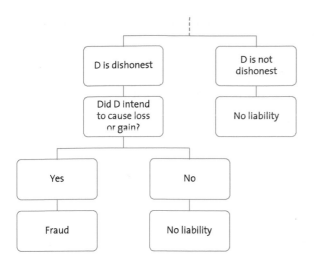

A summary of the points we have covered in this section is:

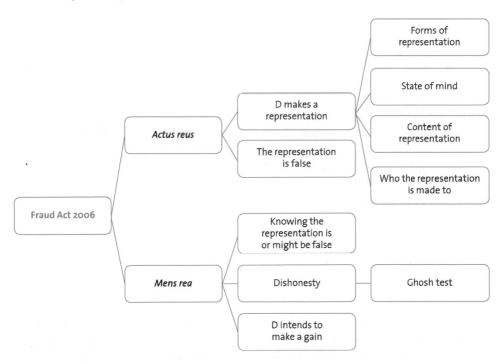

## Fraud by failing to disclose information

The offence of fraud by failing to disclose information is contained in s 3 of the Fraud Act 2006. It provided that a person commits an offence where he:

❖ dishonestly fails to disclose to another person information which he is under a legal duty to disclose, and
❖ intends by failing to disclose the information:

   i. to make a gain for himself or another, or
   ii. to cause loss to another or to expose another to risk of loss.

The *actus reus* and *mens rea* for this offence are:

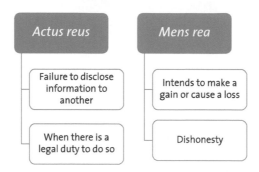

## Failure to disclose information to another

The first element of the *actus reus* of this offence is a failure to disclose information. However, this only applies in circumstances where D is under a legal obligation to disclose.

---

**Case precedent – *R v Frith* [1990] 91 Cr App 217**

**Facts:** D was a consultant who failed to inform the hospital he was working for that a number of patients he was caring for were private patients.

**Principle:** Failure to disclose information

**Application:** The defendant in this case was under a legal duty to disclose this information.

---

## Legal duty to disclose

Whether a duty to disclose information exist, is a question of law for the judge to determine. In a problem question you would need to establish the legal duty for D to inform V. The following situations are likely to give rise to such a duty.

❖ an employment contract;
❖ another type of legal contract;
❖ related to D's work or position;
❖ insurance or financial agreements;
❖ relating to trade or markets;
❖ being a trustee.

It is not necessary for the defendant to know that such a legal duty exists.

## Intends to make a gain or loss

We considered the concept of intention in the section on false representation.

## Dishonesty

We have considered the concept of dishonesty earlier in this chapter and the principles in relation to dishonesty apply here.

A summary of the points we have covered in this section is:

| Failure to disclose information to another | Where there is a legal duty to do so | D intends to make a gain or cause a loss | Dishonesty |
|---|---|---|---|
| • from D to V | • a legal relationship | • permanent<br>• temporary<br>• D retains what D already has | • Ghosh test |

# Fraud by abuse of position

This is a narrower offence in so far as it is limited to circumstances in which a defendant occupies a particular position. For example:

❖  an accountant and their client;
❖  a solicitor and their client; or
❖  an employer and employee.

Within this relationship, D uses his position, trust and power in order to commit fraud.

The offence is set out in s4 of the FA 2006 as:

a)  D occupies a position in which he is expected to safeguard or not act against the financial interest of another;
b)  where D dishonestly
c)  abuses their position

    i.  intending by this to gain for himself or another, cause loss to another, or
    ii.  expose another to the risk of loss.

The *actus reus* and *mens rea* of the offence are:

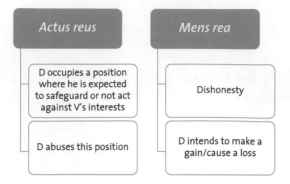

### D occupies a position where he is expected to safeguard, or not act against V's interests

D occupies a privileged position, and because of this D is expected to safeguard another's financial interests, or not act against the financial interests of another. Positions that might give rise to such expectations include: trustee and beneficiary, director and company, professional person and client, agent and principal, employee and employer etc.

If there is any doubt as to whether this relationship exists, the judge will determine this as a matter of law.

### D abuses the position

There is no definition of abuse of power, and it can depend on the individual circumstances of the case, and the nature of the relationship between D and V.

**Aim Higher**

Section 4(2) also stipulates that there can be an abuse of position from a failure to act (omission).

A useful case relating to an omission is the case of *Gale* (2008). In this case D was a baggage handler who accepted a bribe to put cargo in an aeroplane hold, without checking the contents. The cargo was illegal drugs. As D held a position of trust, the court found that he abused this trust.

| D occupies a position of trust with V | This relationship can be determined as a point of law | D abuses this position | By an act or omission |
|---|---|---|---|

It is not however, necessary to prove that D knew he occupied a position of trust in which he was expected to safeguard V's interests or not act against them – this should be determined as part of the *actus reus* (the act) from the type of relationship between D and V, as already discussed.

### Dishonesty

Dishonesty is once again a vital part of this offence. The Ghosh test is applicable here also.

### D intends to make a gain / cause a loss

Again, the discussion in relation to gain/loss in relation to fraud by false representation is applicable here.

A summary of the points we have covered in this section is:

| D occupies a position where he is expected to safeguard or not act against V | D abuses his position | Dishonesty | D intends to make a gain/cause a loss |
|---|---|---|---|
| • Point of law on the type of relationship | • Can be an act or omission | • Ghosh test | • From his position in the relationship with V |

# Obtaining services dishonestly

This offence is outlined within s 11 of the FA 2006, replacing the offence of 'obtaining services by deception'. One of the reasons for this change was to cover offences carried out by using machines, such as chip and PIN machines, or those carried out on a computer and/or on the internet.

## Up for Debate

Note here that the name of the offence focuses on obtaining services, therefore D must obtain the service as part of the *actus reus*.

This is different from the other offences we have considered – think about why this is different as you work through this section.

The *actus reus* and *mens rea* for this offence are:

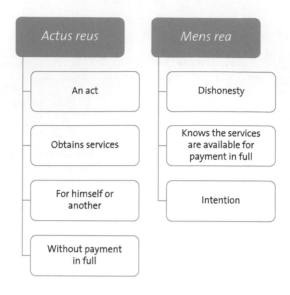

## D performs an act

The first element of the *actus reus* of this offence requires D to perform an act. There must be a causal link between the act and the obtaining of the service. This is because the statutory wording requires that D, by his *dishonest* act, obtains the service. This means that if D honestly obtains the service and then decides to leave without paying, the service is not obtained by the dishonest act. The correct offence in this example would be making off without payment, a separate offence (which is described in the next section).

You can summarise this as:

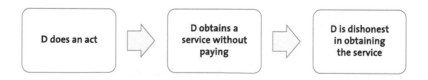

## Obtains services

The term *services* includes:

❖ the provision of board and lodgings;
❖ entertainment;
❖ social and sporting amenities;
❖ repair and decorating;
❖ letting goods on hire and the provision of transport.

These are quite wide definitions, and have been tested and refined through case law over the years.

## Common Pitfall

Be careful here, as D must not have actually obtained the service yet – D would not be liable if he had not watched the festival, or not travelled on the train.

For example, consider the case of *Nabina* (2002), where D dishonestly lied about his personal details to obtain a credit card. This dishonest act allowed him to obtain the card *and* the continued use of the card to purchase services would both amount to a s 11 offence.

But be careful – there are instances which do not constitute a dishonest act. These can include:

> **If another person makes a mistake**

> **Services that do not require payment**

### *For himself or another*
Here D can undertake the dishonest act to gain/use services for himself or another person.

**Example:** Nathan books a holiday for his mother with a card he obtained under a false name. Look at the following steps to work through this case:

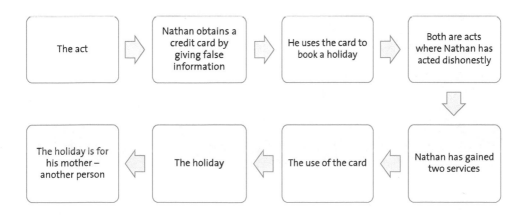

## *Without payment in full*

This is covered by s 11(2)(b) of the FA 2006, which sets out that D must obtain the service without making payment in full.

When you are applying this element to a problem question, remember to check that the services do require payment in full – i.e. that they are not provided free. Otherwise, payment will not be required and this element of the *actus reus* will not be made out.

We are now moving on to consider the *mens rea* for the s 11 offence.

## *Dishonesty*

Once again, as per the previous offences, it must be shown that D acted dishonestly, and this is established through the use of the Ghosh test.

## *D knows the services are available for payment in full*

The next element of the *mens rea* for this offence is that D must know that the services are made available, on the basis that payment has been, is being or will be made. Therefore D knows that the service requires payment in full (s 2(a)).

This is usually obvious given the circumstances or the type of service.

## *Intention*

It must be shown that D did not intend to pay for the service – in full or in part. The intention must be present when the act is committed by D.

Therefore, not only does D avoid payment, but D *intends* to avoid payment, i.e. D does not fail to make payment by mistake, or by thinking he had already paid.

### Aim Higher

What if D changes his mind at the last minute and does make the payment? Or if D changes his mind part way through the act and originally intended to make payment and then changes his mind?

What you need to remember is D's intent to make payment in full, at the time of the act. This should give you the basis to make a decision, and to clearly argue this decision in your answer.

A summary of the points we have covered in this section:

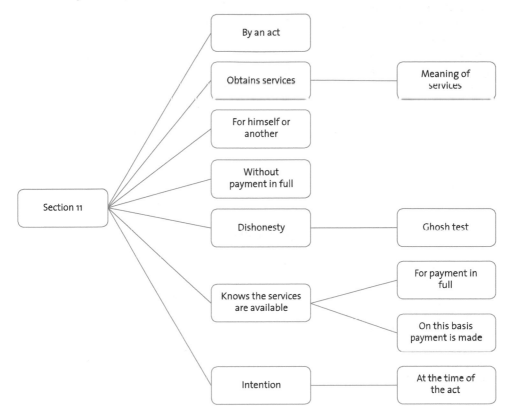

## Blackmail

The offence of blackmail is contained within s 21 of the Theft Act 1968. Section 21 of the Theft Act states:

(1)   A person is guilty of blackmail if, with a view to gain for himself or another or with intent to cause loss to another, he makes any unwarranted demand with menaces; and for this purpose a demand with menaces is unwarranted unless the person making it does so in the belief –

    (a)   that he has reasonable grounds for making the demand; and
    (b)   that the use of the menaces is a proper means of reinforcing the demand.

(2)   The nature of the act or omission demanded is immaterial, and it is also immaterial whether the menaces relate to action to be taken by the person making the demand.

(3)   A person guilty of blackmail shall on conviction on indictment be liable to imprisonment for a term not exceeding fourteen years.

To be liable for blackmail the defendant must:

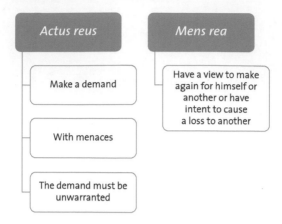

We will now consider each element of the offence of blackmail in more detail.

### D must make a demand

Making a demand is the first essential element for blackmail – without the demand, there can be no blackmail. The demand must require V to do something, or it must require V not to do something. Blackmail is a conduct crime and it is therefore irrelevant whether D's demands are effective.

The demand can include a number of different actions, and the demand can be express or implied: *Collister & Warhurst* (1955).

The way in which the demand is made can be important. For example:

❖ The demand does not need to have been read by or communicated to V, but there must be proof of the demand.
❖ Where a demand is made by post, as soon as the letter is posted, the demand has been made.
❖ The demand can be made in a number of different ways. It can be oral and in a letter, a fax such as a text message, email, on the internet etc.

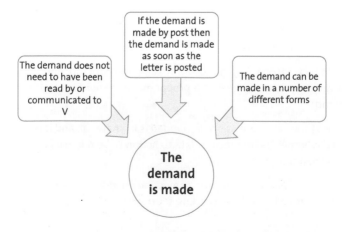

This places the emphasis on D making the demand (which is sufficient), rather than V being aware that the demand has been made.

---

**Case precedent – *R v Hester* [2007] EWCA Crim 2127**

**Facts:** D became involved in a gang. He was instructed by the gang to obtain money by blackmailing the victim. D was convicted of blackmail.

**Principle:** The demand for blackmail

**Application:** The defendant appealed against his conviction on the basis that at the time he joined the gang the demand had already been made by other members of the gang. As such he argued that his conviction was unsound. The defendant's appeal was unsuccessful. The court ruled that the demand was a continuing act.

---

The demand is a continuing act and continues until the demand is withdrawn.

### With menaces

The demand must be accompanied by menaces and similar to the demand, these can also be express or implied. Menaces are serious, or significant threats.

The word *menace* and its meaning are important here. Clearly it extends beyond physical violence (*Tomlinson* (1895)), and D must be aware of the likely effect on V. 'The threat must be of such a nature and extent that the mind of an ordinary person of normal stability and courage might be influenced or made apprehensive, so as to give way unwillingly to the demand' (*R v Clear* (1968), LJ Seller).

---

## Up for Debate

Do you think there is an issue here in terms of the subjectivity of the threat/demand?

A person that is confident and outgoing may not give way as quickly as a timid person? Do you think that the circumstances in which the threat are made may also have an impact? For example: a demand made in a letter may have less impact than a demand made face to face?

For example, if the menace was contained within a letter, it may prompt a different response from V than if they were face to face with D.

---

Consider the case of *R v Lawrence and Pomroy* (1971). Here the menace was implied, but delivered face-to-face by a large intimidating man. The phrase or test used to describe the level of security required to amount to blackmail.

In the case of *R v Garwood* (1987), the victim was of a timid nature, and if D is aware of the impact of his actions on D, this could also be classed as menaces.

When you are working through a problem question there are a few points you will need to consider:

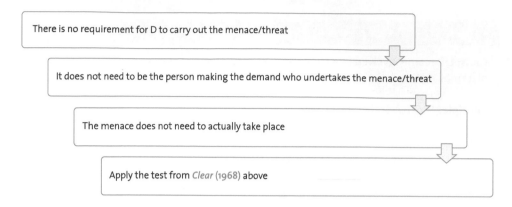

There is no requirement for D to carry out the menace/threat

It does not need to be the person making the demand who undertakes the menace/threat

The menace does not need to actually take place

Apply the test from *Clear* (1968) above

Consider these points as you work through a problem question, and this should help you to determine whether or not the demand is accompanied with menaces.

## The demand must be unwarranted

Section 21(1) of the **Theft Act 1968** outlines that in order for a demand to be warranted the person making the demand believes both:

(a) that they had reasonable grounds for making the demand; and
(b) that the use of menaces is a proper means of reinforcing the demand.

Therefore, if there are no reasonable grounds for making the demand and the menaces are not a proper means of reinforcing the demand, the demand is unwarranted. It is important to note that this is based on the defendant's belief. In other words what D believes to be true. The test is subjective.

This is decided on a subjective basis, and a court would consider both parts of s 21(1).

## Reasonable grounds for making the demand

Remember that this is based on the D's belief. D must believe that there were reasonable grounds. It does not matter whether those grounds were reasonable.

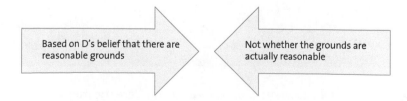

Based on D's belief that there are reasonable grounds

Not whether the grounds are actually reasonable

## The use of menaces is a proper means of reinforcing the demand

This part of the test asks whether D's actions were an appropriate means for re-inforcing the demand.

## Common Pitfall

What D threatens amounts to a criminal offence. It is therefore automatically classed as an unwarranted demand.

A useful case to demonstrate this is *R v Harvey* (1981), where the Ds threatened to harm V's family unless he returned money. The judge ruled that the demand and menace were criminal actions and were not reasonable or proper.

### With a view to make a gain or intent to cause loss

Section 34(2)(a) of the Theft Act 1968 defines a 'gain' and 'loss' as only a gain or loss of money or other property. This would therefore exclude other types of benefits, such as those of a sexual nature (e.g. where D threatens to tell V's employer that V has stolen money from the company unless V has sexual intercourse with D).

In a problem question, double check what the gain or loss for D could be, as this can be included by examiners to check a student's knowledge! For example, consider the case of *R v Bevans* (1988), where D's gain was an injection of morphine. At first you may think that this is not a gain or money or property, but the judge found that D did in fact gain property – the morphine – and as such was liable for blackmail. It is important to note that the gain or loss can also be temporary.

A summary of the points we have covered in this section is:

| Make a demand | With menaces | Demand must be unwarranted | Intend to make a gain or cause a loss |
|---|---|---|---|
| • Type of demand<br>• Communication | • Can be an act or omission | • Reasonable grounds for making the demand<br>• Menaces is a proper means | • Of money or other property |

# Putting it into practice
## Question 1

Ian is a doctor and makes house calls most days. He visits Jane, an elderly woman who collects antique china. While at the house, Ian realises that Jane's vase is very old and valuable, and tells Jane that he really likes it but it is not worth much, if anything. On this basis, Jane tells Ian that he can have the vase, as he has helped her recover from her illness. Ian takes the vase to the local auction house, who sell it at auction for £10,000.

Would Ian be liable for a fraud offences?

## Suggested solution

When approaching this case you should follow the structure that we have practised:

1.  Identify the crime
2.  Define the crime
3.  Deal with all elements of the *actus reus*
4.  Deal with all elements of the *mens rea*
5.  Deal with potential defences
6.  Address lesser or alternative offences

When looking at this case, you would first need to identify which fraud offence has occurred. Here we can see a relationship between two people, one of whom is a doctor who makes a gain, so the offence of fraud by the abuse of position would be the offence to consider.

Work through the *actus reus* and *mens rea* to define whether Ian would be liable for this offence. D occupies a position of trust – here we can see that Ian is a doctor and Jane is the patient, implying a privileged relationship between the two people. Ian's role as a doctor means that Jane would be likely to believe his views, as he is there to help improve her health and safeguard her interests – not to act against her. Remember that if there is a question over D occupying a position of trust, this would become a point of law.

D abuses that position – the question shows that Ian knew the true cost of the vase, but knowingly gave Jane false information. Remember that there is no formal description of 'abuse' as it depends on the circumstances, but you could argue that Ian abused this position of trust by providing false information which Jane believed.

Dishonesty – in this situation you would be referencing and working through the Ghosh test, and applying this to the scenario to demonstrate whether Ian had acted dishonestly.

D intends to make a gain or cause a loss – here Ian makes a clear gain of £10,000, from the abuse of position. Not only this but Jane loses the vase (property), which would constitute a loss for her.

As you argue through your answer, remember to refer to the legislation and how it would be applied to the facts of this question.

# Question 2

Anna and Meera are artists and Meera is very well known. Meera sees a painting by Anna and takes it to her studio, adds her own name to the bottom and sells it in her gallery. James knows that Anna actually painted the picture, and as a friend of Anna is very cross. He confronts Meera and says: 'Pay me £1,000 or I will beat you up for what you did to Anna.' Meera is very scared of James, so agrees quickly and gives him the money.

Would James be liable for any offences?

## Suggested solution

Remember to follow the structure that we have practised:

1. **Identify the crime**
2. **Define the crime**
3. **Deal with all elements of the *actus reus***
4. **Deal with all elements of the *mens rea***
5. **Deal with potential defences**
6. **Address lesser or alternative offences**

The offence you would be focusing on here is blackmail, under the Theft Act 1968. Remember to work through the elements of blackmail, to identify whether James is liable. Provide a full definition for the offence and the source of the offence.

Make a demand – we can see from the question that James made an oral demand from Meera, and that the demand was explicit and specific: 'Pay me £1,000 or I will beat you up for what you did to Anna'. Remember that a demand can take a number of forms, and can also be implied.

With menaces – taken from the position of V (Meera), she is scared of James and quickly agrees, which is how it can be argued that the demand was with menaces. You can also refer to and apply the test established in *Clear* (1968).

The demand must be unwarranted – the examiner would expect to see you discuss the two main parts of this element – reasonable grounds for making the demand, and it is unwarranted if it is a criminal offence. In the question James threatens to beat up Meera, i.e. cause her unlawful harm, which could constitute a criminal act (non-fatal offences), hence this would be the area that you would expect to pull out within the answer.

There must be a gain by D or the victim suffers a loss – clearly within the question James would make a gain of £1,000, which he does not appear to pass on to Anna either. The gain is monetary and passed the test.

Remember to refer to appropriate case law and legislation throughout your answer.

# Key Points Checklist

| | |
|---|---|
| Section 1 of the Fraud Act 2006 creates a single offence of fraud. This offence can be committed in three ways:<br>s 2 fraud by false representation<br>s 3 fraud by failing to disclose information<br>s 4 fraud by abuse of position | ✔ |
| The *actus reus* of fraud by false representation (s 2 of the Fraud Act 2006) is the making of a false representation. The *mens rea* of the offence is that D was dishonest, that D knew that the representation was false and that D's intention was to make a gain or cause financial loss. | ✔ |
| The *actus reus* of fraud by failing to disclose (s 3 of the Fraud Act 2006) is a failure to disclose information to another, where there is a legal duty to disclose information. The *mens rea* of the offence is that D intends to make a gain or cause loss and that D does so dishonestly. | ✔ |
| The *actus reus* of fraud by abuse of position (s 4 of the Fraud Act 2006) is that D occupies a position of trust where he is expected to safeguard the interests of V, and D abuses that position of trust. The *mens rea* for the offence is that D does so with the intention to make a financial gain or cause loss. | ✔ |
| Blackmail is defined in s 21 of the Theft Act 1968. The *actus reus* of the offence is that D makes a demand with menaces and the demand is unwarranted. The *mens rea* of the offence is D intends to make a gain for himself or another, or cause loss to another. | ✔ |

# Table of key cases referred to in this chapter

| Key case | Brief facts | Principle |
|---|---|---|
| *DPP v Ray* [1974] AC 370 | D ate a meal in a restaurant, then realised he could not pay – remained silent and ran out | Type of representation |
| *Harris* [1975] 62 Cr App R28 | D booked into a hotel room, but had no intention of paying | Representation |
| *Metropolitan Police Commissioner v Charles* [1976] AC 177 (HL) | D writes a cheque to V, knowing there are insufficient funds available and the cheque will not go through | Representation |
| *R v Wai Yu-tsang* [1991] 4 All ER 664 | D agreed not to tell his employer about dishonoured cheques | Intent within false representation |
| *Gale* [2008] All ER 130 | D was a baggage handler at an airport, and accepted a bribe to put cargo on an aeroplane | Abuse of position of trust |
| *Nabina* [2002] All ER 733 | D used false information about himself to gain a credit card | Obtaining services dishonestly |

| *R v Collister & Warhurst* [1955] 39 Cr App R100 | D implied his demand to V by asking what he had in his possession | Implied demand in blackmail |
|---|---|---|

@ **Visit the book's companion website to test your knowledge**

❖ Resources include a subject map, revision tip podcasts, downloadable diagrams, MCQ quizzes for each chapter, and a flashcard glossary

❖ www.routledge.com/cw/optimizelawrevision

# 9 Inchoate Offences

**Understand the law**
- Can you identify which sections of the Criminal Law Act 1977 relates to conspiracy?
- Can you identify which section of the Criminal Attempts Act 1981 refers to the offence of attempt?

**Remember the details**
- Can you remember the *actus reus* and *mens rea* for conspiracy and attempt?
- Can you define the *actus reus* and *mens rea* of these offences using case law?

**Reflect critically on areas of debate**
- Do you understand the definition of intention in relation to conspiracy, and how intention is established?

**Contextualise**
- Are you able to contextualise the different inchoate offences and relate them to other substantive offences?

**Apply your skills and knowledge**
- Can you complete the activities in this chapter, using case law and legislation to support your work?

# Chapter Map

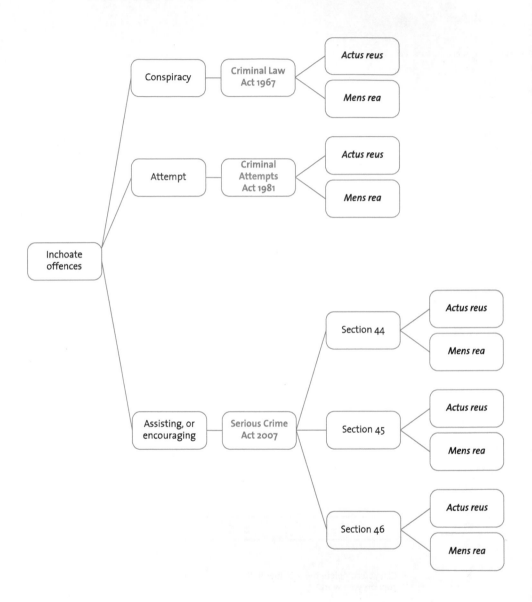

# Inchoate elements

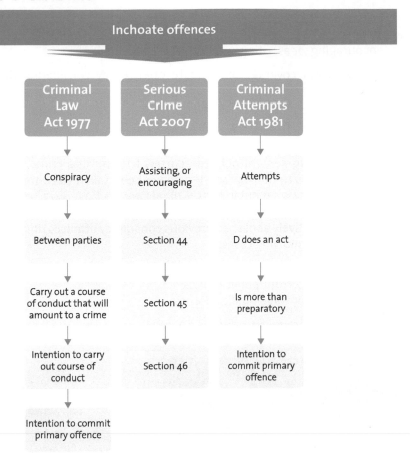

# Inchoate offences

As you work through this chapter, you will notice that inchoate offences are differ-ent from the offences that we have discussed in other chapters, largely because they are committed before the primary criminal act takes place. They cover the time when D progresses his thoughts or plans to commit a criminal offence into a reality, i.e. the preparatory stages in committing an offence.

The focus of inchoate offences is on the activity that takes place before the crime if committed. Therefore, the primary offence is incomplete (inchoate). Conspiracy charges have been used against terrorist suspects in the UK who have been apprehended before carrying out their terrorist objectives.

In this chapter we will consider:

❖ conspiracy;
❖ attempt;
❖ encouraging, or assisting.

We will start our coverage of inchoate offences by considering the offence of conspiracy.

# Conspiracy

Conspiracy is an agreement between parties to commit a crime, and this can be punished even where no positive steps have been taken to commit the intended offence. Conspiracy is set out in the Criminal Law Act (CLA) 1977.

The CLA 1977 effectively abolished previous conspiracy offences under common law, except for in the following cases:

❖ conspiracy to defraud;
❖ conspiracy to corrupt public morals;
❖ conspiracy to outrage public decency.

The above are common law offences.

## Aim Higher

Although the main conspiracy offences are contained within the **CLA 1997**, there are also separate conspiracy offences contained within other Acts; for example, the **Fraud Act 2006**.

Section 1 of the Criminal Law Act 1977 stipulates:

(1) Subject to the following provisions of this Part of this Act, if a person agrees with any other person or persons that a course of conduct shall be pursued which, if the agreement is carried out in accordance with their intentions, either –

    (a) will necessarily amount to or involve the commission of any offence or offences by one or more of the parties to the agreement, or
    (b) would do so but for the existence of facts which render the commission of the offence or any of the offences impossible,

he is guilty of conspiracy to commit the offence or offences in question.

The *actus reus* and *mens rea* for conspiracy are:

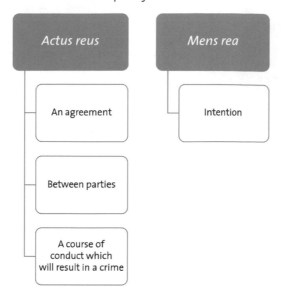

We will now consider these elements in more detail.

### An agreement
The first conduct element in the *actus reus* is the agreement. An agreement can be oral as well as written down. The agreement must be to commit a criminal offence. The parties to conspiracy need not go on to commit that offence. It is sufficient that a general agreement has been reached.

### Between parties
There must be at least two parties to an agreement. This means that in the following situation, there will be no agreement:

❖ When a company director conspires in the company name – this is because the company does not have a separate mind. Therefore the director conspires with himself.
❖ Where the defendant conspires with a person who is mentally disordered and unable to understand the nature and purpose of the proposed course of conduct.

In addition, s 2(2) of the **CLA 1977** stipulates:

| | |
|---|---|
| D is not liable if the only person he agrees with is his spouse | • However, marriage after a conspiracy, or during its continuance, is no defence. A spouse can commit conspiracy where there is an agreement between spouses to conspire with others. |
| D will not commit conspiracy where the agreement is made with an individual under the age of criminal responsibility. | • Section 2(2)(c) |
| A defendant is not liable for conspiracy where they are the intended victim of the offence in question. | • Section 2(1) |

## Aim Higher

When the facts of a problem question involve more than one potential defendant you must remember to consider conspiracy. Look for key words such as 'agreed', 'planned', 'decided'. It is possible that the examiner is asking you to consider conspiracy.

We are now moving on to consider the third element of the *actus reus*, which is that the parties to the agreement must have agreed on a course of conduct that will result in a criminal offence.

### A course of conduct that will result in a crime

The parties must agree that at least one of them pursues a course of action that will result in a criminal offence.

There is no 'result' element within the *actus reus*, so it does not need to be shown that the intended crime was actually committed. In circumstances where the Ds go on to commit the substantive offence it is the substantive offence, not the conspiracy to commit the substantive offence, that should be charged. This is illustrated in the case of *Wright* (1995).

## Common Pitfall

It is important to remember that the offence committed must be linked to the offence that the D conspired to commit. Exercise caution where the offence committed differs significantly from the offence committed. It is not unusual for students to become confused considering the act committed not the act agreed.

**But note** – conspiracy should only be discussed if the agreed offence is **not** committed. If the offence agreed upon **is** actually committed, then both Ds will be joint principals to the offence, or one will be the principal and the other will be the secondary participant.

Remember these key points as:

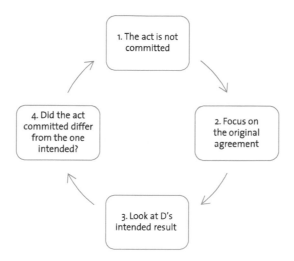

1. The act is not committed

2. Focus on the original agreement

3. Look at D's intended result

4. Did the act committed differ from the one intended?

**Example:** George and Eve agree to traffic heroin from one country to another. However, Eve actually puts cannabis in the bags instead and cannabis is trafficked from one country to another.

Would George be liable for conspiracy to traffic illegal drugs?

Facts very similar to this occurred in the case of *Siracusa* (1989). In this case the defendant was convicted. The court held that the agreement was the essence of the crime of conspiracy – the agreement between the parties must be as to the specific offence. The court held that this could include a lesser offence (in this case trafficking a Class B drug instead of a class A drug.

We are now moving on to consider the *mens rea* for conspiracy.

## Intention

❖ Intention relates to an intention to commit an offence; and
❖ an intention that their agreement will lead to a course of conduct that will lead to the offence.

It is vital that the Ds intend to carry out a course of conduct that amounts to a criminal offence. Recklessness or negligence is insufficient. Intention and intention alone will suffice. The case of *Saik* (2006) identifies and confirms this principle. D must also intend that the offence will occur.

**Case precedent – *McPhillips* [1990] 6 BNIL**

**Facts:** D was guilty of conspiracy to plant a bomb, but was not a party to the conspiracy to murder, because, unknown to his accomplices, he did not intend the result (the evidence being that he intended to give a warning so the area could be evacuated).

**Principle:** Intention

**Application:** This is the correct position, and D was found not guilty of conspiracy to murder.

Now that we have considered the main elements of conspiracy, we will look at other aspects of conspiracy which you would need to consider in an essay question, we will consider in detail the specific conspiracy offences contained in the CLA 1977.

## When does the conspiracy actually occur?

As already noted, the conspiracy 'crystallises' at the point that the parties agree. The conspiracy is a continuing offence, so it continues until it is terminated by the commission of the act, abandonment or frustration. As it is a continuing offence other parties can also join an existing conspiracy. This was established in *Leigh* (1775).

## Aim Higher

A single agreement can involve more than one conspiracy. For example, in the case of *Cooke* (1986), an agreement by rail stewards to sell personal food on a train was a conspiracy to defraud British Rail, *and* also a conspiracy to defraud passengers.

Where there is an agreement to commit offences of a certain type, agreements to commit the particular offences of that type are evidence of a general conspiracy.

For example, in *Hammersley* (1958), police officers in Brighton conspired with suspected criminals by alerting the criminals about police intentions to prosecute or investigate them. The purpose of this was to solicit and obtain reward for these favours. It was held that, although the conspiracy involved a number of illegal agreements over a number of years, there was only one conspiracy (to obstruct the course of public justice), not a series of conspiracies.

**Example:** friends Cho and Harriet talk about defrauding Albert of some valuable paintings he has in his home. They both agree that it is a good plan. However, they are overheard by Bert, who reports their conversation.

Have Harriet and Cho committed a conspiracy?

Work through the steps below to decide.

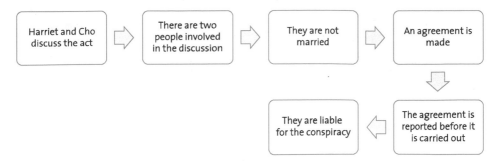

## Conspiracy and impossibility

As seen above, there is no result element in the *actus reus* of conspiracy. The *actus reus* of conspiracy does not require that the offence actually occurs. But what if the crime could never have occurred because the facts render it impossible?

| Case precedent – *DPP v Nock* [1978] AC 979 |
| --- |

**Facts:** D conspired, with others, to produce cocaine from a powder containing the drug. However, there was no actual cocaine in the powder.

**Principle:** Conspiracy and impossibility

**Application:** An agreement to do the impossible can be used as a defence in conspiracy.

The **CLA 1977** was amended by s 5 **Criminal Attempts Act 1981**. This amendment was necessary to deal with the decision in *DPP v Nock* (1978).

Section 5 of the **Criminal Attempts Act 1981** provides that:

(1)   Subject to the following provisions of this Part of this Act, if a person agrees with any other person or persons that a course of conduct shall be pursued which, if the agreement is carried out in accordance with their intentions, either –

   (a)  will necessarily amount to or involve the commission of any offence or offences by one or more of the parties to the agreement, or
   (b)  would do so but for the existence of facts which render the commission of the offence or any of the offences impossible,

   he is guilty of conspiracy to commit the offence or offences in question.

A summary of the points we have covered in this section is:

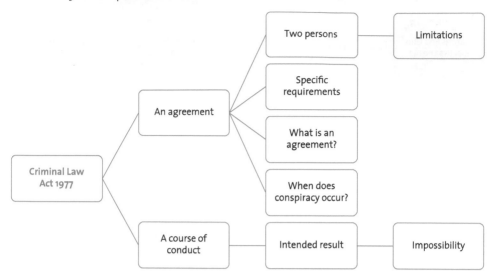

# Attempts

The law on attempts is set out in s 1 of the Criminal Attempts Act (CAA) 1981. It provides:

(1) If, with intent to commit an offence to which this section applies, a person does an act which is more than merely preparatory to the commission of the offence, he is guilty of attempting to commit the offence.

## Aim Higher

The **CAA 1981** effectively turned the previous common law offence of attempt into a statutory offence. This was in response to a report by the Law Commission on the law on attempts, which made a number of recommendations.

The *actus reus* and *mens rea* are:

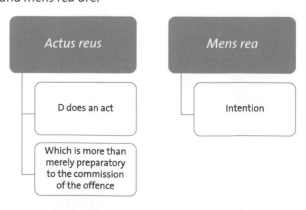

The **CAA (1981)** stipulates that:

**Section 1(4) – only indictable offences**
- Only indictable offences an be attempted. This includes triable-either-way offences.

**Section 1(4) – exceptions**
- There is no offence of attempting to conspire, attempting to aid and abet etc.
- This is with the exception of suicide and attempting to assist after an offence.

**Section 1(4) – location**
- Provides that the offence, if completed, must be one that could have been indicted in England or Wales.

It is clear that there are strict rules regarding the type of offence that can be attempted. It is therefore important that you remember the following checklist when dealing with attempts.

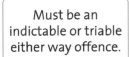

| Must be an indictable or triable either way offence. | Not a participation offence | Indicted in England or Wales |
|---|---|---|

We are now going to consider the second element of the *actus reus*.

## The act is more than merely preparatory to the commission of an offence

In order to establish liability for attempt the D must have done something which is 'more than *merely* preparatory'. Thus the D must have moved from the planning and preparation stages to the active commission of the offence in question. The difficulty here is that the line between preparation and acts which are more than 'merely preparatory' is not all that clear.

Before the **CAA 1981** the courts had developed a series of tests to determine at what stage D was actually 'attempting to commit a crime' – i.e. the difference between preparatory acts and those which are more than 'merely preparatory'.

The following three cases illustrated the distinction between the two:

*Eagleton* (1885)  *Davey & Lee* (1967)  *Jones* (1990)

Look at the cases in the table below and see if you can identify any principles emerging from them

| Case | Facts |
|---|---|
| *Boyle and Boyle* (1987) | The Ds in this case damaged a door whilst attempting to gain entry into a property that they intended to burgle. The court held that this was sufficient to amount to acts that were more than merely preparatory. |
| *Tosti and White* (1997) | The Ds in this case drove to the scene of the intended offence with oxyacetylene equipment, which they hid in a hedge, and then they examined a heavy padlock on a barn door. These were *'essentially the first steps in the commission of the offence'.* |
| *Dagnall* (2003) | Despite not having touched V in any sexual way, the defendant in this case was convicted of attempted rape because he had virtually succeeded in what he was intending to do and had overcome V's resistance. He was only prevented from committing the rape by the arrival of the police. |
| *Campbell* (1991) | In this case police believed D was going to rob a post office. The defendant was observed in close proximity to the post office. He then left the area and returned half an hour later. He was arrested by the police outside the post office. He had in his possession an imitation gun. He admitted when questioned that his intention was to rob the post office but said he had changed his mind and was arrested before he could leave. This was 'merely preparatory' (not 'more than'). |

From these cases, we can see that the point at which acts make the transition from preparatory acts to acts which are more than merely prepartory depends on the circumstances of the case, and the offence in question. What is clear is that the D must be at the beginning of the commission of the offence.

After looking at these cases, consider the example below, and whether an attempt was made.

**Example:** Ed is a burglar. He carefully selects the houses that he burgles, trying to ensure as best as he can that the properties he selects will render a high yield in terms of the items that he steals. Ed has been watching Paul's house for several days in an attempt to establish the owner's daily routine. On Tuesday morning Ed is lurking outside Paul's house waiting for him to leave for work. Amber, Paul's elderly and nosy neighbour, sees Ed and is suspicious and she calls the police. PC Caesar arrests Ed, who has in his possession specialist tools for gaining entry into properties, gloves and an instruction manual for disabling alarm systems and CCTV.

Would Ed be liable for the offence of attempted burglary?

## Up for Debate

Case law is gradually refining the meaning of 'attempt', and as this refinement continues, the line between preparatory actions and attempt will become clearer. Is this an indication that the Act is unclear?.

## Intention

Section 1(1) refers to the defendant acting 'with intent to commit an offence'. Therefore, only intention to commit the offence in question is sufficient. It is worth noting that intention to commit a different offence is insufficient.

### Case precedent – *Fallon* [1994] Crim LR 519

**Facts:** D shot a police officer and the court needed to decide if it was accidental or deliberate.

**Principle:** Intention

**Application:** The Court of Appeal cautioned against the provision of a complicated direction on the meaning of intention.

In order to establish liability for attempt, the prosecution must establish that D possessed intention with reference to the consequences specified in the *actus reus* of the offence. There can be occasions when this does not sit neatly with the *mens rea* for the primary offence. Look at the examples in the diagram below, and think about situations in which this can occur:

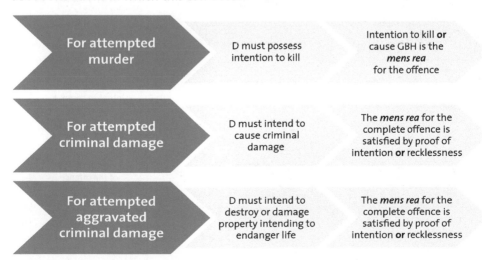

| For attempted murder | D must possess intention to kill | Intention to kill **or** cause GBH is the *mens rea* for the offence |

| For attempted criminal damage | D must intend to cause criminal damage | The *mens rea* for the complete offence is satisfied by proof of intention **or** recklessness |

| For attempted aggravated criminal damage | D must intend to destroy or damage property intending to endanger life | The *mens rea* for the complete offence is satisfied by proof of intention **or** recklessness |

## Attempt and impossibility

It is possible that a defendant may embark on a course of conduct in which they attempt the impossible. Section 1(2) of the **CAA 1981** stipulates that in these a defendant may be still be liable for attempt:

> . . . even though the facts are such that the commission of the offence is impossible.

In the case of *Jones* (2007), a police officer pretended to be a 12-year-old and sent text messages to the defendant D as part of an undercover operation to catch the author of graffiti in a toilet seeking young girls for sex. D replied to the text messages sent by the police officer and was charged and convicted of attempting to intentionally incite a child under the age of 13 to engage in sexual activity contrary to s 8 of the **Sexual Offences Act 2003**. In reality it would have been impossible for the defendant to commit this offence in relation to the 'victim' as the intended victim was not under the age of 13.

A summary of the points we have covered in this section is:

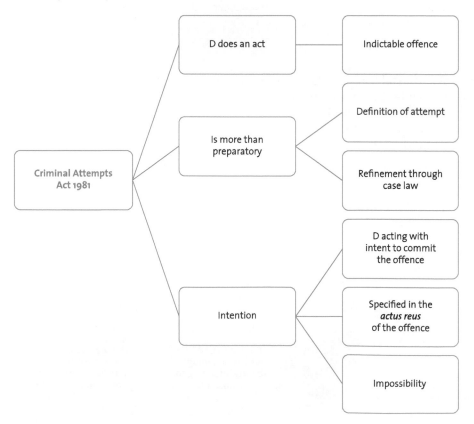

# Encouraging or assisting

Prior to the implementation of the Serious Crime Act (SCA) 2007 there was a common law offence of incitement. Section 59 of the SCA 2007 abolished the common law offences. Sections 44, 45 and 46 of the SCA 2007 create three inchoate offences.

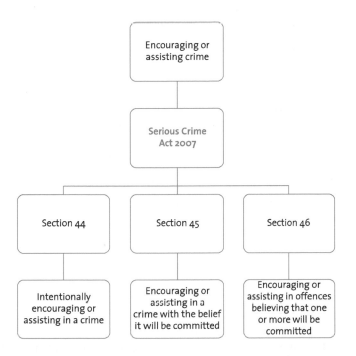

We will consider each of these sections in order.

## Section 44: intentionally encouraging or assisting an offence

(1)  A person commits an offence if –

(a)  he does an act capable of encouraging or assisting the commission of an offence; and

(b)  he intends to encourage or assist its commission.

(2)  But he is not to be taken to have intended to encourage or assist the commission of an offence merely because such encouragement or assistance was a foreseeable consequence of his act.

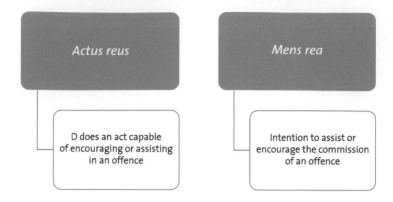

We will now consider each of these elements separately.

### D does an act capable of assisting or encouraging in the commission of an offence

The defendant must do an act which is 'capable' of assisting or encouraging in the commission of an offence. Section 65(2) provides that this offence can be committed by omission where D fails to discharge a duty. The act does not actually have to assist or encourage in the commission of an offence; it is sufficient that it is capable of doing so.

### Intention to assist or encourage in the commission of an offence

Thus a defendant that foresees that their behaviour may encourage or assist in the commission of an offence does not have the requisite *mens rea* for the offence. This does not include where D foresees encouragement or assistance as a likely consequence of his actions.

We will now consider s 45 of the SCA 2007.

## Section 45: encouraging or assisting an offence believing it will be committed

Section 45 of the SCA 2007 provides that:

A person commits an offence if –

(a) he does an act capable of encouraging or assisting the commission of an offence; and

(b) he believes –

    (i) that the offence will be committed; and
    (ii) that his act will encourage or assist its commission.

The *actus reus* and the *mens rea* for this offence are illustrated in the diagram below:

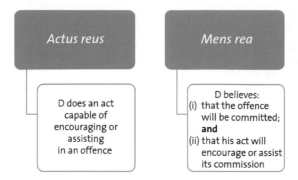

We will now consider each of these elements separately.

### D does an act capable of encouraging or assisting in an offence

As per the s 44 offence, D must do an act which is 'capable' of assisting or encouraging in the commission of an offence. Section 65(2) provides that this offence can be committed by omission where D fails to discharge a duty. The act does not actually have to assist or encourage in the commission of an offence; it is sufficient that it is capable of doing so.

### D must believe that the offence will be committed AND that his act will encourage or assist in the commission of an offence

Thus there are two elements to the *mens rea* requirement for the s 45 offence. In the first place D must believe that the offence will be committed. D must also believe that his act will encourage or assist in the commission of an offence. It is not necessary that his actions actually accomplish this; only that D believes that they will.

It is not therefore, an offence for D to do something that he fears or suspects will assist in the commission of an offence. Nor is it an offence to do something that D fears or suspects will encourage the commission of an offence. D must have a belief that it will encourage or assist in the commission of the offence.

It is irrelevant whether D's belief is a mistaken one; an honest belief is all that is required to construct liability.

We will now consider the s 46 offence.

## Section 46: encouraging or assisting offences believing one or more will be committed

(1)   A person commits an offence if –

    (a)   he does an act capable of encouraging or assisting the commission of one or more of a number of offences; and

(b)  he believes–
    (i)   that one or more of those offences will be committed (but has no belief as to which); and
    (ii)  that his act will encourage or assist the commission of one or more of them.

(2)  It is immaterial for the purposes of subsection (1)(b)(ii) whether the person has any belief as to which offence will be encouraged or assisted.

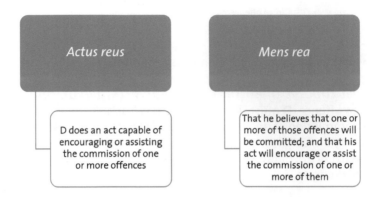

We will now look at the different elements necessary to construct liability for this offence.

## D does an act capable of encouraging or assisting the commission of one or more offence

We have considered this *actus reus* requirement in part under ss 44 and 45, although clearly in this case there is reference to one or more offences. This provision is intended to capture the situation where D anticipates that their actions will assist or encourage in the commission of one or more of a range of offences: *Sadique* (2013).

## That D believes that one or more offences will be committed and D believes that his action will encourage or assist the commission of one or more of them

As with the s 46 offence there are two elements to the *mens rea* requirement for the s 45 offence. In the first place D must believe that the offence or offences will be committed. D must also believe that his act will encourage or assist in the commission of an offence or offences. It is not necessary that his actions actually accomplish this; only that D believes that they will.

Therefore if D does something that he fears or suspects will assist or encourage in the commission of an offence or offences, this will not be sufficient to satisfy the MR requirement for this offence.

# Reform of inchoate offences

There have been calls for further reform of this area of law. The Law Commission considered the question of reform and how the law could be developed in this area. Conspiracy and Attempts (Law Com No. 318, December 2009).

The area of inchoate offences offers a useful case study in the evolution of the law, as in a relatively short space of time it has progressed from:

A common law offence

to a statutory offence

with further reforms recommended

## Conspiracy

The Law Commission in *Conspiracy and Attempts* (Law Com No. 318, December 2009) recommends replacing the offence of conspiracy under the CLA 1977 with the following:

1.  Conspiracy would involve an agreement by two or more persons to engage in the conduct element of an offence and (where relevant) to bring about the consequence of the offence (the result required by the offence).

At present the law requires an agreement to pursue a course of conduct, but there is no mention of the required results (although the case law has implied this).

2.  D must have intended to engage in the conduct and intended to bring about the consequences (result).

Direct and oblique intention would suffice in these situations; however, recklessness would not.

---

### Case precedent – *Anderson* [1986] AC 27

**Facts:** D provided supplies to a prisoner to help his escape from the prison, not believing that it would actually work.

**Principle:** Reform of intention in conspiracy

**Application:** It was held that there need be no intention to bring about the result, only an intention to pursue a course of conduct. This case was criticised because it meant that a conspiracy could exist where no party intended the crime to result. Although this case was largely ignored, the proposed law makes it clear that such a situation would not give rise to conspiracy. D may instead be convicted of assisting or encouraging crime.

---

3.  Spouses would no longer be immune from liability.
4.  D could be found guilty even though the person with whom he conspires is a victim of the offence (abolishing the current rules).

5.  There would also be a defence of acting reasonably in order to prevent crime or harm. This would be along the same lines as the defence in relation to ss 44–46 Serious Crime Act 2007.

## Attempt

The Law Commission in *Conspiracy and Attempts: a consultation paper* (Law Com CP No.183, 2007) recommended two new offences.

❖ An offence of attempt that operates only where D has reached the last acts necessary to complete the offence.
❖ An offence of criminal preparation.

It would need to be shown that D intended to commit the crime, meaning intention (direct or oblique) would suffice as would a conditional intent.

### Up for Debate

These offences were eventually abandoned. Do you agree that this was the right course of action, or is further reform of attempts still required?

# Putting it into practice

## Question

Look at the scenario below and then answer the following question:

Shirley, Debra and Linda are part of a gang at school. Shirley and Linda have been bullying April. Debra did not agree with this, but was too scared to confront the other girls. Shirley sent a text to Linda saying that they should trap April in the toilets at lunchtime and give her a 'good slapping'. Linda agreed and sent a text to Debra telling her of the plan. Debra agreed to keep watch, but then decided that she would disclose the plans to a teacher.

At lunchtime Shirley and Linda trapped April and took her inside the toilets. Debra kept watch outside but immediately told the first teacher that she met what was about to happen. The teacher arrived on the scene just in time.

Both Shirley and Linda were convicted of conspiracy to commit ABH – is Debra also guilty of this offence?

## Suggested solution

Remember to apply the structure that we have practised throughout this book:

1. Identify the offence
2. Define the offence
3. Deal with all aspects of the AR
4. Deal with all aspects of the MR
5. Deal with potential defences
6. Address lesser alternative charges

Remember in relation to inchoate offences that you need to discuss the primary substantive offences too! This should include an accurate legal definition with sources. It should also include brief discussion of the AR and MR.

This case clearly considers conspiracy. You need to work through the *actus reus* and *mens rea* to determine liability regarding Debra. Remember to refer to the correct legislation, noting the evolution of the offence from a common law offence into an Act.

An agreement – first go through the checks: the agreement is made between two or more people, and they do not fall within the exemptions, i.e. they are not married. Further, we can see that a written agreement has been made, i.e. a text message, setting out the agreement, which is then passed onto Debra from another, again indicating that an agreement is in place and is made between two or more people.

A course of conduct – here you first need to check that the agreement relates to the same offence as that attempted, i.e. the offence has not changed. In this case it refers to ABH, and you would need to demonstrate that this is consistent throughout. For example, if the agreement was ABH but the offence attempted was murder, this may affect liability.

The *mens rea* is the key point here – particularly whether Debra intends to reach a decision with the others. Look at the sequence of text and other messages, and see if you can determine whether Debra's intention to make an agreement is clear.

In particular look at her knowledge that the surrounding circumstances are present. Two useful cases to refer to here are *R v McPhillips* (1990) and *Yip Chiu-Cheung* (1994), where D exhibits similar circumstances to D. Consider both cases and their similarities, and apply this to the question.

# Key points checklist

| | |
|---|:---:|
| Inchoate offences include: Conspiracy; attempt; encouraging or assisting in the commission of a criminal offence. | ✔ |
| There are two types of conspiracy: (1) common law conspiracy; and (2) statutory conspiracy. Statutory conspiracy is governed by s 1 of the Criminal Law Act 1971. The *actus reus* for the offence is: an agreement; between parties; to carry out a course of conduct that will lead to the commission of an offence. The *mens rea* for the offence is: an intention to carry out agreed course of conduct; intention to commit the substantive offence. | ✔ |
| Attempt is covered by s 1 Criminal Attempts Act 1981. The *actus reus* of the offence is: an act not an omission; the act must be more than merely preparatory to the commission of the primary offence. The *mens rea* for the offence is that the defendant must have had the intention to commit the substantive offence. | ✔ |
| The final inchoate offence is encouraging or assisting in the commission of a criminal offence. Section 59 of the Serious Crime Act abolished the common law offence of incitement, replacing it with three separate offences in ss 44, 45 and 46 of the SCA 2007. | ✔ |

# Table of key cases referred to in this chapter

| Key case | Brief facts | Principle |
|---|---|---|
| *Griffiths* [1966] 60 Cr App R14 | D ignored the fact that the goods were stolen | Conspiracy – the agreement |
| *Cooke* [1986] 1 AC 909 | D and other conspired to sell their own food on a British Rail train | A case can involve more than one conspiracy |
| *Siracusa* [1989] 90 Cr App R 340 | D agreed to import heroin, but it was actually cannabis that was imported | The agreement must be the same as the result in conspiracy |
| *Yip Chiu-Cheung v R* [1994] 2 All ER 924 | D, an undercover policeman, conspired with another man to traffic heroin | Intention in conspiracy |
| *Saik* [2006] UKHL 18 | D was convicted of laundering money, and appeal was held. | D must intend or know that a fact or circumstance necessary for the commission of the crime will exist |
| *Tree* [2008] | D sold a speedboat which he thought was from the proceeds of crime, but was from tax evasion | D must intend or know that a fact or circumstance necessary for the commission of the crime will exist |
| *DPP v Nock* [1978] AC 979 | D conspired to produce cocaine from a powder, but there was no cocaine in the powder | An agreement to do the impossible |

| Fallon [1994] Crim LR 519 | D shot a police officer – the court had to decide if D intended to kill V | Attempts – intention |
|---|---|---|
| Haughton v Smith [1975] AC 476 | D agreed to meet a van with stolen goods inside, but the police had already intercepted the van | Attempt and impossibility |
| Anderson [1986] AC 27 | D supplied goods to a prisoner, not expecting him to escape | Reform of intention in conspiracy |

---

@ **Visit the book's companion website to test your knowledge**

❖ Resources include a subject map, revision tip podcasts, downloadable diagrams, MCQ quizzes for each chapter, and a flashcard glossary

❖ www.routledge.com/cw/optimizelawrevision

# 10

**Understand the law**
- Do you understand the definitions of non-insane automatism, insane automatism and intoxication?
- Can you identify how the defences have evolved and have been refined through case law?
- Do you understand the difference between general and specific defences?

**Remember the details**
- Can you remember the different elements of non-insane automatism, insane automatism and intoxication?
- Can you remember the key cases law in relation to each of these defences?

**Reflect critically on areas of debate**
- Do you understand the distinguishing features of insanity when compared to diminished responsibility and automatism?
- Do you understand the significance of whether a crime is one of basic or specific intent in relation to the defence of intoxication?

**Contextualise**
- Can you apply the different defences in this chapters to other areas of the law?
- Can you identify the limitations of these defences?

**Apply your skills and knowledge**
- Can you complete the activities in this chapter using the liability charts and relevant case law?

# Chapter Map

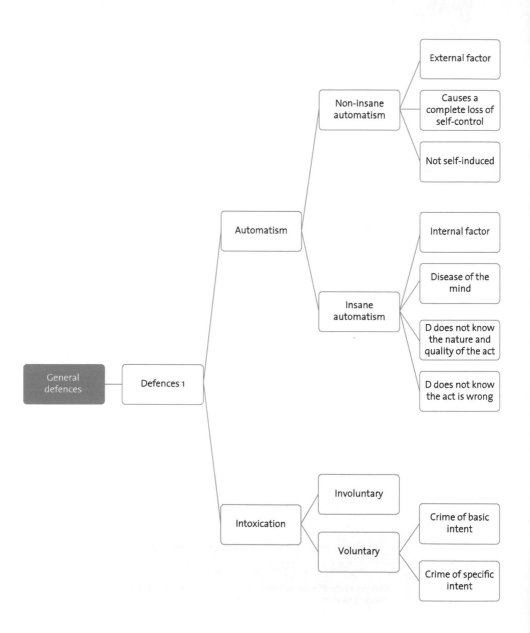

# Defences

In the next two chapters we will consider general defences. Defences form an important aspect of criminal law and when you are constructing liability in a problem question you must always consider whether the defendant will be able to avail themselves of a defence. Defences may be specific or general in nature.

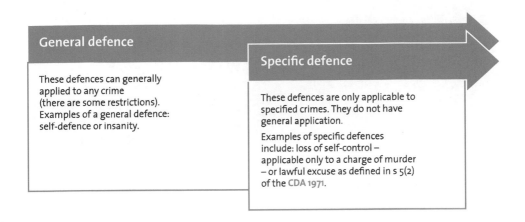

**General defence**

These defences can generally applied to any crime (there are some restrictions). Examples of a general defence: self-defence or insanity.

**Specific defence**

These defences are only applicable to specified crimes. They do not have general application.

Examples of specific defences include: loss of self-control – applicable only to a charge of murder – or lawful excuse as defined in s 5(2) of the CDA 1971.

Defences are important because they can determine whether the defendant should be excused from an offence due to surrounding circumstances, or whether D's actions can be justified. Therefore there are two types of defence: justificatory defences and excusatory defences.

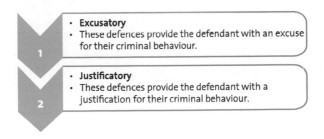

**1**
- **Excusatory**
- These defences provide the defendant with an excuse for their criminal behaviour.

**2**
- **Justificatory**
- These defences provide the defendant with a justification for their criminal behaviour.

In this chapter, we will focus on the following defences:

- ❖ automatism
- ❖ insanity
- ❖ intoxication.

When you are dealing with a problem question and you have finished constructing liability for a criminal offence, you should next consider the availability of a potential defence. The key to remember is that in a problem question you must first construct liability for an offence, **THEN** move on to consider defences.

## Aim Higher

It is not uncommon for students to start their analysis of a problem question with a consideration of available defences for the defendant. You must remember that liability for an offence must always be constructed first. If the defendant is not liable for a criminal offence they have no need for a defence! Therefore defences – by which we mean specific and general defences – should always come after liability has been constructed.

In the event that the defendant may avail themselves of a specific and a general defence we would suggest that you deal with the specific defence before general defences. Therefore the correct order should be:

1. Construct criminal liability.
2. Discuss the availability of specific defences.
3. Discuss the availability of general defences.

We will start our consideration of defences by outlining the definition of the defence. The we will move on to consider the ingredients of each defence before finally examining the legal effect of successfully running the specific defence.

## Aim Higher

When discussing defences it is important in the first instance that you provide an accurate legal definition of the defence. You should also note whether the defence is a common law defence or a statutory defence. You must then remember to consider the elements required to make out the offence. Once you have considered the distinct elements of the defence you can then go on to consider the legal effect of successfully running the defence in question. The consideration of defences in a problem question is as follows:

1. Definition of the defence (with authority).
2. Is the defence a common law or statutory definition (give the source)?
3. Explain each element of the defence (with authorities).
4. Explain the legal effect of successfully running the defence in question.

## Automatism

The first defence that we are going to consider is the defence of automatism. There are in effect two types of automatism: non-insane automatism and insane automatism. Automatism is a claim that the defendant was unable to control their actions, or behaviour as a result of an internal, or external factor. It is important that you understand what differentiates non-insane automatism from insane automatism.

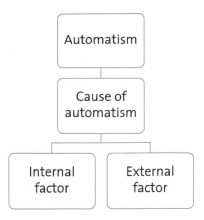

Non-insane automatism is the result of some external factor, whereas insane automatism (often referred to simply as insanity) is the result of an internal factor. Therefore when considering automatism a critical question will be: is the defendant's loss of control the result of an internal or an external factor? This question is crucial because the outcome of successfully running the defence of non-insane automatism is quite different from the outcome of successfully running the defence of insane automatism (insanity). You can see the different outcomes in the diagram below:

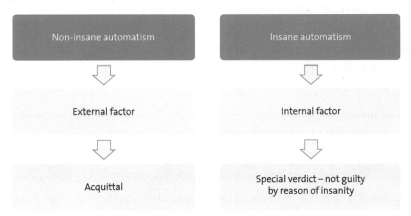

We are now going to consider the defences of non-insane automatism and insane automatism separately.

## Non-insane automatism

In the case of non-insane automatism the defendant is claiming to have been acting involuntarily as a result of some external factor. The defendant is said to have been acting in a state of automatism. In *Bratty v AG for Northern Ireland* (1963) Lord Denning defined automatism as:

An act which is done by the muscles without any control by the mind, such as a spasm, a reflex action or a convulsion or an act done by a person who is not conscious of what he is doing, such as an act done when suffering from concussion . . .

The key ingredients of this defence are:

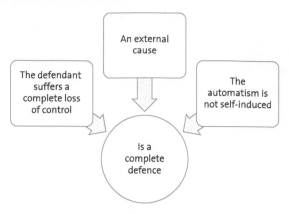

We will now look at each of these ingredients separately.

## The defendant suffers a complete loss of control

In order for the defence of non-insane automatism to succeed the defendant must have suffered a complete loss of self-control. If the defendant has not suffered a complete loss of self-control and has retained some ability, albeit limited ability, to control his or her actions then the claim of non-insane automatism will fail: *Broome v Perkins* (1987).

We will now consider a number of different scenarios which may arise within a problem question, in which you would need to consider whether non-insane automatism can be used as a defence.

### The defendant is conscious

Where D is conscious he must lack complete control over his actions.

| Case precedent – *Broome v Perkins* [1987] Crim LR 271 |
| --- |

**Facts:** D was driving his car in a hypoglycaemic state, but from time to time he exercised control over the vehicle by braking violently.

**Principle:** Automatism and consciousness

**Application:** D was found guilty, because he exercised partial control.

This precedent was then followed in *A-G's Reference (No 2 of 1992)* (1993), where driving without awareness was held to be no answer to a charge of causing death by reckless driving, as the defendant in this case had retained some control over his driving.

This is because the defence of automatism requires a complete loss of control. This is a very strict rule which means where a D retains partial control over their actions, they will not be able to use the defence of non-insane automatism as a defence.

## Common Pitfall

Where D acts in a way that he would not normally act but still retains control, he cannot rely on this defence.

In *Isitt* (1978), D argued that his dangerous driving was due to a previous accident that had led to memory loss. At the time of the offence he could not remember what he had done as his subconscious mind had taken over. The Court of Appeal dismissed D's appeal, as he had control over his bodily actions.

Examiners can often test a student's knowledge with examples of this type, so keep focused on the main elements of the defence and remember to support your answer by reference to authority.

The defence of non-insane automatism will also fail if D's initial voluntary conduct leads up to an involuntary act. Look at the case precedent below, and identify the voluntary conduct and how this conduct led to the act.

### Case precedent – *Ryan v R* [1967] HCA 2

**Facts:** D with one hand pointed a loaded shotgun at V, whom he had robbed, and with the other hand he tried to tie V up. V moved and D argued that he involuntarily pressed the trigger because of a reflex action.

**Principle:** Automatism and voluntary conduct

**Application:** The pointing of the gun and the placing of the finger on the trigger were voluntary acts, so D was responsible whether the pressing of the trigger was involuntary or not.

Remember these key points as:

Non-insane automatism requires a complete loss of control

If D retains full or part control, they cannot rely on non-automatism as a defence

Examples such as cravings do not constitute automatism

D is guilty where voluntary conduct leads to an involuntary act

## *Where D is unconscious or in a state of impaired consciousness*

If the defendant is unconscious, then he lacks control over his actions. Expert medical opinion is normally required to establish the facts, particularly as the argument of a full 'blackout' is usually considered with suspicion: *Cooper v McKenna* (1960).

Total or impaired consciousness may result from the use of drugs, hypnosis or alcohol. But whether D can rely on the defence of non-insane automatism in these circumstances depends on whether the final element of the defence is established.

**Example:** Andy is walking down a busy street when a large shop sign comes loose and falls, hitting Andy on the head. He is in a semi-conscious state and stumbles into Tai, who falls over and severely cuts his head.

Could Andy use the defence of non-insane automatism here?

In this situation, Andy is hit on the head by an object. This is an unexpected external factor, which causes a state of semi-consciousness in which Andy is arguably unable to exercise voluntary control over his actions. As a result of the semi-conscious state Andy bumps into Tai, who cuts his head:

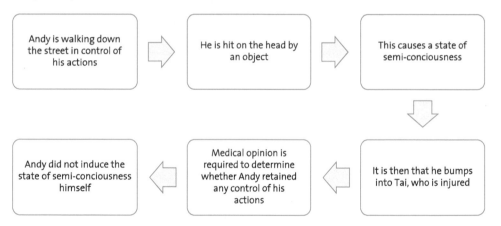

## *The cause of the automatism/loss of control must be external*

The factor that causes the defendant to suffer a complete loss of self-control must be an external factor. This might include a blow to the head or a reflex action caused by a swarm of bees. Look at the case precedent below.

| Case precedent – *Hill v Baxter* [1958] 1 QB 277 |
| --- |

**Facts:** D was driving when he was attacked by a swarm of bees, causing involuntary movement to his arms and legs. As a result of the involuntary movements he crashed the car.

**Principle:** The automatism must be the result of an external factor.

**Application:** Automatism was a complete defence to the offence of driving without due care and attention.

Examples of external factors include:

* the consumption of alcohol;
* an insulin injection;
* concussion from a blow;
* the administration of an anaesthetic or other drug; and
* hypnosis.

It is important to note that a hypoglycaemic state that is caused by the intake of insulin is considered to be an external factor. Thus the appropriate defence in the case of hypoglycaemia (low blood sugar levels) is automatism: *Quick* (1973).

In contrast hyperglycaemia, is often the result of an internal factor such as diabetes. Where it is the result of a disease or another internal factor the correct defence would be insanity: *Hennessy* (1989).

## Aim Higher

The treatment of diabetics in relation to the operation of this defence is a useful way of illustrating the distinction between internal and external factors.

Sleepwalking is also considered to be the result of an internal cause, as held in the case of *Burgess* (1991).

However, in *T* (1990), D's defence of automatism was successful in relation to a charge of robbery where the D was suffering from post-traumatic stress disorder (she had been raped). The rape was held to be an extraordinary event and as such the post-traumatic stress disorder was an external factor.

## *The defendant must not have caused the loss of self-control*
The final element of the defence is that the automatism must not be self induced. In circumstances where the automatism is self-induced the defence will fail.

The defence will apply only if the defendant is not at fault. The defendant will be at fault if he has induced the state of automatism through the misuse of alcohol or drugs. However, sometimes the distinction is not always as clear as this.

## *D voluntarily consumes alcohol or dangerous drugs*
Self-induced automatism is no defence to crimes of basic intent (i.e. a crime that can be committed recklessly or intentionally). The reason for this is that

a person who has self-induced a state of automatism is considered by the courts to be a person that has been reckless in getting into this condition in the first place. In these circumstances a person should not be able to plead the defence of non-insane automatism.

However, where D is voluntarily intoxicated but has committed a crime of specific intent (one for which intention and intention alone will suffice), provided that they lacked the ability to form the *mens rea* for the offence they may be able to avail themselves of the defence. It will depend on whether they formed a drunken intent and whether the other elements of the defence are present.

Remember this as:

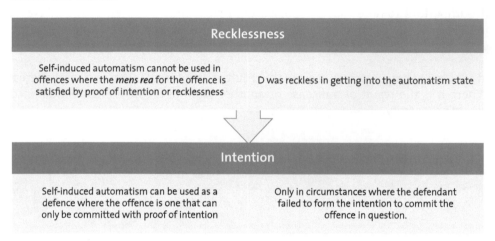

### Recklessness

| Self-induced automatism cannot be used in offences where the *mens rea* for the offence is satisfied by proof of intention or recklessness | D was reckless in getting into the automatism state |

### Intention

| Self-induced automatism can be used as a defence where the offence is one that can only be committed with proof of intention | Only in circumstances where the defendant failed to form the intention to commit the offence in question. |

Therefore, when answering a problem question where the defendant is voluntarily intoxicated and is claiming non-insane automatism, you will need to consider the offence that D is alleged to have committed, and you will need to consider the *mens rea* for the offence to determine whether D can be held liable for the offence.

## Aim Higher

There is some overlap here between automatism and intoxication. Voluntary intoxication is a defence to crimes of specific intent provided the intoxication has prevented the formation of the necessary intent.

This point was confirmed in the case of *Bailey* (1983), which concerned the commission of a crime of specific intent by D, who was diabetic and had attacked a man with an iron bar. D had taken insulin and consumed alcohol but he had not eaten. These combined factors can lead to an unconscious and aggressive state. The Court of Appeal held that if the state of automatism was self-induced it can provide a complete defence to a crime of specific intent provided the prosecution cannot prove the necessary intention.

However, if D's state of automatism was brought about by the voluntary consumption of alcohol or illegal drugs, it would be no defence to a crime of basic intent.

Another useful example of this principle can be seen in the case of *Lipman* (1970).

---

**Case precedent – *Lipman* [1970] 1 QB 152**

**Facts:** D killed his girlfriend by stuffing a bed sheet down her throat whilst under the influence of LSD (an illegal drug).

**Principle:** Subjective recklessness

**Application:** It was accepted that D could not have formed the specific intent required for murder (intention to kill or cause GBH), because of his drug-induced state. D was, however, liable for reckless manslaughter, because he was reckless in voluntarily taking the LSD in the first place.

---

## D voluntarily consumes prescription drugs

If the defendant takes prescription drugs and this produces unexpected or unforeseen behaviour that leads to the commission of a crime then D may be able to rely on the defence of automatism or intoxication. This is summarised as:

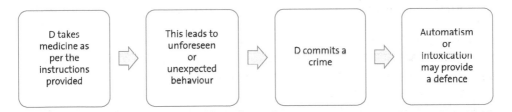

Thus in these circumstances a defendant has a defence to a crime of basic intent and to a crime of specific intent. This was confirmed in the following case.

---

**Case precedent – *Hardie* [1984] 1 WLR 64**

**Facts:** D was depressed about having to move home. He took a non-prescribed drug (some of his girlfriend's Valium) to calm his nerves and then started a fire in a wardrobe. He was convicted of damaging property with intent to endanger the life of another or being reckless as to the endangerment of life contrary to s 1(2) **Criminal Damage Act 1971**.

**Principle:** Automatism and medicinal drugs

**Application:** The Court of Appeal quashed the conviction. D had not been reckless because he did not know the Valium would make him unpredictable or aggressive.

Now test your understanding of automatism with this example.

**Example:** Sheila is driving her car when she feels a sharp pain in her neck. A rare poisonous spider has bitten her neck and Sheila momentarily loses control of the car, the car veers off the road and kills two people waiting at a bus stop.

Could Sheila use the defence of non-insane automatism here?

In the first instance you would provide a definition of non-insane automatism. Then you should ask:

1. Did Sheila suffer a complete loss of self-control?
2. Was this the result of some external factor?
3. Did D induce the state of automatism?

If the defence of non-insane automatism is established Sheila will have a complete defence.

We are now moving on to consider the second form of automatism, insane automatism. This is often referred to as the defence of insanity.

## Insanity

It is crucial to note that in the context of this defence, that the definition of insanity is concerned with criminal insanity, and that the definition of criminal insanity does not correspond with the medical definition of inanity. The justification for this distinction is that insanity in this context is a legal, not a medical term and involves considerations of public protection as well as individual responsibility. It is worth noting that many academics have called for reform of this area of law and as such the defence of insane automatism or insanity is a popular topic with examiners.

> ### Common Pitfall
>
> Insanity is sometimes referred to as 'insane automatism' and automatism is sometimes referred to as 'non-insane automatism'. Make sure that your use of these terms is accurate!

There are essentially two different ways in which the defendant's alleged insanity may be relevant to his or her criminal liability for an offence. These are:

1. Where the defendant's mental state renders them unfit to stand trial. In reality this may have nothing to do with the commission of the offence itself (e.g. the illness/condition may have developed after the commission of the offence).
2. Where the defendant was legally insane at the commission of the offence. In such circumstances this may give rise to the defence of insane automatism/ insanity. If the defendant successfully runs the defence of insanity this gives rise to a special verdict of not guilty by reason of insanity.

## Special verdict

It is important to remember that the successful use of the defence of insanity does not result in an acquittal as is the case in non-insane automatism. The legal effect of successfully running the defence of insanity is a finding of 'not guilty by reason of insanity'. This in many cases means that the defendant is not free to leave court. In reality the defendant may be subject to detention in a mental health facility. As a result this defence is very rarely utilised by defendants, as they are understandably anxious about the consequences of a finding of not guilty by reason of insanity.

It is vital to remember that insanity will be the appropriate defence where D's mind is affected by an **internal** factor, for example diabetes or epilepsy. Non-insane automatism will be the correct plea where the malfunctioning of D's mind is caused by an **external** factor.

In a problem question where liability for murder has been established and the defendant is suffering from mental health issues you should consider the special partial defence of diminished responsibility. You may also want to consider the defence of insanity. It should be remembered that diminished responsibility is only available where D is charged with murder, whereas insanity is available as a defence to all offences.

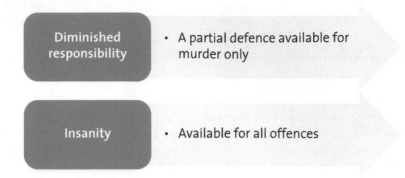

Diminished responsibility
- A partial defence available for murder only

Insanity
- Available for all offences

## The test for insanity – the M'Naghten rules

Insanity is a common law defence and as such the definition of insanity is not located within a statute – the definition derives from the M'Naghten rules, and in their interpretation by the courts. The rules are derived from the case of *M'Naghten* in 1843. The rules state: Every man is presumed sane, but this can be rebutted by evidence that he was

> 'labouring under such a defect of reason, from disease of the mind, as not to know the nature and the quality of the act he was doing, or, if he did know it, or that he did not know he was doing wrong.'

In the case of this defence the burden of proof rests with the defence to prove on the balance of probabilities. The prosecution may of course attempt to disprove the defence once it has been raised.

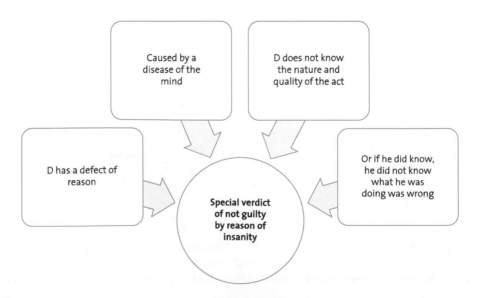

The elements of the defence of insanity are:

1. D has a defect of reason
2. Caused by a disease of the mind
3. Which in turn means that D does not know the nature and quality of his act. Or?
4. If he does know the nature and the quality of the act, he does not know that it is wrong.

We will now consider these elements in more detail.

## The defendant has a defect of reason

The defence of insanity will only apply to defendants whose cognitive powers of memory, reason and understanding are defective. Thus a defendant must be incapable of exercising normal powers of reasoning. A defect of reason will not be established in circumstances where D simply fails to use his powers of reasoning: *Clarke* (1972).

## Caused by a disease of the mind

The defect of reason must be caused by a disease of the mind – this is a legal question, not a medical one, and it is established where an internal factor causes a defect of reason. A defect of reason will be established in circumstances where *Kemp* (1957). It is the internal nature of the source of the defect of reason which separates insanity from the defence of non-insane automatism.

## Internal factors

The defence of insanity tends to be used by defendants suffering from serious mental health issues, but it can also be utilised by individuals who are suffering from a change in the physical state of the brain. For example in *Sullivan* (1984), the defendant committed ABH while suffering from an epileptic seizure. Insanity was the appropriate defence, because the defect of reason had been caused by an internal factor, amounting to a disease of the mind.

A degeneration of the brain is not always required.

---

### Case precedent – *Kemp* [1957] 1 QB 399

**Facts:** D attacked his wife with a hammer. It appeared he suffered from arteriosclerosis, which caused a congestion of blood in his brain. As a result, he suffered a temporary lapse of consciousness, during which he made the attack.

**Principle:** Insanity and internal factors

**Application:** The judge held that the disease must affect the cognitive or intellectual capacities of the mind in the sense of reason, memory and understanding.

---

In the next section we are going to consider a range of factors and whether or not they are deemed internal or external in nature. We will consider:

❖ sleepwalking
❖ diabetes
❖ normal stress and strain.

### Sleepwalking

One issue that the courts have had to consider is whether acts done while sleeping are the result of an internal factor and as such captured by the defence of insanity, or whether they are the result of an external factor and captured by the defence of non-insane automatism. For example, the cases of *Tolson* (1889) and *Lillienfield* (1985) both deal with situations where the defendant was alleged to have committed a crime whilst sleepwalking.

The case of *Burgess* in 1991 confirmed that sleepwalking is the result of an internal factor and therefore the appropriate defence to a crime that has been committed whilst sleepwalking is insanity. The timeline for these important cases is:

| Tolson (1889) | Lillienfield (1985) | Burgess (1991) |

From this, we can see that in a problem question, you should first consider whether the cause is internal (insanity) or external (automatism), and this will lead you in the right direction, even if the outcome is not as you might have expected!

### Diabetes

Earlier in this chapter we considered the application of law in relation to individuals who commit criminal offences whilst suffering from a diabetic episode.

Whether or not a diabetic episode is considered an internal or external factor will depend on whether the episode was caused by the condition itself, or the use of insulin. In the case of *Quick* (1973), the defendant, who had diabetes, inflicted ABH. The defendant submitted that at the time of his conduct he was suffering from hypoglycaemia (low blood sugar) and was unaware of what he was doing. The Court of Appeal held that this was caused by his use of insulin, not by his diabetes. Therefore the cause was an external factor (insulin) and the defence of non-insane automatism should have been left to the jury.

Remember that:

| Too much insulin (external) causes low sugar level | ⟶ | Hypoglycaemia (defence = automatism) |
| Too little insulin (internal) causes high sugar level | ⟶ | Hyperglycaemia (defence = insanity) |

### The ordinary stresses and strains of life

It could be argued that the daily stress of life, particularly for a person experiencing problems, could be an internal factor.

For example, in the case of *Rabey* (1977), the defendant, who had become infatuated with a girl, found out that the object of his infatuation did not feel the same way. The defendant hit the victim on the head with a rock. The defendant submitted that where a person's defect of reason results from a 'dissociative state' caused by an stress resulting from a rejection, this should give rise to the defence of automatism. The judge at first instance accepted the argument and allowed the defence of non-insane automatism. On appeal it was held that it did not constitute an external cause, and insanity was the appropriate defence.

## The defect of reason means that D does not know the nature and quality of his act
and/or

## He did not know that what he was doing was wrong
Either the defect of reason must be responsible for the defendant failing to appreciate the nature and quality of his act, or the defect of reason must result in the defendant not knowing what he was doing was wrong.

Thus there are two important aspects to this element, which are set out in the diagram below:

| Not knowing the nature and quality of his act or its consequences | • The concern here is with the physical nature and quality of the act, not its legal or moral quality<br>• e.g. D cuts a woman's throat thinking that he is cutting a loaf of bread<br>• In relation to consequences, D knows that he has cut off a person's head but does not realise the consequences of this |
|---|---|
| And/or not knowing the act is wrong | • Whether D is able to appreciate the legal as opposed to the moral wrongness of the act he does at the time |

Therefore a defendant may know the nature and quality of the act that he is doing but he may still avail himself of the defence of insanity if he does not know what he is doing is legally wrong. Wrong in this context means legally wrong as opposed to morally wrong, as illustrated in the case of *Windle* (1952).

**Let us consider the following example:** Tim is told by voices in his head to shoot his mother. Would Tim be able to use insanity as a defence?

If Tim is suffering from a defect of reason that is caused by a disease of the mind but he knows that shooting his mother is a crime, then the defence of insanity would not apply. However, if Tim has a defect of reason caused by a disease of the mind and does not appreciate that shooting his mother is a crime, then insanity may be a suitable defence.

A summary of the ingredients for the defence of insane automatism:

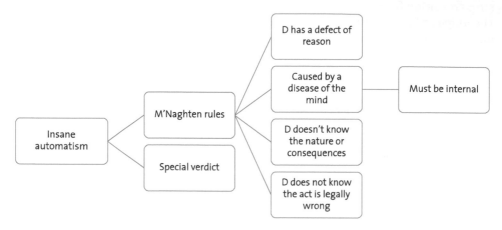

In the next section we are going to consider the defence of intoxication.

# Intoxication

Intoxication can occur when a defendant consumes drugs or alcohol. Where intoxication is used as a defence, it is important to understand how far D is impaired by the intoxicant, and how this may impact upon their conduct. The defence is far more complex than simply acknowledging that the defendant was drunk and therefore did not know what he/she was doing.

## Common Pitfall

Intoxication rarely provides a defence, as it is limited in nature and is only available where the intoxication prevents the *mens rea* of the offence from being established. It is never a defence where D knows what he is doing but is simply less inhibited or more aggressive because of the intoxicant.

The basic principles with regard to intoxication are as follows:

1. In crimes of specific intent, voluntary intoxication may provide a partial defence where the *mens rea* is not formed.
2. In crimes of basic intent, voluntary intoxication does not provide a defence.
3. **Involuntary intoxication** (i.e. this includes the unforeseen consequences of medication and where V's orange juice has been laced with vodka or drugs by another person) may provide a complete defence to crimes of specific intent and crimes of basic intent provided that the *mens rea* for the offence has not been formed.

4.  **A drunken intent is sufficient** – where a defendant is involuntarily intoxicated but still forms the *mens rea* for the offence in question this is sufficient to establish liability.

The first two principles derive from the case of *DPP v Majewski* (1976) and are known as the rule in *Majewski*. The third and fourth principles derive from the case of *Kingston* (1994).

We will now consider these rules in more detail.

## Voluntary intoxication: the rule in Majewski

Intoxication will be classed as voluntary where D knowingly consumes intoxicating substances, provided of course that they are generally known to be intoxicating; this includes alcohol and drugs.

D is voluntarily intoxicated if he knows he is ingesting a drug or alcohol, even though he may underestimate its strength. In *Allen* (1989), D intentionally drank wine and was voluntarily intoxicated even though he had not been aware of its high alcoholic content.

Remember this summary as:

## D must lack the mens rea of the offence

The 'defence' of intoxication will only succeed where D failed to form the *mens rea* for the offence because of the intoxication. For example, if Leah intentionally stabbed Rosia in a pub, could Leah argue that she was intoxicated and therefore have a defence?

The answer to this is no. Leah will not be able to plead the defence of intoxication even to an offence of specific intent. The reason for this is that the example clearly states that she intended to stab Rosia. A drunken intent is still intent: *Kingston* (1995); *DPP v Beard* (1920).

Therefore D must lack the *mens rea* for the offence. He does not have a defence where he took the intoxicant (usually alcohol) in order to give himself 'Dutch courage' so that he could commit the crime. This is because D did have the *mens rea*, albeit at an earlier time. This principle was confirmed in *A-G for Northern Ireland v Gallagher* (1963).

---

### Case precedent – *McKnight* [2000]

**Facts:** D killed V and claimed she was drunk, but not 'legless'.

**Principle:** Intoxication and 'Dutch courage'

**Application:** The Court of Appeal held that where a defendant claims to have been so intoxicated that he lacked the intention to commit a specific intent crime, there has to be some evidential (factual) basis for saying that he was too drunk to form the intent, before it becomes appropriate for the judge to even consider putting intoxication to the jury.

---

The key principle here is that the intoxication (through drink, drugs or other intoxicating substance) must prevent the defendant forming the *mens rea* for the offence.

Try to remember these key points as:

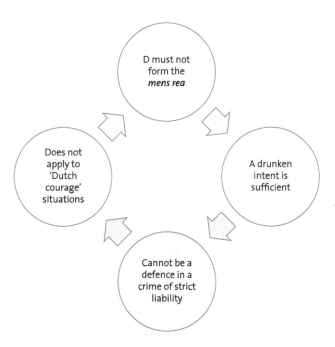

## Intoxication and crimes of basic and specific intent

As has been noted previously, where D is charged with a crime of specific intent, voluntary intoxication may provide a defence, provided that the intoxication prevented the D from forming the *mens rea* for the crime in question. However, it should be remembered that where the defendant does escape liability for a specific intent crime, he may be liable for a lesser offence that can be made out by proof of recklessness. For example:

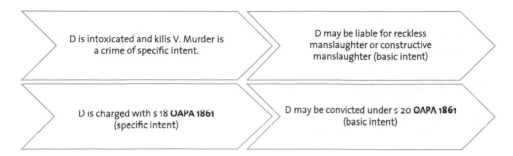

In a problem question, you will therefore need to consider related offences when dealing with a defendant who is claiming intoxication as a defence. It may be that the defendant is liable for an offence to which there is no appropriate lesser charge – such as theft. In such cases, intoxication would provide a complete defence.

It is important to differentiate between crimes of basic and specific intent when applying this defence, and discussing the distinction between these different types of crime demonstrates a good level of knowledge to the reader.

## Crimes of specific intent

Where the defendant is charged with a crime of specific intent, such as murder, voluntary intoxication may provide him with a defence. However, as already noted, this will only be the case where D, because of his intoxicated state, is unable to form the necessary intention: *Majewski* (1976).

Remember this key point:

> There mere fact that D is drunk will not necessarily mean that he is unable to form the intention

For example, consider the case below and you can see that, despite being drunk, D still had the *mens rea* – 'a drunken intent is still intent'.

### Case precedent – *Kingston* [1995] 99 Cr App R 286

**Facts:** D had his drinks spiked and was then put in a room with a boy (who was also drugged). D then sexually assaulted the boy.

**Principle:** Intoxication and specific intent

**Application:** D admitted that he had paedophilic tendencies, which he could normally resist and that, during the assault, he knew what he was doing. The effect of the drugs was merely to reduce his ability to resist such temptations. It was held that D should not be permitted the defence of intoxication.

## Crimes of basic intent

Voluntary intoxication will not provide a defence to a crime of basic intent (one for which recklessness will suffice: *DPP v Majewski* (1976).

The rule in *Majewski* (1976) does not, however, apply to all basic intent crimes. If D commits a crime of negligence such as gross negligence manslaughter, *DPP v Majewski* (1976) will not apply because there is no requirement of recklessness. The prosecution is likely to argue that D is still liable because his getting drunk was negligent, given that a reasonable person is not an inebriated person and that the negligence was gross. Conversely, the defence could argue that if the reasonable sober person would have acted as such, then D is not guilty despite his drunkenness.

## Involuntary intoxication

The basic principle is very similar to voluntary intoxication: if D has the *mens rea* for the crime, he will be liable. However, if he lacks the *mens rea* because of involuntary intoxication, he may have a complete defence regardless of the type of crime, whether basic or specific intent. See the illustration below:

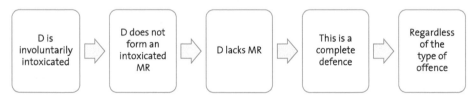

**Example:** Harry's food is spiked with drugs without his knowledge, and while intoxicated Harry strikes William. Could Harry use intoxication as a defence? Harry will have a defence to all offences provided that he has not formed a drunken intent, because he lacks the *mens rea* and his state has been induced by involuntary intoxication.

In such circumstances, there is no need to draw a distinction between basic intent and specific intent crimes, as intoxication will form a complete defence.

present before the involuntary intoxication. As the *mens rea* was present before, D may then be liable for the offence, despite the involuntary intoxication.

Note here that criminal law is not concerned with moral blame – it is concerned with the *actus reus* and *mens rea*, and if both can be proved, D has no defence. Do you think this is the correct approach to take in these circumstances?

In a problem question ensure that you consider the facts of the case, including:

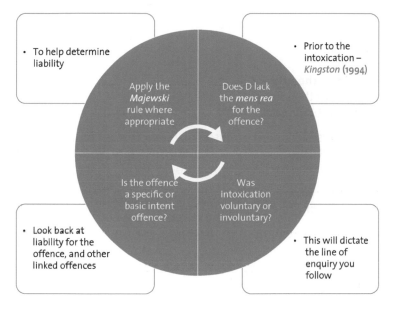

- To help determine liability

Apply the *Majewski* rule where appropriate

Does D lack the *mens rea* for the offence?

- Prior to the intoxication – *Kingston* (1994)

Is the offence a specific or basic intent offence?

Was intoxication voluntary or involuntary?

- Look back at liability for the offence, and other linked offences

- This will dictate the line of enquiry you follow

A summary of the points we have covered in this section is:

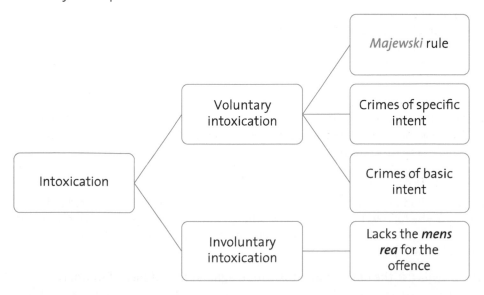

- *Majewski* rule
- Crimes of specific intent
- Crimes of basic intent

Voluntary intoxication

Intoxication

Involuntary intoxication

- Lacks the *mens rea* for the offence

# Putting it into practice

## Question 1

Andrew is in hospital, and the nurse gives him an antibiotic that Andrew has never had before. Andrew suffers a fit, and his arms and legs move uncontrollably, hitting the nurse in the face. Assess whether Andrew could use the defence of automatism against the offence of battery.

## Suggested solution

Remember that it is crucial that you construct liability for an offence before moving on to consider the availability of any defence!

Follow the normal process for constructing liability:

1. **Identify the crime**
2. **Define the crime**
3. **Explain the AR of the offence**
4. **Explain the MR of the offence**
5. **Consider relevant defences**

When examining this scenario, it is reasonably clear that automatism is a potential defence. However, it is key that you identify the right species of automatism. Remember that automatism can be broken down into:

❖ non-insane automatism; and
❖ insane automatism.

Non-insane automatism requires the following:

1. An external factor
2. That causes the defendant to suffer loss of control
3. The loss of control is not self-induced.

By contrast insane automatism requires the following:

1. A defect of reason
2. Caused by a disease of the mind
3. Which results in the defendant not knowing the nature and quality of the act he is performing and/or
4. The defendant did not realise that what he was doing was wrong.

The critical issue in relation to non-insane automatism and insane automatism is whether the cause is an internal or external factor. In this case Andrew's fit is caused by a drug, which is administered by a nurse. The drug is an external factor and it causes the fit, which causes the uncontrollable movements by Andrew: *Hill v Baxter* (1958).

## Question 2

Lydia has had an argument with Paula about her boyfriend, and decides to seek revenge. She follows Paula to the pub, where Paula is meeting her friends. Lydia has three strong alcoholic drinks for courage, and then stabs Paula with a broken bottle, killing Paula.

Could Lydia use the defence of intoxication against the offence of murder?

## Suggested solution

Once again you will need to establish liability for an offence before considering the availability of any defence. You should follow the normal structure:

1. **Identify the crime**
2. **Define the crime**
3. **Explain the AR of the offence**
4. **Murder is a result crime so you must address causation**
5. **Explain the MR of the offence**
6. **Possible defences**

Intoxication is a defence which can be quite difficult to demonstrate. To do so, you would work through the main elements of the defence, noting that this is voluntary intoxication, as opposed to involuntary intoxication. The general rule laid down in *Majewski* is that voluntary intoxication is a defence to a crime of specific intent.

However, intent is crucial here. Remember that a drunken intent is still intent: *Kingston* (1995). It is also clear that intoxication cannot be used where the defendant became intoxicated for 'Dutch courage'. In this case it would seem that Lydia possessed the *mens rea* for murder prior to the intoxication: *McKnight* (2000).

# Key Points Checklist

| | |
|---|---|
| When dealing with defences in the context of a problem question, you must ensure that you have constructed potential liability for an offence first! | ✔ |
| Automatism can be divided into two forms of automatism: non-insane automatism and insane automatism. The outcome of successfully running these defences differs significantly and you must acknowledge this in any answer that you produce. Non-insane automatism can lead to a complete acquittal, whereas insane automatism (also known as insanity) results in a special verdict of not guilty by reason of insanity. | ✔ |
| Another key distinguishing feature of the defences of non-insane automatism and insane automatism is the cause. In the case of non-insane automatism the cause is an external factor. In the case of insane automatism the cause is an internal factor. | ✔ |
| There are two stages in the criminal proceeding process at which the defendant's mental state may be of relevance. The first is the point at which the defendant stands trial. The defendant must have the capacity to enter a plea and participate/understand the trial process. The second point at which the defendant's mental capacity is relevant is where the defendant was criminally insane at the commission of the crime. | ✔ |
| The M'Naghten rules lay down the test for criminal insanity. It is important to note that the definition of criminal insanity differs considerably from the medical definition of insanity. | ✔ |

| For the purposes of criminal law, intoxication as a defence can be broken into: (1) voluntary intoxication; and (2) involuntary intoxication. As a general rule individuals voluntarily intoxicated cannot use intoxication as a defence to a crime of basic intent, although it may be a defence to a crime of specific intent provided that the defendant has not formed a drunken intent. In the case of involuntary intoxication the general rule is that this form of intoxication can constitute a defence to any crime, provided that the defendant has not formed a drunken intent or used alcohol for 'Dutch courage'. | ✔ |
|---|---|

## Table of key cases referred to in this chapter

| Key case | Brief facts | Principle |
|---|---|---|
| *Hill v Baxter* [1958] 1 QB 277 | D was driving a car, and was attacked by bees, causing him to crash the car | Automatism as a defence |
| *Broome v Perkins* [1987] Crim LR 271 | D was driving his car when in a hypoglycaemic state, but exercised some control | Automatism and conscious state |
| *Ryan v R* [1967] HCA 2 | D pointed a gun at V and tied up V. V moved and D pulled the trigger | Automatism and voluntary conduct |
| *Lipman* [1970] 1 QB 152 | D killed his girlfriend when high on drugs | Automatism – intention and recklessness |
| *M'Naghten* [1834] 10 Cl | D murdered Sir Robert Peel's secretary, but was acquitted due to insanity. | M'Naghten rules |
| *Kemp* [1957] 1 QB 399 | D attacked his wife with a hammer, and was suffering from a disease which affected his mind | Insanity and internal factors |
| *DPP v Majewski* [1976] AC 443 | Set out the rules for voluntary intoxication as a defence | Rules of intoxication as a defence |
| *McKnight* [2000] | D killed V and claimed she was drunk, but not 'legless' | Intoxication and *mens rea* |
| *DPP v Morgan* [1975] AC 182 | V was raped by two of her husband's friends, whom he had invited home to have sex with his wife. He said her protests were a sign of her pleasure. | Mistaken belief |

@ Visit the book's companion website to test your knowledge

❖ Resources include a subject map, revision tip podcasts, downloadable diagrams, MCQ quizzes for each chapter, and a flashcard glossary

❖ www.routledge.com/cw/optimizelawrevision

# 11

# Defences 2

**Understand the law**
- Do you understand the similarities and differences between duress by threats, duress of circumstances and necessity?
- Do you understand how the defences in this chapter have evolved, and how they have been refined through case law?

**Remember the details**
- Can you remember the different elements of duress by threats and duress of circumstances?
- Can you remember the different elements of necessity?
- Can you remember in what circumstances mistake can operate as a defence to criminal liability?

**Reflect critically on areas of debate**
- Do you understand the distinguishing features of these defences when compared to the defences in the last chapter?

**Contextualise**
- Can you apply the defences in this chapter to other areas of the law, and provide examples for these?

**Apply your skills and knowledge**
- Can you complete the activities in this chapter using authorities to support your answers?

# Chapter Map

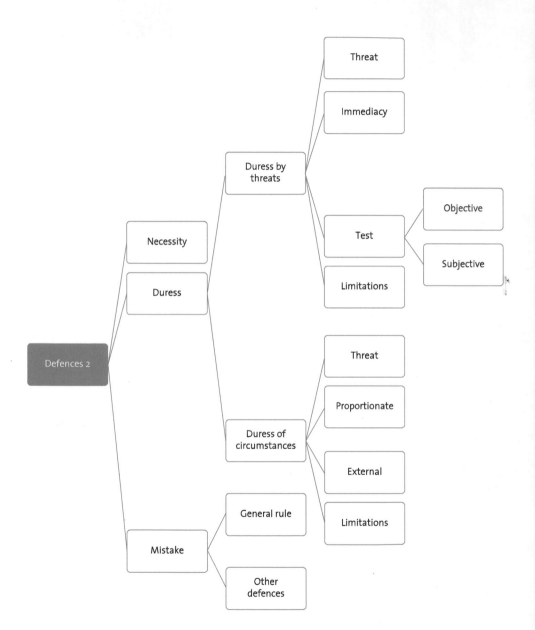

# Introduction

In this chapter we are continuing our consideration of defences. In this chapter we are going to consider:

❖ necessity
❖ duress
❖ mistake.

# Necessity

The defence of necessity is based on the notion that, in some situations, it may be justifiable for a defendant to engage in criminal conduct in order to avoid a greater harm.

One of the difficulties with the defence of necessity is that it is somewhat unclear as to whether it exists as a distinct defence, or whether it is, in reality, simply a form of duress. This uncertainty causes problems for law students because this defence lacks a widely accepted definition and clear boundaries.

The concept of necessity operates extensively in medicine, where it is used as a justification for medical treatment that takes place without a patient's consent. It is not unusual for the medical profession to be presented with a patient that is unconscious or unable for other reasons to agree to medical treatment that is necessary to save the patient's life. It is unsurprising therefore that many of the leading authorities in relation to this defence have their origins in the practice of medicine. For example, in *Re F (Mental Patient: Sterilisation)* (1990), the judge granted doctors permission to sterilise a patient who lacked the mental capacity to understand the consequences of unprotected sexual activity.

## Aim Higher

There are many examples of a defence of necessity being successfully utilised, although the courts have tended to avoid using the term 'necessity', preferring instead to declare that D's conduct was 'not unlawful'. For example, in *Bourne* (1939), it was not an offence under the OAPA 1861 to perform an abortion on a 14-year-old girl who had been raped. It is important to note that at the time in question abortion was unlawful in England and Wales.

In this case the court held that the defendant, who was a doctor, had acted lawfully given that he had acted in good faith and in the best interests of the patient.

One of the most memorable cases in English criminal law is the case of *R v Dudley and Stephens* (1884). In this case the defendants were shipwrecked and adrift in a lifeboat for several days. Before long their supply of food and fresh water ran out and Dudley and Stephens agreed to kill the cabin boy in order to eat his flesh. This would ensure that they did not starve to death. Shortly after they had committed the murder they were consequently put on trial for the murder of the cabin boy. They claimed 'necessity': that the murder of the cabin boy was a necessity if they were both to survive. The court rejected the defence of necessity and the defendants were convicted of murder.

Over the passage of time there have been a number of unsuccessful attempts to run the defence of necessity for example *London Borough of Southwark v Williams* (1971). Thus many commentators have suggested that the defence of necessity is rarely acknowledged in English Law. Although it is important to note that does not mean that the circumstances surrounding the commission of an offence are not considered at all, but in most cases these arguments feed into arguments that mitigate the defendant's sentence. In the case of *Re A* (2000), however, the court appear to have clearly accepted the existence of a defence of necessity.

> **Case precedent – Re A [Children] (Conjoined Twins: Surgical Separation) [2001] 2 WLR 480**
>
> **Facts:** Twins Mary and Jodie were conjoined, and their parents' religion opposed the doctors' advice that the twins should undergo an operation to separate the two children. The hospital applied to the courts for permission to perform the operation without the parents consent. The case was very controversial because the doctors know that if the operation to separate the children took place the weaker twin would certainly die. However, if the operation was not performed both twins would certainly die.
>
> **Principle:** Necessity and homicide
>
> **Application:** The Court of Appeal ruled that it would be lawful for the hospital to perform the operation in the absence of the parents consent. The doctors in this case would be afforded the defence of necessity.

Following the case of **Re A** it would appear that the defence of necessity consists of the following elements:

❖ D commits the offence in order to avoid inevitable and irreparable evil;
❖ no more is done than is necessary to avoid the evil;
❖ the evil inflicted is proportionate to the evil avoided;
❖ the offence is one that attracts the defence.

It is helpful to know that the defence of duress (which we will consider next), has expanded to such an extent that the development of the defence of necessity is to all intents and purposes restricted to cases which are extreme or extraordinary in nature. In reality, the development of the defence of duress of circumstances has reduced the scope of necessity. Any future development of the defence is likely to be restricted to extreme or extraordinary cases.

In the next section of this chapter we are going to consider a related defence, the defence of duress. A key distinction between these two related defences is illustrated in the diagram below.

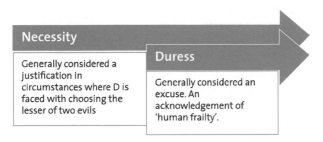

# Duress

There are two types of duress: duress by threats and duress of circumstances. When answering a question in which consideration of duress is necessary you must distinguish between the two species and not simply use the term duress. The examiner will need to see that you understand the defence in detail in order to award high marks.

## Duress by threats

The defence of duress applies in situations where the defendant is overborne by threats to himself, or another person. The defendant commits a criminal offence to avoid those threats being carried out.

In the case of duress by threats the defendant is admitting that he committed the *actus reus* of the offence with the requisite *mens rea* for the offence. However, the defendant is claiming that at the commission of the offence there were circumstances in existence that excuse the defendant's actions. In essence this defence is a recognition of human frailty. In the case of *Hasan* (2005) Lord Bingham said that a defendant acting under duress is 'morally innocent'. This defence is one which recognises human frailty.

In the case of *Hasan* (2005) the House of Lords confirmed that the defence operates on the basis of excuse rather than justification. In order for the defence to succeed the following elements need to be present.

| A threat | ⇨ | Which is immediate | ⇨ | The defendant's will is overborne | ⇨ | The offence in question is not excluded |

### A threat

The threat must be one of serious bodily harm or death: *Dao* (2012). A threat of serious psychological injury will not suffice: *Baker* (1997). The threats may be directed at the defendant or the defendant's family. The D can rely on this defence even if he is not in the presence of those making the threats; for example, if D's partner is being held hostage and has been threatened. This was established in the case of *Hurley and Murray* (1967).

### The threat must be immediate

The defendant must believe that the threat of death or serious physical harm will occur immediately, or almost immediately, unless he commits the offence: *Quayle* (2005). It is important to exercise caution here, because duress does not provide a defence to a person who unreasonably fails to escape or avoid the threat. The key question here is what is reasonable in the circumstances. This will depend on the nature of the threat and the D's reasons for not going to the police, for example. The opportunity to escape, or go to the police must be assessed at the time at which the threat is made.

---

### Case precedent – *R v A* [2003]

**Facts:** D was charged with possession of heroin and crack cocaine with intent to supply. She was caught with her boyfriend, and said that she had acted under duress by threats from J, a gang member, who had threatened to kill her in the past.

**Principle:** Duress by threats – immediacy

**Application:** On appeal, it was held that whether there was an opportunity to escape was a question that arose when the defendant committed the crime. Whether she had an earlier opportunity to escape.

## Test

It is important to note that in order for the defence to succeed the defendant must have believed that the threat will be carried out. This in itself is not sufficient and a person of reasonable firmness sharing the same characteristics as the D would have also given in to the threat: *Howe* (1987).

| The subjective element | • D honestly believes that unless he commits the crime the threat will be carried out |
| The objective element | • A reasonable person sharing the same characteristics as the defendant would have given way to the threat |

## *A person of reasonable firmness would have responded as the defendant did*

A defendant can only rely on the defence if he meets an external, objective standard, which is that person of reasonable firmness sharing the defendant's characteristics would have acted as the defendant did: *Graham* (1982).

❖ Evidence that D was unusually pliable or vulnerable is irrelevant: *Horne* (1994); *Hegarty* (1984).
❖ Age, sex, pregnancy, disability and serious mental illness are relevant characteristics: *Bowen* (1997).
❖ Post-traumatic stress disorder was accepted as a relevant characteristic in *Sewell* (2004).

**Don't forget** – that the reasonable person is sober and possesses reasonable fortitude. If a D cannot reach the standard of reasonable fortitude because of alcohol or drugs, the defence will not be available: *Flatt* (1996).

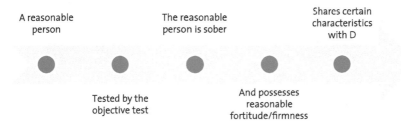

## Limitations

The defence of duress is limited in certain situations. We will now explore these limitations. It is important that you are able to articulate the limitations of this defence in a problem or essay question.

## *Voluntary association with known criminals or criminal gangs*

D cannot rely on this defence if he voluntarily assumed the risk of being compelled to do something against his will, by associating with criminals or criminal gangs.

In *Fitzpatrick* (1977), duress by threats was not a defence to a charge of robbery committed as a result of threats from the IRA, because D had voluntarily joined that organisation.

In the case of *Sharp* (1987), D was party to a conspiracy to commit robbery. He said that he wanted to pull out when he saw that the others had guns. E threatened to 'blow his head off' if he did not carry on with the plan. In the course of the robbery, E killed V. It was held that where a person has voluntarily and with knowledge of its nature, a criminal organisation or gang which he knew might bring pressure on him to commit an offence, and was an active member when he was put under pressure, he cannot avail himself of the defence of duress by threats. D's conviction for manslaughter in this case was upheld.

## Murder and attempted murder

The defence of duress is not available to a charge of murder: *Howe* (1987). Similarly, it is not available to a charge of attempted murder: *Gotts* (1992). Following the case of *Ness* (2011), it would seem that a claim of duress is available to a defendant charged with conspiracy to murder.

A summary of the points we have covered in this section is:

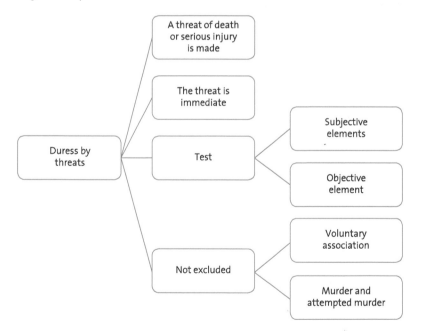

## Duress of circumstances

The defence of duress of circumstances arises when a defendant commits an offence as a result of a threat of death or serious injury from the existing circumstances. The threat may come from others, or as a result of the circumstances. What is significant about duress of circumstances is that although there may be threats from others the defendant in this case has not been threatened to comply with a threat.

| Duress by threats | • Threats come from a person or persons<br>• There is a threat to comply |
| --- | --- |

| Duress of circumstances | • Threat from person(s) or circumstances<br>• No threat to comply |
| --- | --- |

## Aim Higher

In recent years there has been some discussion about the relationship between necessity and duress of circumstances. It was decided in *Pommell* (1995) that duress of circumstances is governed by the same principles as duress by threats. This means that the harm sought to be avoided must be death or serious injury. Significantly, it was held that duress of circumstances should be a general defence to all crimes except murder, attempted murder and treason.

### Case precedent – *Martin* [1989] 1 All ER 652

**Facts:** D, who was disqualified from driving, drove his stepson, who had overslept to work. He said that he did so because his wife feared that the son would lose his job, and she threatened to commit suicide if D did not drive him.

**Principle:** Duress of circumstances

**Application:** The defence of duress of circumstances should have been left to the jury, although this is actually a case of duress by threats: *'drive or else'*.

The elements of the defence are as follows:

In the next illustration you can see a case law timeline through which the parameters of the defence have been refined.

We will now consider the different elements of the defence.

### There must be a threat
The threat posed to the defendant must be one of death or serious injury: *Martin* (1989). The threat can be to the accused or to others.

### The threat is caused by the circumstances, or posed by others
In the case of duress of circumstances the duress is a result of the circumstances the defendant finds himself in, or as a result of a threat posed by other persons. It is not, however, the result of a direct threat to comply: *Cole* (1994).

### The threats must be external
In order for the defence of duress of circumstances to succeed the threats must be external to the defendant. So the suicidal thoughts of the defendant cannot amount to duress of circumstances: *Rodger* (1998).

### D must only do what is reasonably necessary to avoid the threat
There is an expectation that the D would do everything possible to avoid the threat or circumstances which put D under duress. If D does not act on these, then this could impact on the success of the defence.

### The defendant must meet the requirements of the test
In the case of duress of circumstances the test is whether the defendant acted as he did because of what he reasonably believed to be the situation. The defendant must have had good reason to fear that death or serious injury would result, and a sober person of reasonable firmness would have acted as the defendant did. Once again there is an objective and subjective element to the test.

### The response of the defendant is proportionate
In the case of *DPP v Bell* (1992), D escaped a threat of serious harm by driving, despite having consumed alcohol. It was held that if D drives off in fear of his life when he has consumed alcohol, he does not commit an offence if he stops driving after the threat has ceased. This was the case here. Thus the defendant's response must be proportionate to the risk posed.

### Limitations to the defence
The defence of duress of circumstances is not available to a charge of murder or attempted murder: *Pommell* (1995). In *S(C)* (2012) the defence was unavailable to a charge of removing a child from England and Wales contrary to the **Child Abduction Act 1984**.

Now look at the example below, and consider how this would apply:

**Example:** Archie has a party at his house. Three men he has not met before turn up, and one starts flirting with Archie's girlfriend. Archie is upset and asks them to leave. Later that evening, Archie receives a phone call to say that the three men are coming back to the house 'to get him'. Archie fears that the men will kill him or cause him serious harm, so he gets into his car and drives to his grandmother's house, seven miles away, passing the men on the road. They are walking away from the house and do not try to chase him. Further up the road Archie is stopped by the police and found to be drink driving.

Could Archie use duress of circumstances as a defence? Work through the steps below:

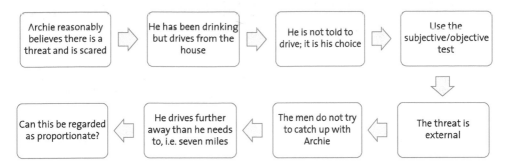

This case situation arose in *Crown Prosecution Service v Brown* (2007). The court found that when the police stopped D, he was not acting under a threat from the men, as he knew they were not pursuing him. The threat had passed, the defendant's response was not proportionate as the threat had passed, and the defendant no longer had reasonable grounds for suspecting the threat still existed. D could have stopped the car as soon as the threat passed.

A summary of the points we have covered in this section is:

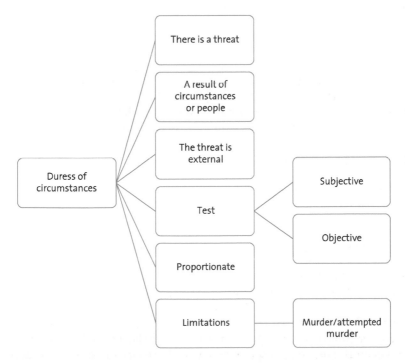

# Mistake

In this section we are going to consider the impact that mistake can have on a defendant's criminal liability. In essence this is an argument that D has made a mistake and that the mistake should either excuse or justify D's actions.

The following points should be borne in mind in relation to this defence.

❖  The vast majority of mistakes do not impact on criminal liability.
❖  A mistake as to the law is no defence.

Generally, the plea of mistake is either a denial of the *mens rea*, or an assertion that, had the facts been as the defendant believed them to be, he would have had a defence to the crime with which he is charged.

This defence is unlike the other defences that we have considered in this chapter and the previous one, as there are no particular elements of the 'defence'. Put simply, it depends on the type of mistake and the circumstances.

## Mistake of fact negating *mens rea*

Think about the offence of theft – suppose the defendant mistakes another's property for his own when he appropriates it. This would affect liability for the offence. In this situation the defendant has made a mistake in relation to the *actus reus* for the offence of theft (in this case D believes that the property belongs to him). This mistake of fact in relation to the *actus reus* invalidates D's *mens rea*. In other words, the defendant in this case does not make a dishonest appropriation of property belonging to another and there is no intention to permanently deprive the owner of it.

The authority on this defence is *DPP v Morgan* (1975), which is considered below.

---

### Case precedent – *DPP v Morgan* [1975] AC 182

**Facts:** V was raped by two of her husband's friends, whom he had invited home to have sex with his wife. He said her protests were a sign of her pleasure.

**Principle:** Mistake

**Application:** D claimed mistaken belief in consent, and the House of Lords held that D would not be guilty of rape if he honestly, albeit mistakenly, believed that V consented to sexual intercourse.

It is important to note that this case is no longer good law in relation to sexual offences and consent.

---

## Mistake and self-defence

It is settled law that a defendant who mistakenly believes that he is under attack may still rely on the defence of self-defence. In these circumstances the defendant is judged on the facts as he believed them to be: *Williams (Gladstone)* (1987).

Now look at the two cases of *Williams (Gladstone)* (1987) and *Beckford v R* (1987). In both cases it was held that D is to be judged on the facts as he believed them to be, thus emphasising the subjective nature of the test. In both of these cases the defendants made honest mistakes as to whether force was necessary.

According to Lord Lane in *Williams*, the reasonableness of a defendant's belief is only relevant in deciding whether he actually held that belief. The more unreasonable a belief, the less likely it is that D would have held it.

## Mistake induced by alcohol or drugs

We have already discussed intoxication in the previous chapter. If a defendant makes a mistake as a result of voluntary intoxication, he cannot rely on the defence of mistake: *O'Grady* (1987); *O'Connor* (1991).

A summary of the points we have covered in this section is:

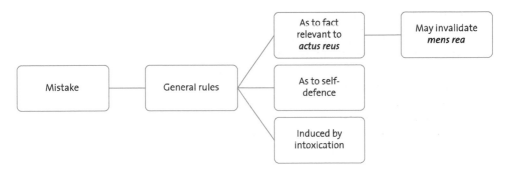

# Putting it into practice

## Question 1

Tamar is frightened of Emily, who regularly bullies and abuses Tamar. One evening Emily tells Tamar that she will kill Tamar if she doesn't drive to the shop to buy Emily more vodka. Tamar, who has been drinking, fears that Emily will carry out her threat if she does not comply. Tamar gets in her car and drives to the local shop to buy more alcohol. Tamar loses control of the car and hits a pedestrian, who is killed instantly.

## Suggested solution

Remember that it is crucial that you construct liability for an offence before moving on to consider the availability of any defence!

Follow the normal process for constructing liability:

1. **Identify the crime**
2. **Define the crime**
3. **Explain the AR of the offence**
4. **Explain the MR of the offence**
5. **Consider relevant defences**

In this question there are two primary offences: one which relates to driving under the influence of alcohol and one that relates to the death of the pedestrian. In a case like this we would suggest that you start with the most serious offence. This is a homicide offence. You can discount murder because Tamar does not have an intention to kill or cause GBH. This factor also rules out voluntary manslaughter because that is a charge of murder reduced to voluntary manslaughter through the existence of a special partial defence. This leaves involuntary manslaughter. You can consider both constructive manslaughter and gross negligence manslaughter. You will need to work your way through the elements of each offence, applying the principles of law to the question. Once you have constructed liability for one of the offences you can then consider the existence of a defence.

You could start by explaining that duress can take two forms: duress by threats and duress of circumstances. In this case we have a threat to comply, therefore duress by threats would seem to be the appropriate species of duress. The elements that you will need to consider are:

1. Is there a threat – is it of death or serious injury?
2. Is the threat one of immediate harm – did Tamar have an opportunity to escape the threat?
3. Did the threat cause Tamar to commit the offence?
4. Test – she will need to satisfy the subjective and objective elements of the test for duress.
5. Does the scenario fall into one of the exceptions/limitations?

## Key Points Checklist

| | |
|---|---|
| There is a lack of clarity regarding whether the defence of necessity exists and, if it does, what its parameters are. The key cases in relation to necessity are *Dudley v Stephens* and *Re A*. Following *Re A* it would appear that a defence of necessity does exist but only in extreme circumstances. | ✔ |
| The defence of necessity involves a claim by the defendant that they were forced to act as they did to avert a greater harm occurring. | ✔ |
| Duress may be as a result of threats or circumstances. These are general defences although they are limited in applicability. Duress of either type is not available to a charge of murder or attempted murder. | ✔ |
| Duress by threats requires: a threat of death or serious injury; the threat is immediate and provides little opportunity for the defendant to alert the authorities or escape the threats; D must reasonably believe that the threat will be carried out (subjective); it must also be demonstrated that a man of reasonable firmness sharing the characteristics of D would have been unable to resist the threats; D must not fall into one of the excluded categories or be charged with committing an excluded offence. | ✔ |

| | |
|---|---|
| Duress of circumstances requires: a threat of death or serious injury; from a person or circumstances; the threat must be external; D must meet the subjective and objective test; D's response must have been proportionate; it must not be an excluded offence. | ✔ |
| In relation to mistake, the general rule is that mistake does not affect liability and mistake as to the law is no defence. Mistake as to fact where it impacts on *actus reus* may invalidate *mens rea*. Mistake as to self-defence may operate as a defence. Mistake induced by intoxication is no defence. | ✔ |

# Table of key cases referred to in this chapter

| Key case | Brief facts | Principle |
|---|---|---|
| *DPP v Morgan* [1975] AC 182 | V was raped by two of her husband's friends, whom he had invited home to have sex with his wife. He said her protests were a sign of her pleasure. | Mistaken belief as to AR |
| *Re A [Children] (Conjoined Twins: Surgical Separation)* [2001] 2 WLR 480 | Doctors requested permission from the court to separate twins who may otherwise die | Necessity and homicide |
| *R v A* [2003] | D was found in possession of illegal drugs, and said she was scared of J, who had threatened to kill her some time ago | Duress by threats – immediacy |
| *Martin* [1989] 1 All ER 652 | D was disqualified from driving, but drove his stepson to work after his wife threatened to kill herself | Duress of circumstances |

@ Visit the book's companion website to test your knowledge

❖ Resources include a subject map, revision tip podcasts, downloadable diagrams, MCQ quizzes for each chapter, and a flashcard glossary

❖ www.routledge.com/cw/optimizelawrevision

# Index